Women and Leadership in Distance Education in Canada

Issues in Distance Education
Series editor: George Veletsianos

Selected Titles in the Series

The Theory and Practice of Online Learning, Second Edition
Edited by Terry Anderson

Online Distance Education: Towards a Research Agenda
Edited by Olaf Zawacki-Richter and Terry Anderson

Teaching Crowds: Learning and Social Media
Jon Dron and Terry Anderson

Emergence and Innovation in Digital Learning: Foundations and Applications
Edited by George Veletsianos

25 Years of Ed Tech
Martin Weller

The Finest Blend: Graduate Education in Canada
Edited by Gale Parchoma, Michael Power, and Jennifer Lock

Metaphors of Ed Tech
Martin Weller

Critical Digital Pedagogy in Higher Education
Edited by Suzan Köseoğlu, George Veletsianos, and Chris Rowell

Principles of Blended Learning: Shared Metacognition and Communities of Inquiry
Norman D. Vaughan, Deborah Dell, Martha Cleveland-Innes, and D. Randy Garrison

Troubles Online: Ableism and Access in Higher Education
Edited by Chelsea Temple Jones, Fady Shanouda, and Lisanne Binhammer

Feminist Pedagogy for Teaching Online
Edited by Jacquelyne Thoni Howard, Enilda Romero-Hall, Clare Daniel, Niya Bond, and Liv Newman

Women and Leadership in Distance Education in Canada

Edited by Cindy Ives, Pamela Walsh, and Rebecca E. Heiser

AU PRESS

Published by AU Press, Athabasca University
1 University Drive, Athabasca, AB T9S 3A3

https://doi.org/10.15215/aupress/9781771994439.01

Cover design by Kyle Flemmer
Printed and bound in Canada

Library and Archives Canada Cataloguing in Publication

Title: Women and leadership in distance education in Canada / edited by Cindy Ives, Pamela Walsh, and Rebecca E. Heiser.
Names: Ives, Cindy A., 1954- editor | Walsh, Pamela, editor. | Heiser, Rebecca E., editor.
Series: Issues in distance education series.
Description: Series statement: Issues in distance education series | Includes bibliographical references.
Identifiers: Canadiana (print) 20250267268 | Canadiana (ebook) 20250267276 | ISBN 9781771994439 (softcover) | ISBN 9781771994446 (EPUB) | ISBN 9781771994453 (PDF)
Subjects: LCSH: Women in higher education—Canada. | LCSH: Leadership in women—Canada. | LCSH: Distance education—Canada.
Classification: LCC LB2332.34.C3 W63 2025 | DDC 378.0082—dc23

We acknowledge the financial support of the Government of Canada through the Canada Book Fund (CBF) for our publishing activities and the assistance provided by the Government of Alberta through the Alberta Media Fund.

Canada Alberta Government

Contents

Women and Leadership in Distance Education in Canada

Acknowledgements

We are inspired by the dedication and perseverance of women distance educators worldwide. Some are recognized in this book, but many remain unheard or underacknowledged. We especially value the contributions of the pioneers and visionaries who designed distance education services and programs to serve students' learning needs. We recognize the authors who have shared their stories, contributing to a rich narrative tradition of leadership in Canadian distance education, which continues to evolve.

Introduction

The impetus for this book emerged from our experiences as women students, scholars, practitioners, and leaders of distance education and from the history of distance education in Canada. We view ourselves as women-centred leaders who advocate for women's perspectives, needs, and experiences in leadership by creating inclusive environments, promoting gender equity, and supporting women's personal and professional development. We consider this book an act of feminist leadership and aim to inspire future leaders to reflect critically on their own inclusive leadership practices.

Our research and practice have convinced us that the perspectives of women leaders in Canadian higher education are inadequately documented and understood. Caplan (1995) and Blackmore (2013), for example, outlined issues in women's leadership in education that in our experience have not improved satisfactorily. In this book, we focus exclusively on current women's stories of their leadership in university distance education to address a familiar aspect of the gap. Our intention is to share the stories of our colleagues and amplify their voices to describe what too often is invisible and unheard (Coulter, 1988; DeFrank-Cole & Tan, 2021).

Drawing from our formal work experiences, our research, and our leadership practices, we believe that we have a unique perspective on the critical importance of women and leadership in university-level distance education to facilitating change and overcoming ill-structured challenges.

Conceptual Framing

Women, distance education, and leadership comprise an interdisciplinary intersection that encompasses the roles, experiences, and contributions of women in the evolving landscape of distance education. To explore this intersection comprehensively, we adopt an integrative framework (Mark et al., 1999) that acknowledges and examines the diverse identities and experiences of Canadian women leaders in university distance education to position the significance of this underexplored area of study.

Women in Distance Education

Women embody multi-dimensional identities and characteristics such as race, socio-economic status, and cultural values that shape and influence their educational journeys and leadership roles. Within distance education globally, women play a significant role as both learners and educators. As learners, historically, they have comprised the majority of the distance education student population, citing the flexibility of distance learning as an opportunity to access education while balancing personal, professional, and academic responsibilities (Gnanadass & Sanders, 2018; Von Prümmer, 2000). In response to this primary learner demographic, Burge and Lenskyj (1990) suggested that feminist principles of teaching and learner-centred instructional approaches are inherent to distance education contexts and delineate that feminist approaches are learner centred. However, despite women constituting the student population, women-centred approaches are not fully recognized in distance education theories and practices (Coulter, 1988; Kramarae, 2003), highlighting a dearth of research on the gendered aspects of distance education (Patterson, 2012). Summarized by Faith and Coulter (1988, p. 197), "it is only by applying conscious attention to gender issues that problems can be identified and resolved so that all students . . . find their education to be an enabling and empowering experience."

As distance educators, women serve in diverse roles as instructors, faculty members, instructional designers, professional specialists, and administrators in their university systems. Early advocates such as Von Prümmer et al. (1988) brought to light issues faced by women in distance education organizations, such as respect, representation, and access, and called for a greater focus on women learners' needs in course design and administration. Scholars suggest that nearly 70% of the instructional design workforce is composed of women (Bond et al., 2021). Despite the efforts of early advocates and growing representation, however, the experiences of women leaders and their practices in higher education—including distance education contexts—are still under-represented in research or documented in other ways, a trend prevalent across most sectors (Cook & Glass, 2014). For example, women remain under-represented in associate (42%) and full professor (32%) positions at Canadian universities. Furthermore, their representation in tenured faculty ranks is mirrored by their limited participation in academic administrative leadership positions (Messcar, 2025). These gaps call for a closer examination of the challenges and contributions of women as leaders in higher education, highlighting their significant yet unacknowledged impacts.

Leadership Challenges and Contributions

With the conceptual backdrop of women as majority stakeholder learners and educators in distance education, women leaders encounter unique systemic challenges such as gender bias, limited access to leadership roles, and a critical need for more inclusive policies and practices (Shava & Ndebele, 2014). This disparity highlights an imbalance of power since most of those who participate are not seated at decision-making tables to prioritize issues and practices inclusive of and responsive to the varied needs, expectations, and experiences of all stakeholders in the educational community, suggesting a misalignment in values and effective continuous practices of improvement. While women leaders in distance education navigate intricate challenges and systemic conditions, frequently they find themselves at the forefront during crises or in roles overlooked and disregarded, a symptom of being affiliated with an educational model perceived as less than the in-person gold standard (Heiser, 2024; Jung, 2022). Nevertheless, women distance education leaders, like those whose stories appear in this collection, extend their services across university systems and contexts to integrate solutions and foster connectivity through relational practices aimed at prioritizing and supporting others.

Often through their communication strategies—a practice valued as both a leadership attribute and an effective approach in distance learning environments (Ekren, 2014; Saks, 2009)—women distance education leaders inject positive and long-term changes in their systems to enhance experiences and expand opportunities for others, making distance education more accessible, inclusive, and transformative (Olcott, 2020). By utilizing stories as an effective communication strategy to convey and document their experiences as leaders, women can find their voices to enact change and pave the way for future women leaders to thrive (Gourley, 2013). Maintaining a narrative tradition, which Coulter (1988, p. 16) claims offers opportunities for empowerment through the "importance of hearing and validating women's experiences," this collection of shared stories presents a previously uncharted but rich landscape of distance education.

As we consider the intersection of women, distance education, and leadership, it is essential to acknowledge and recognize the significant roles that women play in this field. The importance of women in distance education is underscored not just by their presence but also by the distinctive perspectives that their experiences provide, which can differ from the seminal theories and organizational frameworks generated by their male counterparts. Therefore, it is crucial to comprehend women's stories and utilize their experiences in leadership to foster positive change and innovation in distance education. Shaped by this conceptual framing, we turn to an examination of the literature to explore how research on this complex intersection has been applied in practice.

Distance and Higher Education

Global participation in higher education has steadily increased in recent decades, more than doubling in the past two decades (UNESCO, 2021, p. 218); Canada experienced significant growth during the same period (Statistics Canada, 2020, para. 2). A 2023 report on Canadian postsecondary education states that, "by 2021–22, full-time enrolments were 82% higher than they were in 2000–01" (Usher & Balfour, 2023, p. 7). Worldwide participation in online learning has also increased (Palvia et al., 2018), with evidence suggesting that this is especially the case for women (World Economic Forum, 2022). In Canada, it was reported that 83% of universities offered online courses for credit in 2018, up from 68% in 2010 (CDLRA, 2019, p. 3). As an example of women's participation in distance education, Coulter (1988) reported that Athabasca University enrolled 60–62% women in the late 1980s, whereas the participation rate of women undergraduates in Canada was 52%, and suggested that distance education was a preferred mode for women learners. This trend continues today, with women comprising approximately 66% of undergraduate students and 77% of graduate students (Athabasca University, 2024).

Universities are among the earliest providers of distance education and online learning; traditional learning and teaching practices are changing, and distance education methods are influencing these changes. The acknowledged resistance to change in universities (Marshall, 2010) has not affected women positively (Smith-Carrier et al., 2021). Research examining the transition to online learning in seven Canadian universities with historical mandates for distance education (Ives & Walsh, 2021) identified access, revenue generation, and technology as drivers of online learning and explored aspects of changing practices in learning and teaching. Resistance to change, the lack of dedicated resources, and the need for effective, visionary leadership emerged as critical factors for success. We proposed that lessons from the experiences of distance educators who were early adopters of online learning could help others to address challenges and opportunities. We still believe this. Working with doctoral students investigating aspects of distance education opportunities in their own professional contexts, we are strongly motivated to share the "experiential wisdom" (Burge, 2008, p. 5) that we have uncovered.

An early adopter of new technologies for adult learners, Canada has an established reputation for leadership in educational approaches that address geographic and demographic challenges in rural and remote areas. For example, the CBC broadcast an interactive and innovative distance education program to rural areas from 1941 to 1965. Called the National Farm Radio Forum (Parks Canada, 2008), this initiative enabled story sharing among neighbours and fostered local leadership initiatives. Exploiting "the power of radio technology to pioneer interactive distance education," this model was adopted by UNESCO to provide opportunities for adult education in remote populations worldwide. Building upon this history, Canada's low population density of only 4.24 people per square kilometre led to the widespread introduction of correspondence education or self-study programs by the early 1990s.

Inspired by feminist scholars before us, we continue in this book the tradition of narrative descriptions of women's experiences in higher and distance education leadership (Piper & Samarasekara, 2021; Schnackenberg & Simard, 2019). Focusing on distance education specifically, Bainbridge & Wark (2022) and Kanwar et al. (2013) offer stories of women pioneers in the advancement and development of distance education globally. As evidence of our commitment to add to this narrative and to background the stories that follow, we include in this introduction a brief chronological list of examples in the literature of this rich foundation of women's achievements, challenges, needs, and perceptions, beginning with the trailblazers and then moving to more recent accounts. We then connect this research to similar collections of stories about and from women students related to their experiences of distance education. Leadership issues figure prominently in all of these narratives.

Faith (1988) layered the perspectives of women distance educators and thought leaders on the historical context of the practice. She included chapters from Canadian women forerunners and argued that women were not only significant contributors to the field of distance education but also "central figures in developing appropriate theory and practice for a growing female learner population" (p. 331). In a study for the Council of Ontario Universities Committee on the Status of Women, Caplan (1995, p. 217) documented experiences of "general maleness and heterosexism of the [university] environment" that illustrated a lack of incentives, harassment and safety issues, devaluing of women and their work, exclusion and isolation, double standards, and stereotyping. She provided some advice for women academics struggling to survive in universities. Burge (2008) described lessons learned by 44 pioneer distance educators, 15 of whom were women. Interviewees recounted their stories, from which Burge identified personal and professional characteristics of institutional leadership and management effectiveness. She gathered as well their concerns about the future. Patterson (2012, p. 1) critically reviewed "the largely North American literature on feminist pedagogy and distance education within the discipline of women's studies and . . . suggest[ed] ways to better integrate these two perspectives."

Kanwar and her colleagues (2013) collected stories of women leaders in distance education in Commonwealth countries. Recognizing underutilized leadership practices of women, they provided recommendations for institutions regarding organizational barriers and the provision of support systems for women. Fitzgerald (2013) shared her perspectives and those of other women in senior leadership positions in higher education in Australia and New Zealand, pointing out that women are consistently under-represented in leadership positions in higher education, particularly at senior levels. She emphasized the need to conceptualize leadership in democratic, inclusive, and socially just ways as opposed to gender-based, stereotypical frameworks. Similarly, Clover et al. (2016) documented the achievements of women researchers, activists, and students in adult education and leadership in Canada, further extending feminist and activist scholarly traditions.

More recently, Schnackenberg and Simard (2019) collected the stories of women and their challenges in higher education leadership in the United States. Their final chapter ("Women in Leadership: Summary for Success," pp. 277–297) provides evidence-based strategies for success and asserts that women themselves need to address persistent gender inequities by enhancing awareness of the realities of leadership, including historical salary and responsibility gaps; developing grit and confidence; taking advantage of opportunities; ensuring readiness through study and experience; harmonizing aspirations and goals; explicitly articulating personal and professional vision and mission; preparing an entry plan that includes strategic actions for championing change; creating effective, collaborative teams; and taking care of themselves. They concluded that successful instructional leaders are focused on and visibly support student learning outcomes in all that they do. Parchoma and colleagues (2020) published a range of evidence from multiple authors (many of them women) on blended and online learning within graduate university contexts in Canada. They proposed that collaborative teams of faculty members with instructional designers, educational technologists, and other skilled professionals can lead traditional university programs toward greater openness, flexibility, and access. Graduate offerings that combine technological and pedagogical principles will be more focused on effective, quality learning and support for students. Finally, Bainbridge and Wark (2022) shared career profiles of and interviews with 30 pre-eminent academics (seven Canadians) who contributed before 1980 to the development of open and distance learning around the world. The impact of their encyclopedic collection is meaningful evidence of women's contributions to distance education theory, design, practice, management, and policy.

Feminist scholars have also published stories of women's experiences as students in distance education. Faith and Coulter (1988), pointing out that feminist scholarship had not yet studied distance education environments, explored some of the negative impacts of home study–style distance education on homebound women students, including isolation and invisibility. They concluded that "research to date surely indicates that a reconsideration of our approaches to curriculum development, instructional design and evaluation, course delivery and institutional research is in order so that distance education can become gender-inclusive" (p. 197). Coulter's (1988) chapter not only described the classic characteristics of distance education, which allows for flexible, less threatening learning, but also made the point that home study has the potential to exacerbate the systematic silencing of women. Berge and Lenskyj (1990) described the design and implementation of an Ontario Institute for Studies in Education graduate women's studies course and offered guidelines for improved woman-centred teaching based on student evaluations of the distance learning environment, advocating for the application of a feminist andragogy in future courses.

May (1994) interviewed nine women learners and analyzed their personal accounts of access and technology in a women's studies undergraduate course from a feminist perspective, demonstrating the "richness and range" (p. 82) of perspectives. She proposed further research to explore interactions, barriers, services, technology, and tutor training, all in support of women's learning needs. Von Prümmer (2000) published an institutional evaluation case study of women distance students at Fern Universität in Germany, devoting a chapter to the challenges and opportunities inherent in distance teaching and learning. She concluded with observations about necessary improvements, including an increased focus on learning rather than teaching and the enhanced use of information and communication technologies. Vaskovics & Smith (2015) described four Canadian women graduate students at Athabasca University, "framed within a Postmodernist-Feminist context" (p. 12), focusing on their multiple roles, learning preferences, and general satisfaction with online learning.

We conclude that one of the strengths of this narrative tradition of women's lived experiences in distance and higher education leadership is that women are writing for women, illustrating the experiences of the overlooked, and sharing stories of success and challenge. The authors' stewardship demonstrates commitment to a vision of a more equitable future. By offering practical advice for personal and professional approaches to leadership, these authors collectively champion current and prospective colleagues.

In our book, we aspire to uncover the contributions of Canadian women and reveal how they enact their leadership in an effort to enhance awareness and inform future practice. We collect the ideas of current women distance educators who describe their leadership challenges, explain why the issues are pervasive in their contexts, and offer strategies for how to improve their practice based on their experience. We now turn to foundational and theoretical literature that describes dimensions of leadership to illustrate the systemic challenges that women leaders face in higher education.

Leadership Approaches

Feminist scholars assert that leadership theories are foundationally and systematically gender biased. Fletcher (2004), for example, described post-heroic leadership models that de-emphasize individualism found in traditional heroic models. Instead, post-heroic models favour leadership shared and distributed through networks and dynamic interactions among individuals. However, Fletcher emphasized that these models are not inherently gender neutral. She argued that, though post-heroic models represent a shift from individual to collaborative and relational leadership, they "cannot flourish in structures and systems organized around beliefs in individualistic meritocracy" (p. 658) associated with old models.

The focus on interactions between and among individuals and groups portrays leadership as relational, a process that is complex, organic, and networked. Relational forms of leadership are evident in conceptual models such as distributed (Gronn, 2000), complexity (Clarke, 2013), and inclusive leadership (Chrobot-Mason & Roberson, 2022). Insights from complexity theory aid in conceptualizing how crisis leadership is enacted. Drawing from global experiences during the COVID-19 pandemic such as the move to online learning, Uhl-Bien (2021, pp. 1401–1402) explained how complex pressures allowed leaders to "open up adaptive space," thereby freeing and enabling people and "systems to develop and advance new ways of thinking" and doing. Aspects of complexity, relational, and inclusive leadership approaches—including listening to diverse perspectives, maintaining a culture of trust, and communicating and sharing information in a timely manner—are deemed integral during crisis events. These models recognize that the capacity for leadership and innovation is dispersed within organizations, including universities (Bolden, 2011). Context specific, a relational approach focuses on "communication as the medium in which all social constructions of leadership are continuously created and changed" (Uhl-Bien, 2006, p. 665). Therefore, leadership (wherever it occurs) is enacted through communication.

The literature confirms that women have been underrepresented in academic and administrative leadership roles in higher education, reporting that the female experience is invisible and that others are blind to women's achievements, needs, and perspectives in distance education (Caplan, 1995; Faith, 1988). Fitzgerald (2013, p. 26) observed that "women are underrepresented in leadership positions in higher education, particularly at senior levels." She added that breaking through gendered structural and cultural barriers to senior positions is challenging but that retaining women in "middle and senior levels in roles where agency and leadership can be exercised" (p. 114) is also daunting.

Furthermore, the World Economic Forum's 18th Global Gender Gap annual report (Pal et al., 2024) highlighted gender gaps in labour market outcomes across 146 economies (p. 12). Leading the index for 15 years, Iceland is ranked first, closing over 90% of its gender gap (p. 5), whereas Canada is ranked 37th (p. 12), closing approximately 76% of its gender gap (p. 135). However, the proportion of women in senior (leadership) roles was only 35.5% (p. 24).

Peterson (2014, p. 40) found an increased risk of failure among women leaders, a phenomenon known as the "glass cliff." She argued that the metaphor highlights that academic management positions in higher education are sometimes viewed as problematic or precarious and a less attractive option compared with research track positions. Fitzgerald (2013, p. 9) noted that women frequently have been located in "institutional housekeeping roles" that take time away from other academic work. Among the challenges that she acknowledged are ensuring the retention of women leaders and understanding the circumstances that support women in leadership positions. Fitzgerald was influenced by the power of women's stories and how they demonstrate the contextual, adaptive, and personal nature of leadership.

Harvey and Jones (2022) pointed out that women demonstrate exemplary leadership in higher education, especially in teaching and learning domains. They suggested that distributed leadership, in which individuals collaborate and assume responsibility for leading action for change, allows women to claim their expertise. They described the process as flexible, multi-level, iterative, and reflective. Rosa and Clavero (2022) emphasized that, though universities can be powerful in promoting gender equity, inclusion, and diversity in both higher education and society, salary gaps and gender imbalances within the academic hierarchy persist. For example, Smith-Carrier and colleagues (2021) provided a conservative estimate of the gender wage and pension gaps over the course of an academic career and retirement at Canadian universities. Whereas in 2019 male professors earned an average of 10% higher than female professors for the same work, the gender pension gap is an additional 48% to 64% more than the gender pay gap, leading to greater long-term inequities for women. The authors concluded that "previous work has substantially underestimated the long-term effects of the existing gender pay gap within, and outside of, academia" (p. 82). Reflecting on her 2015 PhD research, Cafley (2021) provided a description of the continuing struggle for gender equity in university senior leadership in Canada. She observed that, over a three-year period, four of five Canadian university presidents who "experienced abbreviated terms" (para. 4) were women.

Moving past the systemic challenges and resistance to change in universities, this book highlights women leaders who apply effective leadership strategies, enabling change and transformation from within and forging new pathways in the field of distance education. Chapter authors recognize leadership dimensions and competencies consistent with informal and middle leadership, often serving in roles such as dean, director, instructor, instructional designer, program coordinator, educational developer, and others. Their contributions provide practical examples of the vast level of influence that they wield across their organizations by implementing evidence-based practices in their contexts.

Sections and Chapters

Informed by our conceptual framework, the scholarship of women's leadership, and the advancement of distance education, this convergence fosters conditions for change and innovation. Pointing to the transformation of teaching and learning methods, Beaudoin (2016) claimed that distance education has affected the evolution of higher education. The 19 stories that we collected for this book were submitted in response to a national call for proposals and underwent a rigorous review and editorial process with the intention to demonstrate the expansive scope of Canadian women leading distance and online education at Canadian universities. Contributing authors' narrative accounts offer perspectives and insights through descriptions of influences and challenges that they have encountered in their leadership practices.

These accounts illustrate actual examples of inclusive, relational, and complexity leadership models, demonstrating how these approaches have shaped experiences and contributions in distance education. Their reflections offer practical strategies and lessons of resilience, creativity, and hope for the future, in relation not only to distance education but also to innovative and effective leadership in postsecondary education more generally. The stories offer a wide variety of perspectives, narrative styles, and experiences, addressing many aspects of women's leadership in university distance education in Canada. Some are very personal; others are more academic. Taken together they offer an authentic glimpse of some women's experiences with leadership, in keeping with the tradition that we have already introduced.

We have combined the narratives in three sections, bookended by the reflections of long-time and well-respected distance educators from across the country: Lori Wallace and Lorraine Carter,

Diane Janes, and Katy Campbell. Their decades of experience in the field connect the pioneers with today's practitioners. These authors corroborate most of the topics discussed by other established and emerging scholars represented in this book.

In the first section, "Planning Learning," five stories demonstrate the power of strategic program and course design and educational development to influence both innovation in university teaching and resources and transformation of cultures. The authors are instructional designers or faculty members and represent six universities in six provinces. The chapters include common threads related to agency and intentional instructional leadership that focus on students' needs and quality learning outcomes. They illustrate that values such as trust among colleagues, common vision, and accessibility can lead to inclusive processes that integrate systems and quality design perspectives for social justice and other aims. The narratives demonstrate feminist approaches to teaching and learning, including prioritizing relationship and community building through collaboration and communication within courses and programs. These stories suggest middle-level leadership approaches that counter historical gender-based and colonial practices, helping to disrupt the traditional undervaluing of women's contributions in academia.

The second section, "Communicating and Collaborating," extends examples of women-centred, principles-based leadership in course and program design to university-wide organizational development. Some of the five stories document approaches to helping universities manage continuity in times of crisis or organizational change. The authors include experienced administrators and faculty members at universities in four provinces. Some chapters emphasize the contributions of distance and online leaders to university responses to the pandemic and other crises as exemplars of how middle-level leaders collaborated with colleagues to enable the unplanned move to online teaching. Other chapters offer strategies for successful collaborative leadership of initiatives to establish access for Indigenous, rural, and remote students. All speak to the importance of aligning values and consulting on solutions to unexpected or disruptive organizational challenges—an expression of relational leadership. The narratives highlight trust as an essential value, expressed through transparency, collegial relationships, and pragmatic, problem-solving approaches to multiple challenges of stakeholder buy-in and innovation. These stories are reflective accounts, demonstrating the importance of expertise and experience and describing the multiple roles of women leaders in universities.

In the third section, "Reflecting on Experiences," seven stories portray the lived experiences of leaders at institutions in four provinces and one territory. The authors describe their experiences as students, faculty members, instructional designers, senior and mid-level administrators, and agents of change. These reflections are poignant, candid commentaries on how the authors respond to a range of systemic, personal, and other barriers that they face on their leadership journeys. In some cases, they recount experiences of inappropriate behaviour; gendered, racist, and dismissive attitudes; and occasionally hostile treatment by colleagues and contemporaries. The authors share explicitly feminist, social justice perspectives on their struggles against invisibility, discrimination, and imposter syndrome. They offer practical strategies for finding creative solutions and establishing safe spaces for women and other minorities within the academy through equity, diversity, and inclusion initiatives and communities of practice. Although the narratives differ widely in style and content, all of them include common threads of respect, inclusiveness, and collaboration. They advocate dialogue, self-growth, and persistence and recommend intentional instructional leadership, networking, and mentorship for helping others into successful leadership opportunities.

These stories of Canadian women's leadership—shared by students, professionals, faculty members, and other educators—are shaped by their foundation in distance education values. The chapters reflect the persistence of the authors in the pursuit of their goals and their resilience in the face of formidable systemic and personal barriers. For example, all express commitment to access to higher education. And all advocate women-centred or feminist approaches to learning and teaching. But the lessons learned are not exclusive to distance education. Rather, they can inform women and leadership across higher education worldwide. By continuing the tradition of narrative descriptions of women's experiences and voices, this collection further illustrates that women have been paving the way for innovative and inclusive approaches to education and demonstrating that diverse perspectives and experiences are essential components of systemic change.

We recognize the need for ongoing dialogue and action focused on promoting values-based, inclusive, and socially just leadership. This feminist leadership should employ relational and decolonizing practices, such as fostering mentorship, creating spaces, providing freedom for everyone to contribute, and maintaining openness to diverse ways of thinking and knowing. Additionally, it is crucial to identify and confront issues such as gender bias, racism, and other forms of discrimination that hinder inclusivity and justice.

References

Athabasca University. (2024). Athabasca University at a glance. https://www.athabascau.ca/about-au/glance.html

Bainbridge, S., & Wark, N. (2022). *The encyclopedia of female pioneers in online learning*. Routledge.

Beaudoin, M. (2016). A primer for higher education decision makers. *New Directions for Higher Education, 173*, 9–19. https://doi.org/10.1002/he.20175

Blackmore, J. (2013). A feminist critical perspective on educational leadership. *International Journal of Leadership in Education, 16*(2), 139–154. https://doi.org/10.1080/13603124.2012.754057

Bolden, R. (2011). Distributed leadership in organizations: A review of theory and research. *International Journal of Management Reviews, 13*, 251–269. DOI: 10.1111/j.1468-2370.2011.00306.x.

Bond, J., Dirkin, K., Tyler, A. J., & Lassitter, S. (2021). Ladders and escalators: Examining advancement obstacles for women in instructional design. *The Journal of Instructional Design, 10*(2). https://doi.org/10.51869/102/jb

Burge, L. (2008). "Crafting the future": Pioneer lessons and concerns for today. *Distance Education, 29*(1), 5–17. https://doi.org/10.1080/01587910802004811

Burge, E., & Lenksyj, H. (1990). Women studying in distance education: Issues and principles. *International Journal of E-Learning & Distance Education, 5*(1), 20–37. https://www.ijede.ca/index.php/jde/article/view/369

Cafley, J. (2021, October 27). The struggle for gender equity in university leadership. *University Affairs*. https://universityaffairs.ca/features/the-struggle-for-gender-equity-in-university-leadership/

Canadian Digital Learning Research Association (CDLRA). (2019). *Tracking online and distance education in Canadian universities and colleges: 2018*. https://www.cdlra-acrfl.ca/wp-content/uploads/2020/07/2018_national_technical_en.pdf

Caplan, P. J. (1995). *Lifting a ton of feathers: A woman's guide to surviving in the academic world*. Council of Ontario Universities.

Chrobot-Mason, D., & Roberson, Q. M. (2022). Inclusive leadership. In P. G. Northouse (Ed.), *Leadership: Theory and practice* (9th ed.), 322–351. Sage.

Clarke, N. (2013). Model of complexity leadership development. *Human Resource Development International, 16*(2), 135–150. https://doi.org/10.1080/13678868.2012.756155

Clover, D. E., Butterwick, S., & Collins, L. (2016). *Women, adult education, and leadership in Canada: Inspiration. Passion. Commitment.* Thompson.

Cook, A., & Glass, C. (2014). Women and top leadership positions: Towards an institutional analysis. *Gender, Work & Organization, 21*(1), 91–103. https://doi.org/10.1111/gwao.12018

Coulter, R. (1988). Women and distance education: Towards a feminist perspective. In R. Sweet (Ed.), *Post-secondary distance education in Canada: Policies, practices and priorities* (pp. 11–22). Canadian Society for Studies in Education and Athabasca University Press.

DeFrank-Cole, L., & Tan, S. J. (2021). *Women and leadership: Journey toward equity*. Sage.

Ekren, G. (2014). Women's perceptions of leadership in distance education. *International Women Online Journal of Distance Education, 3*(3), 27–41.

Faith, K. (Ed.). (1988). *Toward new horizons for women in distance education: International perspectives*. Routledge.

Faith, K., & Coulter, R. (1988). Home study: Keeping women in their place? In D. Sewart & J. Daniel (Eds.), *Developing distance education* (pp. 195–197). International Council for Open and Distance Education.

Fitzgerald, T. (2013). *Women leaders in higher education: Shattering the myths*. Routledge [VitalSource Bookshelf version]. vbk://9781135048662

Fletcher, J. K. (2004). The paradox of post heroic leadership: An essay on gender, power, and transformational change. *The Leadership Quarterly, 15*, 647–661.

Gnanadass, E., & Sanders, A. Y. (2018). Gender still matters in distance education. *Handbook of Distance Education, 4th edition*, 79–91.

Gourley, B. (2013). Helping other women to become leaders in open and distance higher education. In A. Kanwar, F. Ferreira, & C. Latchem (Eds.), *Women and leadership in open and distance learning and development* (pp. 47–58). Commonwealth of Learning.

Gronn, P. (2000). Distributed properties: A new architecture for leadership. *Educational Management Administration & Leadership, 28*(3), 317–338. https://doi.org/10.1177/0263211X000283006

Harvey, M., & Jones, S. (2022). Challenge accepted: Women claiming leadership in higher education learning and teaching. *Journal of University Teaching & Learning Practice, 19*(1), 68–91. https://doi.org/10.53761/1.19.1.05

Heiser, R. E. (2024). *Quality transnational distance education: A mixed-methods study on internationalization of higher education* [Doctoral dissertation, Athabasca University]. Athabasca University Digital

Thesis and Dissertation Collection. https://dt.athabascau.ca/jspui/handle/10791/447

Ives, C., & Walsh, P. (2021). Perspectives of Canadian distance educators on the move to online learning. *Canadian Journal of Higher Education, 51*(1), 28–40. https://journals.sfu.ca/cjhe/index.php/cjhe/article/view/188971

Jung, I. (2022). Quality assurance in online, open, and distance education. In Zawacki-Richter, O. & I. Jung, (Eds.). *Handbook of open, distance and digital education* (pp. 1–16). Springer Singapore.

Kanwar, A., Ferreira, F., & Latchem, C. (2013). *Women and leadership in open and distance learning and development.* Commonwealth of Learning. http://oasis.col.org/handle/11599/24

Kramarae, C. (2003). Gender equity online, when there is no door to knock on. *Handbook of Distance Education, 18*, 261–272.

Kusum, K., Piaget, K., & Zahidi, S. (2024). *Global gender gap report.* World Economic Forum. https://www3.weforum.org/docs

Mark, M. M., Henry, G. T., & Julnes, G. (1999). Toward an integrative framework for evaluation practice. *The American Journal of Evaluation, 20*(2), 177–198. https://doi.org/10.1016/S1098-2140(99)00025-9

Marshall, S. (2010). Change, technology and higher education: Are universities capable of organisational change? *ALT-J, Research in Learning Technology, 18*(3), 179–192. https://doi.org/10.14742/ajet.1018

Messacar, D. (2025, February 26). Women's representation and compensation in full-time faculty positions: A statistical analysis of Canadian universities from 1970 to 2022, *University Affairs/Affaires Universitaires.* https://universityaffairs.ca/features/womens-representation-and-compensation-in-full-time-faculty-positions/

May, S. (1994). Women's experience as distance learners: Access and technology. *The Journal of Distance Education, 9*(1), 81–98. https://www.ijede.ca/index.php/jde/article/view/208/619

Olcott, D. (2020). In search of leadership: Practical perspectives on leading distance education organisations. *Asian Journal of Distance Education, 15*(2), 48–57. https://www.asianjde.com/ojs/index.php/AsianJDE/article/view/472

Pal, K., Piaget, K., Zahidi, S., & Baller, S. (2024, June 11). *Global gender gap: Insight report.* World Economic Forum. https://www.weforum.org/publications/global-gender-gap-report-2024/

Palvia, S., Aeron, P., Gupta, P., Mahapatra, D., Parida, R., Rosner, R., & Sindhi, S. (2018). Online education: Worldwide status, challenges, trends, and implications. *Journal of Global Information Technology Management, 21*(4), 233–241.

Parchoma, G., Power, M., & Lock, J. (Eds.). (2020). *The finest blend: Graduate education in Canada*. Athabasca University Press. https://doi.org/10.15215/aupress/9781771992770.01

Parks Canada. (2008). National Farm Radio Forum. https://www.pc.gc.ca/apps/dfhd/page_nhs_eng.aspx?id=12571

Patterson, N. (2012). Distance education: A perspective from women's studies. *International Women Online Journal of Distance Education, 1*(2), 1–12. https://www.wojde.org/FileUpload/bs295854/File/01_12.pdf

Peterson, H. (2014). An academic "glass cliff"? Exploring the increase of women in Swedish higher education management. *Athens Journal of Education, 1*(1), 33–44.

Piper, M., & Samarasekara, I. (2021). *Nerve: Lessons on leadership from two women who went first*. ECW Press.

Rosa, R., & Clavero, S. (2021). Gender equality in higher education and research. *Journal of Gender Studies, 31*(1), 1–7. https://doi.org/10.1080/09589236.2022.2007446

Saks, D. L. (2009). Education at a distance: Best practices and considerations for leadership educators. *Journal of Leadership Education, 8*(1), 137–147.

Schnackenberg, H. L., & Simard, D. A. (2019). *Challenges and opportunities for women in higher education leadership*. Advances in Higher Education and Professional Development (AHEPD) Book Series. IGI Global. https://www.igi-global.com/gateway/book/202751

Shava, G. N., & Ndebele, C. (2014). Challenges and opportunities for women in distance education management positions: Experiences from the Zimbabwe Open University (ZOU). *Journal of Social Sciences, 40*(3), 359–372.

Smith-Carrier, T., Penner, M., Cecala, A., & Agócs, C. (2021). It's not just a pay gap: Quantifying the gender wage and pension gap at a post-secondary institution in Canada. *Canadian Journal of Higher Education, 51*(2), 74–84. https://doi.org/10.47678/cjhe.vi0.189

Statistics Canada. (2020, February 19). Canadian postsecondary enrolments and graduates, 2017/2018. *The Daily*. https://www150.statcan.gc.ca/n1/daily-quotidien/200219/dq200219b-eng.htm

Uhl-Bien, M. (2006). Relational leadership theory: Exploring the social processes of leadership and organizing. *The Leadership Quarterly, 17*(6), 654–676.

Uhl-Bien, M. (2021). Complexity leadership and followership: Changed leadership in a changed world. *Journal of Change Management, 21*(2), 144–162. https://doi.org/10.1080/14697017.2021.1917490

United Nations Educational, Scientific and Cultural Organization (UNESCO). (2021). *Higher education figures at a glance*. https://uis.unesco.org/sites/default/files/documents/f_unesco1015_brochure_web_en.pdf

Usher, A., & Balfour, J. (2023). *The state of postsecondary education in Canada, 2023*. Higher Education Strategy Associates. https://higheredstrategy.com/wp-content/uploads/2023/09/SPEC-2023_v4.pdf

Vaskovics, C., & Smith, F. (2015). Canada—Inclusive distance education: Experiences of four Canadian women. *International Women Online Journal of Distance Education, 4*(3), 11–23. https://www.wojde.org/FileUpload/bs295854/File/02_43.pdf

Von Prümmer, C. (2000). *Women and distance education: Challenges and opportunities*. Routledge.

Von Prümmer, C., Kirkup, G., & Spronk, B. (1988). Women in distance education. In D. Sewart & J. Daniel (Eds.), *Developing distance education* (pp. 56–62). International Council for Open and Distance Education.

World Economic Forum. (2022, July 13). *The upward trend in online learning*. https://www3.weforum.org/docs/WEF_GGGR_2022.pdf

1 An Old Buffalo Speaks

Reflections on My Years of Leadership in Distance Education and Online Learning

Lori Wallace

As I reflect on my 40-year career in university distance education (DE), I realize that I've been in the field longer than many (perhaps most) of our current students have been alive. However, I'm certainly not an ancient oracle, stroking my flowing white beard and presenting myself as an expert in all things distance education. Rather, I use the term "old buffalo" simply to reflect the fact that I have been around for quite a while now, have faced many challenges, some more daunting than others, and have gained useful experience along the way. I hope that sharing some of this experience will be of interest to the younger or less experienced buffalo in the herd.

I am now retired (or at least off the payroll) and enjoying what psychologist Erik Erikson (1950) would classify in his theory of psychosocial development as the "generativity stage" (a focus of which is mentorship). It occurs to me that the development of "distance education" as a field (my use of the term includes everything from correspondence to online learning) might be seen to have worked through some of the earlier stages of Erikson's framework, such as the stages of "autonomy vs. doubt" and "identity vs. role confusion."

Background

The growth of distance education at the University of Manitoba (UM) has been part of an ongoing national and international trend, and online courses have become a strategic part of the offerings of most universities in Canada (Johnson, 2019). When I began working in distance education at the university in 1985, there were 495 students enrolled in degree courses (then titled the Correspondence Program), and no full DE degree programs were offered. In 2013 (my last year of direct involvement), DE enrolment had grown to over 8,500 students, with three degree programs offered and twice the number of units participating. The University of Manitoba also introduced the first MOOC, "Connectivism and Connectivity Knowledge," in 2008, facilitated by Stephen Downes and George Siemens, with over 2,300 learners participating.

The Accidental Distance Educator

I don't know anyone of my vintage who had planned distance education as a career goal. I fell into it, as did most of my colleagues. Our work was often undervalued, as was the field itself. My colleagues at other institutions were mostly women, drawn into distance education from other teaching fields, many of them having been distance learners themselves. Those colleagues were far more likely to share stories about their disasters than crow about their accomplishments, and their generosity, energy, and openness were essential to my development as a practitioner and leader.

In 1984, during my first year in an academic position, I was approached to move into the role of director of the Correspondence Program. That approach came, I believe, not only because of my university background but also because of the instructional design experience that I had gained in the private sector.

Lessons from the Private Sector

In the late 1970s, I worked in a human resources development firm that used Robert Mager's Competency-Based Instructional Design model. I am struck that, 40 years after Mager's model was popular in the training sector, these frameworks are increasingly being used to build measurable outcomes and micro-credentials for university programs.

Working in the private sector provided me with two important pieces of learning that put me in good stead: first, projects always had tight timelines and were focused on results; second, any topic can be designed for successful adult and distance learning. The former piece of learning helped me to move projects along and focus on results when I led university units, and the latter helped to carve the enduring dent in the middle of my forehead formed from having content specialists insist that their curricula simply wouldn't fit a DE design model.

Working to Achieve Parity of Quality and Esteem for Distance Education

In the early days, a colleague at the Open University of the United Kingdom spoke about the need for distance education to achieve parity of quality and esteem with conventional face-to-face teaching and learning. It seems that we've been doing that work for too many years, but progress has been made. Some of that progress has been fuelled by research and scholarship, lobbying and policy change, development of graduate programs in instructional design (ID) and distance education, as well as appropriate adaptation of technology for teaching and learning.

At my institution, developing partnerships with other academic units and collecting data were key to raising the esteem and quality of distance education. I had a sign in my office that read "you can't manage what you don't measure," and with commitment to that principle our unit collected, analyzed, and shared with other academic units comparative data on every course (withdrawals, student and unit evaluations, revision history, etc.). In some cases, departments did not analyze similar data on their on-campus courses, so they found the reports useful, and the process fostered credibility and confidence in the quality of our DE programs. This underscores the fact that change, especially in policy and attitude, requires not only powerful stories but also solid quantitative data and analysis.

Student Support

Student support was different before the internet: we developed student networks, offered toll-free telephone numbers and calling cards, and insisted on office hours for instructors. One episode in the late 1980s illustrates how important it was to understand learners' needs. I received a phone call from an Indigenous student in northern Manitoba. He told me that he had been trying unsuccessfully to reach his instructor during office hours. I offered to track down the instructor. The student asked if that could be within 30 minutes because he had walked through the bush to use a telephone and still had to walk back to his home before dark. Similar issues arose with our incarcerated students since telephone privileges in prisons can be precarious.

Although the internet has changed for the better many aspects of the geographically distant student experience, access to reliable and affordable high-speed internet is still an issue, especially in northern and remote communities. Indigenous learners in particular face barriers in terms of technology, geography, financial resources, access to high school courses in their communities, equity in K–12 school funding, a first language other than English, dislocation, racism, and the colonial culture of the university and its bureaucracy.

Back in the day when our support staff mailed all course materials, assignments, and feedback via Canada Post, there was always the risk of delays. If there was a strike or labour disruption, then the process became very challenging indeed. For example, in 1987, rotating strikes at Canada Post meant long delays in the delivery of course materials (print manuals, audiotapes, videotapes—in both Beta and VHS!), assignments, feedback, and exams. Students' academic progress was threatened. My colleagues across the country shared contingency plans and strategies. As I was figuring out how I might arrange delivery of the rock samples that we had purchased from the Geological Survey of Canada, I spoke with a colleague at another university who wondered how the frogs that had been ordered for dissection might look after spending weeks stuck in a Canada Post facility. Suddenly, my rocks seemed to be a much easier problem to deal with.

Consortia and Formal Collaboration

By 1984, Athabasca University was booming. Provincial governments had awakened to the benefits of distance education in reducing barriers to postsecondary learning, and funding to expand distance education was available (the largest provincial grant ($250,000) that we received for UM DE course development was in 1985).

Distance educators have always been a very collaborative bunch, and the bilingual Canadian Association for Distance Education (CADE, created in 1984) and the subsequent development of the *Journal of Distance Education* provided great opportunities for sharing practice and scholarship. CADE conferences offered both formal professional development and many informal huddles in which we swapped issues and strategies and offered much affectionate support. In a reflection, a former CADE president, Joan Collinge, spoke to "CADE's power for collegiality and sustenance, especially for the lone practitioner who does not have a local critical mass of colleagues" (quoted in Roberts & Umbriaco, 2007, p. 199).

My CADE colleagues were a vital professional network for me. Women leaders and colleagues who come to mind include Liz Burge, Joan Collinge, Margaret Haughey, Margaret Landstrom, Betty Mitchell, Grace Milashenko, Ruth Epstein, Margareth Pederson, Anna Sawicki, and Barb Spronk, and UM colleagues include Anne Percival, Kathleen Matheos, Bonnie Luterbach, and Cheryl McLean.

In the days when course materials were print-based with audio and video components, we were able to develop course leasing protocols that allowed us to adapt courses developed at another university to be offered as one of our own courses. Leased courses allowed us to test the market for new topics, expand majors by leasing courses that had enrolments too low to justify in-house development, or fill short-term gaps when one of our courses was undergoing revision. Leasing fees were kept low (quid pro quo) and charged on a per-student-enrolled basis. When courses went online, such arrangements became less attractive because students from across the country could easily be recruited as opposed to just those in one's own province. We worked instead to reduce barriers to course transfer and credit recognition.

The First Year by Distance Education Program (FYDE, now Campus Manitoba) was a Manitoba government initiative that began in the 1990s with the objective of increasing access to university via distance education and through a consortium of all publicly funded Manitoba universities. The project supported course development, consortia infrastructure, a single student portal, and student service centres in rural Manitoba. A key student mobility policy was that all participating universities recognize for credit and residency requirements DE courses successfully completed by Campus Manitoba students. Government grants rarely come without political compromises, but the FYDE/Campus Manitoba programs nudged universities to collaborate and resulted in policy changes previously resisted.

Similar policies in the UM Canadian Forces University Program allowed members of the Canadian Forces and their families to complete degrees despite career transfers and international deployments. Other DE consortia in the 1980s and 1990s in which we were involved included the Prairie Horticulture Certificate Program and the Certificate Program in Adult and Continuing Education consortium.

At the national level, the creation of the Canadian Virtual University (CVU) consortium in 2000 brought together the expertise and offerings of public universities with large DE programs. Innovations included an online course and program database, the development of common forms for visiting student application and letters of permission (we considered this quite an accomplishment given that we worked with registrars' offices at 12 universities!), the waiving of all non-tuition fees, student advising, and a national and an international exam invigilation network. The consortium also conducted research projects, and its work highlighted both domestically and internationally the quality of Canadian DE programs. Vicky Busch, the executive director from the inception of the CVU until 2014, deserves particular mention here for her outstanding commitment and skill in running and representing the consortium. The CVU was dissolved in 2019, its work promoting distance education on national and international stages deemed complete, as evident from the increased prevalence of online learning programs in Canada.

It has certainly been my experience that women in university distance education in Canada (undervalued professionals working in an undervalued area) form strong support networks and achieve exceptional cooperation and results. That is also true of my experience with international projects. In the 1990s, distance education was a primary vehicle for education development projects. With the exception of education ministers or university presidents, each of the projects in which I participated was run by a woman, with women being the target learners. A distance education project in Southeast Asia trained teachers in Teaching English as a Second Language, and the coordinators—Audrey Ambrose-Yeoh and Rachanee Senisrisant—worked tirelessly in support of the project. We remain close to this day—pulling the plow together does that! Likewise, my nursing colleagues at the South West China University of Medical Sciences, led by Li Jiping and Li Xialing, somehow carved out time from heavy work and family responsibilities to develop China's first distance Bachelor of Nursing degree. The trust and commitment brought by leaders and participants to these projects created relationships that strengthened the projects, achieved results, and fostered great learning for everyone involved.

UM Organizational and Policy Trends

At the University of Manitoba, since its inception and until recently, the Correspondence (DE/Online) Program was a centralized unit, housed within the academic unit of Continuing Education (later Extended Education). Double-digit increases in UM distance education enrolment began in the late 1990s, driven largely by students enrolled concurrently in DE and on-campus courses. In 2004, a tuition-sharing agreement was developed in which tuition revenue was shared with participating academic units. It was the first such agreement in Canada and increased interest in developing new distance and online courses and programs.

In our unit in the 1980s and 1990s, instructional designers were in great demand for external consulting. We agreed that any consulting work that came to any of us as a result of our university positions would be brought through our unit, and the resulting income would develop our unit. That would be a much harder sell these days, but at the time it contributed to a very cohesive team.

Our centralized DE unit was well established and efficient with high-quality results. However, after internal consultation, the unit was disbanded in 2015, and staff and functions were transferred to other units. In my view, two issues contributed to the decision: first, control of tuition revenue; second, faculty control of development processes. Regarding the latter point, I can see that our systems for quality control sometimes frustrated last-minute revision to and individualization of courses by each term's instructors, and in retrospect I think that we could have done a better job of developing more flexible processes. However, we also had the experience of instructors revising their courses just before the term began. This strained our staff (e.g., copyright clearance and video production don't happen overnight), caused grief for staff of the bookstore and library, and sometimes weakened the integrity of the design. Nevertheless, user-friendly educational technology has facilitated just-in-time course development and revision, funding models have changed, and perhaps the trend toward decentralization can be seen as evidence of distance education becoming mainstream in universities' strategic priorities and having achieved the parity of esteem and quality that we sought in earlier days.

Until decentralization, all instructional designers were members of academic staff, putting them on an equal footing with content specialists: both the instructional designer and the department head of the content area had to approve the course before it could be offered. This reinforced that the design of the course for student learning was as important as other aspects of curriculum content. Advances in educational technology and budgetary constraints over the years have meant that instructional design work is done increasingly by non-academic staff at our institution and elsewhere. My concern about this trend is that the focus might shift more to the mechanics of educational technology with less expert learning design knowledge being brought into the process. When in 2020 the COVID-19 pandemic thrust all courses into virtual/online learning, I felt for both instructors and students. I know how much work and time go into successful online courses, and resources were in short supply in the early months of the pandemic. Although the exposure to online learning might have been a help in some ways to students and instructors, I can't help but worry that Zoom lectures and voice-over PowerPoint presentations did little to support student learning, ignite enthusiasm, or meet instructional design quality benchmarks.

National Trends

In the 1980s, DE development and delivery often occurred in centralized units, especially in universities, where distance education originated in the "extension" unit to meet the needs of rural learners (e.g., University of Manitoba, University of Saskatchewan, University of British Columbia) (Haughey, 2013). However, distance education and online learning are now supported more typically by teaching and learning centres.

A demographic trend that became a piece of critical learning for my unit came to light in 1989 when one of our staff, Darleen Courrier, mentioned to me that many more students were dropping by to pick up course materials rather than having them mailed. That casual observation became a major research project for me, and the results demonstrated that in universities across Canada distance education no longer served a homogeneous student population of adult learners (over age 25), primarily female, part-time learners, at a geographic distance from the university and with full-time work and/or family responsibilities (Wallace, 1996). The DE student population had become heterogeneous, with a growing cohort of younger, urban, full-time students who enrolled in distance education not because of the barriers of geography, full-time work, or family responsibilities but because they were working an average of 20 hours a week in "McJobs" in which they had little control over their shifts. This new group of learners had geographic access to courses on campus but needed flexibility in the time and place of their learning. They often combined DE courses with on-campus courses to have that flexibility and stay on track to graduate. This demographic shift represented something of a distance education "black market" with word-of-mouth between students rather than any marketing generating enrolment. The trend also generated some resistance from academic departments that considered distance education inferior and believed that urban students should be compelled to enroll in on-campus courses. Thankfully, those attitudes changed over time as distance education continued to demonstrate high-quality results.

Another trend relates to copyright. Over the past two decades, there has been a shift in some universities from copyright ownership of DE courses held by the institution to copyright ownership held by course authors. Historically, copyright was owned by the university to ensure access to courses in which it invested considerable resources. However, that model also limited flexibility in revisions, and some instructors felt hobbled by having to teach courses that gave them few opportunities to add their perspectives. The adoption of technology and the move to online courses have also facilitated the personalization of courses by instructors, and ownership of online courses is now vested in some faculty collective agreements.

Thanks to the leadership of Rory McGreal, Michael Geist, and others such as the ABCopyright group, the grip (and expense) of universities' contracts with Access Copyright have been loosened, and some institutions have begun to deal directly with copyright holders or to use open educational resources.

Reflections on Leadership

I've reflected on my leadership experiences as well as the qualities of leaders whom I most admired, qualities that I try to instill in myself. Some of these qualities might seem at first glance to be self-evident, but I believe that they warrant mention.

Having a DE leadership position did not always bring respect or recognition. In 1985, the dean of Continuing Education and I were interviewed for a piece in the *Winnipeg Free Press* on how our unit was extending access to students. Not only were none of my comments included in the article, but also the caption under my photo read "Lori Wallace is all set for a correspondence course from the U of M." I was in fact the director! I had refused to have my photo taken pushing a course package into a mailbox, but the result in the published article was even more humiliating. Dealing with the media is something that most leaders learn by trial and error, and I was a rank beginner at that time. As time went by, I learned to ask interviewers to share drafts with me for fact checking and was pleased that many of them obliged.

Lots of grey matter is needed of course for leadership, but leaders also need strong moral compasses and stiff spines. That type of leadership is hard under the pressures of politics and resources and harder still if your values aren't always in sync with those of the organization. Your teams can also become insular. That's why I found it vital to have people who were sympathetic, informed listeners but, most importantly, incorruptible judges of my ideas and actions.

Leading means working harder than you ask your staff to work and putting your unit first. Early on, I developed an understanding that the teams we lead often have Teflon or Velcro members. One challenge of leadership is to find ways to make work stick to our Teflon staff members and ensure that the Velcro folks don't collapse from overwork.

I've learned that keeping your sense of humour, especially about yourself, is key: "Blessed are they who can laugh at themselves, for they shall never cease to be amused." I now laugh at my rather unsuccessful attempts to achieve record levels of efficiency in my personal and professional lives. I even bought a book entitled *Life's Too Short to Fold Fitted Sheets*, which had a section listing 17 meals that could be made from a deli chicken.

Another key aspect of leadership is to lead without ego or self-interest: "At the feast of ego, all leave hungry." Teams are just another form of relationship, and in all great relationships we know that we are stronger together than we are separately. Leadership is about achieving collective goals, and to do so, we must recognize the moral role of a leadership position.

I've seen discussions, decisions, and projects usurped by ego or self-interest, and the results rarely have been good. 'Academic politics produce such bitter squabbling because the stakes are so meagre,' is a classic phrase on the matter–usually attributed to Henry Kissinger but reiterated by many–and I would add that some of the egos are *so* large. Projects sometimes have been derailed because the funders lost confidence that their interests were being placed first, and too much attention was paid to the "elevator pitch" and "branding" and not enough to honouring the relationship. It's worth remembering the adage that "people may forget what you accomplished, but they will never forget how you made them feel."

Conclusion

Our workplaces and learners certainly have changed over the decades. We have addressed many challenges and had many successes, perhaps the greatest of which have been to put a dent in pious notions of the superiority of face-to-face learning and to support faculty members and instructors to improve teaching and learning, wherever and whenever they take place. We are now less likely to hear statements that riled Postman and Weingartner (1969) such as teachers declaring "I taught them that, but they didn't learn it," to which these authors retorted that we don't hear salespeople saying "I sold it to him, but he didn't buy it" (p. 34). The fact that *Teaching as a Subversive Activity* is still in print suggests that there's still more work for us.

This old buffalo is enjoying remaining in our DE and ID herd within a more relaxed time frame and without any requirement to "dress for success." Mentorship is such a great way to share and learn.

References

Erikson, E. (1950). *Childhood and society*. W. W. Norton.

Haughey, M. (2013, December 15). Distance learning. *The Canadian encyclopedia*. https://www.thecanadianencyclopedia.ca/en/article/distance-learning

Johnson, N. (2019). *Tracking online education in Canadian universities and colleges: National survey of online and digital learning 2019 national report*. Canadian Digital Learning Research Association. http://www.cdlra-acrfl.ca/wp-content/uploads/2020/07/2019_national_en.pdf

Postman, N., & Weingartner, C. (1969). *Teaching as a subversive activity*. Delta.

Roberts, J., & Umbriaco, M. (2007). CADE: Looking forward by glancing back. *International Journal of E-Learning and Distance Education, 21*(3). https://www.ijede.ca/index.php/jde/article/view/33

Wallace, L. (1996). Changes in the demographics and motivations of distance education students. *Journal of Distance Education, 11*(1), 1–31. https://www.ijede.ca/index.php/jde/article/view/245

Section I
Planning Learning

2 Decolonization in Distance Education

Trying to Lead through Possibility and Good Relationships

Kristine Dreaver-Charles

I live and work on the Treaty 6 territory and the homeland of the Métis; this is the land of my ancestors. As an Indigenous woman working in higher education, I have been constant in my desire to build good relationships as I learned about and tried to offer leadership in decolonizing distance education.

This work is centred on Indigenous story and auto-ethnography. Archibald (2009, p. 2) wrote that "sharing what one has learned is an important Indigenous tradition. This type of sharing can take the form of a story of personal life experience and is done with a compassionate mind and love for others." Auto-ethnography is a process that "involves the writer or researcher in crafting creative narratives shaped out of a writer's personal experiences within a culture and addressed to varied (mostly academic) audiences" (Poulos, 2021, p. 5). This auto-ethnography is also acknowledged as Indigenous auto-ethnography since it is centred on my Indigeneity.

Reconciliation, Indigenization, and Decolonization

Reconciliation, Indigenization, and decolonization are interconnected, often in unique ways. Their presence in distance education is needed. Reconciliation is defined by the Truth and Reconciliation Commission (TRC) of Canada (2015, p. 154) "as an ongoing process of establishing and maintaining respectful relationships." The legacy of intergenerational trauma and disparities of Indigenous Peoples in Canada stems too often from the atrocities committed in residential schools. Reconciliation must be a mutual and ongoing effort involving all Canadians.

Indigenization can be reflective of reconciliation when it stems from the TRC and the 94 Calls to Action. Pidgeon (2016, p. 79) wrote that, "from Indigenous perspectives, Indigenization of the academy refers to the meaningful inclusion of Indigenous knowledge(s), in the everyday fabric of the institution from policies to practices across all levels, not just in curriculum." That weaving in of Indigenous knowledges can be responsive to the Calls to Action and can decolonize.

Decolonization is a shift in power and perspective away from the colonial positioning and the constant whiteness too often privileged in academia and toward Indigenous perspectives and ways of knowing. The shift in epistemologies and the valuing of Indigenous knowledges are acknowledged as being uncomfortable for some concerned about their loss of privilege. Lavallee (2020, p. 127) stated that "ensuring Indigenous knowledges are recognized and valued in the academy and that Indigenous people are free from anti-Indigenous racism in the academy are two objectives that should be the focus of the reconciliation, decolonizing, and Indigenizing exercise." We need to acknowledge that distance education has a place in the academy and a responsibility to participate in the discourse of reconciliation, Indigenization, and decolonization.

The Framework

Medicine wheels are frameworks that centre Indigenous perspectives and ways of knowing, often established with the four directions and teachings that reflect balance, wellness, and cyclical perspectives. My stories are shared through a framework based on a medicine wheel. I am centred in this Indigenous assessment framework, and I share these stories *beginning* in the east, *emerging* in the south, *becoming* in the west, and *inspiring* in the north. The framework was originally created for assessment in a study abroad class and informed by Indigenous cyclical concepts of seasonality (spring, summer, fall, and winter) and life stages (child, youth, adult, and elder) to denote evolving stages and states of mastery. These foundational Indigenous cyclical concepts were connected with the standardized university assessment descriptions in a way to bring together Indigenous and Western perspectives (Cottrell & Dreaver-Charles, 2022).

Through this framework, I examine my own experiences and growth in trying to lead decolonization in distance education. I start in the east.

Beginning/East

I was hired as an instructional designer at the University of Saskatchewan in 2014. I had completed my first education degree at the university, and I had a connection to it. I was not hired to focus on Indigenizing online courses. My position took me across campus to various colleges to meet mostly non-Indigenous instructors and to design online courses with them.

When I started working as an instructional designer, so much was once again new for me. I had to learn to navigate in my position in a very colonial place. Cote-Meek (2014, p. 63) wrote that "the structures that hold together the academy are colonial and therefore influence what is taught, how it is taught and who teaches it." It is a place where standardization is valued and change is slow, and, honestly, it can feel so linear.

This was a year prior to the 2015 release of the report of the Truth and Reconciliation Commission of Canada and our 94 Calls to Action. I watched the news stories of Indigenous people from across Canada as they shared their pain and trauma through their own stories as the commission listened to and documented their words. It was personal for me because my late husband had attended residential school with his siblings, as had both his father had his grandfather.

The divide between policy and implementation can seem vast. I could sometimes see the disconnect between the aspirations of university leadership and those of the instructors with their online classes. In the *beginning*, I had to learn to be an instructional designer, and I had to learn about reconciliation. Occasionally, I would encounter questions from instructors who recognized the need to include Indigenous content in their courses. These conversations made me cognizant that I needed to be part of reconciliation in higher education, and through my position I could contribute to leading and supporting change in distance education. I did not have an instructional design practice inclusive of decolonization yet, but it would come.

I realized early that my priority was to ask good questions and listen to instructors as they told me about the essential aspects of their face-to-face classes. As a lifelong learner, I was fortunate to have one-on-one time with instructors. They often told good stories as they shared their knowledge and experiences, and these stories helped me to understand who they were. By listening to and learning about them and their positions, I felt more capable of leading them through the instructional design process.

I can remember one of my first summers working on campus. I was heading to one of the colleges for a meeting, and along the way I saw three instructors with whom I had worked. I stopped and visited for a few minutes with each of them, shaking hands, and as I mentioned it to my director afterward it made me happy because I knew them. Wilson (2008, p. 84) wrote that, "if we step outside of the community of Indigenous scholars, we can see the importance of relationship building in the everyday lives of most Indigenous people." I could recognize my need as an Indigenous woman to build good relationships with instructors through my instructional design practice.

Emerging/South

A few years after starting my job at the university, I began a second master's degree. I could not find a place in a PhD program, and working at the university made me want to study once again. A university is a place so full of knowledge that I wanted to be in the midst of it. I never heard what went on in the college in the background, but eventually it found me a seat in a PhD program, and I transferred. I gained knowledge and skills, which helped me to navigate better the academy in which I was working. I was reading the literature, gaining an academic perspective, and because of the works of many Indigenous scholars learning about and recognizing my own Indigeneity through their words.

I struggled in those graduate classes. I remember going home one Saturday after a difficult day of class and telling my late husband that I should not have enrolled in a mainstream graduate program. I told him that I should have found an Indigenous program. I had a lot of turmoil being there. Imposter syndrome was always something with which I struggled. The positioning that seemed to go on also challenged me. But eventually I started to find my way and make friends, both Indigenous and non-Indigenous, and I realized that most of us were struggling.

Emerging from my studies was a desire to bring Indigenization into my instructional design practice. I started visiting with my instructional design colleagues to talk about how we could weave an Indigenization approach into our instructional design practices. We began with a single question included in our course design plans. In what areas of your course/modules might Indigenous perspectives be authentically included?

It was a question that we could all ask and needed to ask. The responsibility for Indigenizing distance education was not mine alone. Sometimes after visiting with instructors, I could see that their courses were steeped in Indigenous perspectives, and the question was unnecessary. Instructors had room to respond to the question in various ways. We were asking them to Indigenize their teaching, not telling them that they had to do so. It was an invitation, and we were moving in the right direction.

Chief Mistawasis was my great-great-great-grandfather. During Treaty 6 negotiations, the chiefs needed time to consider the commissioner's offer, and Chief Mistawasis said that "when a thing is thought of quietly, it was the best way" (quoted in Morris, 1880, p. 184). There is a benefit to trying to lead quietly, with subtlety. Sometimes having bold visions and grand plans are important and necessary. But sometimes trying to lead quietly by asking that one question can create a conversation on possibilities. I am hopeful that this approach has engaged instructors and offered my colleagues inspiration.

Becoming/West

After my comprehensive exam, I realized that I needed to shift my focus. Although Indigenization remained significant, I was learning about decolonization, and I could see that it better reflected what I was doing. What was *becoming* important to me was how I was navigating the academy and my desire to be part of changing it in a good way. While I struggled to move forward with my PhD during this time, I still found many good experiences of and opportunities for growth.

The academy is thick and heavy with colonialism. It has permeated it for too long. Tuhiwai Smith et al. (2019, p. 6) noted that, "as scholars, we are not immune to, or above, the historic trauma of our peoples and we have to work purposively to create healthy decolonized academic spaces." It is challenging to be an Indigenous woman. Lateral violence and others' insecurities can surface, wreaking havoc, and I needed to shift away from it. I wanted to create good relationships and support people in a way that we would be able to uplift one another.

I could recognize reciprocity in my instructional design practice as I led faculty members through the design of their online courses, offering feedback and suggestions while asking many questions. They were often uncertain of the possibilities of distance education pedagogy, and I did my best to explain it and encourage them. As we worked together, they often checked in on the progress of my studies and offered insights and stories of their experiences that a first-generation Indigenous graduate student really needed to hear.

My first scholarly publication was in a biomedical science journal. A department head with whom I was working to design an online course recognized, before I did, that as a PhD student I needed publications. It was a valuable experience because I was able to see firsthand what was involved in publishing an article. This publication also made me realize that my contributions to academia could take me in many different directions, and I liked that prospect. Mostly, I appreciated that our publication did not hinge on my Indigeneity. I was not the token

Indigenous person included to give credibility to Indigenous-focused research.

I began working with one of my professors after taking a study abroad class with him in Ireland. He wanted to leverage my instructional design skills and the tools of distance education with his next study abroad class in Jamaica. We brought together open pedagogy and Indigenous epistemologies in a way that would support the transformative learning of study abroad and decolonization. The Indigenous assessment framework, as described earlier, came out of this shared effort and was first utilized in the class. During the remote teaching of the COVID-19 pandemic, we again worked to design a virtual study abroad course incorporating much from our initial designs.

Through our longer-term collaborations, we have presented both nationally and internationally. Our first publication, titled "Indigenizing Internationalization and Internationalizing Indigenization: Insights from a Virtual Study Abroad to Ireland, Jamaica, and Aotearoa/New Zealand" (Cottrell & Dreaver-Charles, 2022) was with the Open/Technology in Education, Society and Scholarship Association. We have also contributed a chapter to *Rethink Learning Design*, an open textbook collection, titled "Decolonizing and Opening the Academy via Study Abroad" (Dreaver-Charles & Cottrell, n.d.).

Inspiring/North

Since I started working in higher education, I have presented at conferences with faculty members. An important part of trying to lead in distance education is recognizing those good opportunities to share knowledge, and I enjoy making contributions to the academy with them. But in 2022 I was invited to speak on my own to the Canadian Association of Instructional Designers on instructional design and decolonizing approaches. I was gathering quotations and ideas as I internalized what I needed to say to and ask instructional designers from across Canada. My goal was to be *inspiring*, and I hoped that they would be able to see themselves as having a role in the decolonization of distance education.

I spoke about some of my experiences designing courses with faculty members. I tried to offer ideas on where instructional designers could begin and how they might build their own community of supports. I challenged them to recognize the uncomfortableness for some of them in shifting away from their positioning as experts when trying to decolonize their course designs. That uncomfortableness can lead to avoidance and hinder the efforts to decolonize distance education. Recognizing those uncomfortable moments requires leadership to support and encourage faculty in moving beyond this barrier.

A quick checklist with standard steps to decolonize distance education was not an outcome of this presentation. The uniqueness of decolonizing distance education had to be made obvious. Near the end of my presentation, I told the participants that we all need to lead the work of decolonization through our instructional design practices and that it was not only up to me because I am Indigenous.

I was so spent after finishing that presentation, but I thought that it had gone well. I reflected on it for more than a few days afterward, trying to remember what I had said and of course noting what likely needed to be revised. My presentation was the culmination of my experiences as an instructional designer and my PhD journey as I tried to lead decolonization in distance education. I hope that the participants thought that the time I spent with them was worthwhile and that I offered them some possibilities for decolonizing their course designs.

Conclusion

This journey within my Indigenous assessment framework has been invaluable. In the *beginning*, I could recognize my need to learn a new practice and understand more about reconciliation. From my PhD studies, I could see a focus on Indigenization *emerging* in my instructional design practice. As I gained experience, my need to be impactful in academia was *becoming* apparent. By sharing my experiences and insights with other instructional designers, I hope that I was *inspiring* them to see their own role in decolonizing distance education.

I acknowledge that my time as an instructional designer was not without challenges. I had much to learn along the way, and I did not always find success. A few years ago, I was sharing with my professor some of the good things that people were saying to me. He encouraged me to hold on to their words. So I have tried to remember this and to share what I have held on to from my time in distance education.

It takes a strong community to support an Indigenous woman trying to decolonize distance education. I need to remember the efforts of faculty members able to try something often new and possibly uncomfortable. I am fortunate to know some who still want to connect and collaborate with me on their projects and sometimes just to visit over tea. I am hopeful that my time in distance education has been well spent and that the relationships I have built will continue to support meaningful decolonization in higher education.

Kovach (2009, p. 94) identified the importance of stories: "Stories remind us of who we are and of our belonging. Stories hold within them knowledges while simultaneously signifying relationships." That sense of belonging through good relationships is essential to me and my place in higher education. So, once again, I am *beginning* in the east with a new position as an academic innovation specialist with information and communication technology at the University of Saskatchewan. I am again hoping to build good relationships as I try to incorporate my perspective and my desire to decolonize higher education with a new group of colleagues.

References

Archibald, J. (2009). *Indigenous storywork: Educating the heart, mind, body, and spirit*. UBC Press.

Cote-Meek, S. (2014). *Colonized classrooms: Racism, trauma and resistance in post-secondary education*. Fernwood Publishing.

Cottrell, M., & Dreaver-Charles, K. (2022). Indigenizing internationalization and internationalizing Indigenization: Insights from a virtual study abroad to Ireland, Jamaica, and Aotearoa/New Zealand. *OTESSA Conference Proceedings, 2*(1), 1–7. https://doi.org/10.18357/otessac.2022.2.1.135

Dreaver-Charles, K., & Cottrell, M. (n.d.) Decolonizing and opening the academy via study abroad. In *Rethink Learning Design*. https://rethinkld.trubox.ca/chapter/decolonizing-and-opening-the-academy-via-study-abroad/

Kovach, M. (2009). *Indigenous methodologies: Characteristics, conversations, and contexts*. University of Toronto Press.

Lavallee, L. (2020). Is decolonization possible in the academy? In S. Cote-Meek & T. Moeke-Pickering (Eds.), *Decolonizing and Indigenizing education in Canada* (pp. 117–134). Canadian Scholars.

Morris, A. (1880). *The treaties of Canada with the Indians of Manitoba and the North-West Territories and Kee-wa-tin*. Belfords Clarke.

Pidgeon, M. (2016). More than a checklist: Meaningful Indigenous inclusion in higher education. *Multidisciplinary Studies in Social Inclusion, 4*(1), 77–91. https://doi.org/10.17645/si.v4i1.436

Poulos, C. (2021). *Essentials of autoethnography*. American Psychological Association.

Truth and Reconciliation Commission of Canada. (2016). *A knock on the door: The essential history of residential schools from the Truth and Reconciliation Commission of Canada*. University of Manitoba Press.

Tuhiwai Smith, L., Tuck, E., & Yang, K. (2019). Introduction. In L. Tuhiwai Smith, E. Tuck, & K. W. Yang (Eds.), *Indigenous and decolonizing studies in education: Mapping the long view* (pp. 1–23). Routledge. https://doi.org/10.4324/9780429505010

Wilson, S. (2008). *Research is ceremony: Indigenous research methods.* Fernwood Publishing.

3 Not Just a Pretty Course
Aesthetic Leadership in Distance Education

Cynthia Eden, Natalie Green, Sandy Hughes, Victoria Kennedy, and Megan Pickard

Aesthetic details have long been perceived to be in the feminine domain. Schor (1987, p. 4) notes that aesthetic details are typically classified along a spectrum as being either ornamental with "connotations of effeminacy and decadence" or "everyday" and thus "rooted in the domestic sphere . . . presided over by women." From needlework to makeup applications to setting tables, it is easy to see how aesthetic details are often associated with women's work. However, Schor readily acknowledges that there is no biological basis for the gendering of details (p. 97). Rather than a biological basis, it is the discursive gendering of details as feminine that Schor considers and that we apply here to the field of instructional design.

In 2005, Parrish wrote that there had been a "prevalent reluctance" to discuss or draw attention to the aesthetic aspects of instructional design. Ten years later Carroll and Kop (2016) maintained this stance, noting that learning designers needed to harness the power of visual design in online learning rather than leaving it as an "indifferent though 'beneficial' random occurrence" (p. 99). If the aesthetic design of an online course can enhance learning, then why is there reluctance to discuss or draw attention to it? Could it be because of the connotations of "decadence" and superficiality that Schor (1987) noted? In this chapter, we draw attention to the aesthetic qualities of online learning environments and argue that they matter significantly. In the pursuit of elevating considerations of instructional design aesthetic work as influential and powerful, we, five women working in online instructional design in Open Learning and Educational Support at the University of Guelph in Canada, offer insights into how aesthetic details in our work are inextricably connected to the pedagogical aspects of the work and how we exercise leadership through our attention to aesthetic details.

Context

The field of instructional design emerged in the first half of the 20th century as a response to behaviourism before it matured through its use in military training and promotion by male scholars who were military alumni or funded by the military (Campbell, 2015). Although its roots are in the masculinized sphere of the military, instructional design has now become a female-dominated profession. In 2016, Intentional Futures released a report on instructional design in higher education that noted 67% of its international survey respondents identified as female (p. 6). Similarly, Zippia (2022) reported that 58.2% of all instructional designers in the United States were women ("Instructional Designer Statistics by Gender" section, para. 1). Campbell (2015, p. 238) noted a change in pedagogy from the master-apprentice relationship to one of constructivist epistemology during the 1960s, leading to the emergence of feminist pedagogy and the emphasis on "learning and teaching as egalitarian, learner-focused, democratic, participatory, relational, collaborative, inclusive, empowering, interactive, and experiential." It is within this realm of feminist pedagogy that we situate ourselves and our argument that the aesthetic details of an online course are just as crucial to its overall quality and effectiveness as the content and the facilitation style of the instructor. As Rose (2001, p. 1) put it, "what we see is as important, if not more so, than what we hear or read."

The instructional design of an online course should be integrated solidly with its aesthetics. Carroll and Kop (2016, pp. 93–94) describe visual aesthetics as "something that is sensually attractive/arousing in itself, an object that then goes on to generate feelings to inform a greater sense of what the object is about and means," and "in terms of learning and the building of learning environments, aesthetics can enable us to become 'engaged' through the senses to play integral parts in the environment itself." David and Glore (2010, p. 5) also argued that the visual and instructional design of a course can have a profound impact on how learners "perceive information, learn, judge credibility and usability and ultimately assign value to a product" and that "to dismiss design as merely visual is to make a fundamental mistake." Al-Mahmood (2012) noted that learning online in higher education is a visual practice and that aesthetic details, such as the use of colour, matter to students. As one student from Al-Mahmood's research asked, "why don't they ask some people who really learnt about art and about the design to design this beautifully?" (p. 28).

The following five narratives represent our experiences as women working in the field of distance education development and demonstrate the aesthetic leadership that we bring to individual courses and programs and even across the online learning platform.

Setting the Stage

NATALIE GREEN

Aesthetic and Usability Standards for Online Learning Environments

Our team works cross-functionally to design and develop interactive online asynchronous courses, which we also refer to as "distance education" or "DE" courses. This work leverages the expertise of instructional designers and web and multimedia developers who work collaboratively using a production model. During my years with this team, I have led multiple initiatives to develop aesthetic and quality standards for online learning environments. For a team with diverse and overlapping skill sets to be effective and efficient, it is vital to develop a common language and practice. Although our collective work supports continuous improvement, we need to be intentional about practices and standards to ensure that we are consistent in supporting faculty in creating engaging learning experiences through the lenses of pedagogy and learning theory, aesthetics, usability, and technology.

Early in my career as an instructional designer, I leveraged my background and expertise in art and design to provide leadership in the development of a style guide that would inform our visual design and navigation, focusing on elements such as font, colour, graphics, organization, page layout, and naming conventions. Later, as I moved into management, the opportunity arose to revisit this work and lead the team to develop new conventions, not only at the course level but also across the online learning environment for our DE courses, to ensure that learners have a consistent, effective, and enjoyable experience within the learning management system (LMS). This work included developing a broader set of aesthetic, instructional design, and web quality standards to fit a new visual experience driven by the

LMS vendor. The result was a learning environment prototype, which included a simple and clean aesthetic and intuitive and streamlined navigation.

The home or landing page of a course website is the first impression of the learning experience, so it is vital that the visual aesthetics encourage the learner to continue through the site. Our prototype included a course home page that values white space and includes bold graphical elements and a grid-like structure that organizes a variety of key information. We also streamlined the organizational and navigational features, creating a consistent and uncluttered appearance for the navigation bar and course contents, supporting consistency across offerings, and lessening the cognitive load of students so that they can focus on learning instead of finding materials.

In practice, I have seen how the aesthetics, navigation, and usability of the learning environment set the stage for the design of effective learning experiences. This approach gives one the ability to onboard faculty members much more quickly and ensure that the output meets a high standard, reducing the burden to refine presentation and aesthetics for those developing courses. Since the aesthetic standards and visual appearance of learning environments affect how students experience and interact within courses, these are not just pretty courses but high-quality environments in which both faculty members and students can focus on the discipline and enjoy teaching and learning.

MEGAN PICKARD

Styling Learning Environments through Democratic Leadership

Fifteen months after I started working at the University of Guelph, I became part of a research team tasked with assessing a new software upgrade to the institution's LMS. During this time, I was an online learning quality assurance specialist, and my role on the team involved researching and writing a new style guide that would establish the aesthetic design of the upgraded system and enhance the overall usability and quality of our online courses. Like its predecessor, the new style guide included information on proper navigation, organization of content, accessibility best practices, and page layout examples, as well as instructions on how to use fonts, icons, and colour to ensure a consistent look and feel for all DE courses at the institution.

My biggest challenge in creating this new style guide was getting all potential users on board. As a young woman new to the field of instructional design, I was not in an official leadership position. Many of my colleagues were men and had worked in the department for several years. In early initiatives to implement aesthetic and quality assurance standards, I experienced significant pushback from colleagues because they disagreed with certain aspects of the standards, even though these standards were evidence-based. This disagreement resulted in my colleagues not following the standards, causing inconsistencies in the navigation, organization, and visual design of our course websites. To avoid past experiences, I used a democratic leadership approach to create the new style guide, and I met with my colleagues and listened to their opinions and suggestions.

In their recent meta-analyses of gender differences in leadership behaviour, Shen and Joseph (2021) found that women are more likely to use a democratic leadership style. In writing the new style guide, using an approach that involved my colleagues in the decision-making process proved to be an effective strategy. Once the system upgrade was in place, my colleagues used the new style guide and started to provide me with unsolicited but welcomed feedback on what was working for them and what was not. It became clear that listening to their feedback and involving them in the development process helped them to view the new style guide as a positive experience rather than an authoritative encroachment on their professional agency.

VICTORIA KENNEDY

Putting It in Practice: Course-Level Design Aesthetics

The first time that a course author submits draft content for a new distance education course, it is typically either a text document containing a written lecture or a slide deck from the in-person version of the course. "You're just going to upload this to the course website, right?" the course author sometimes asks or refers to the work that I will do as "formatting" the content. But my work goes beyond formatting; it is a type of instructional leadership by which I guide both how the course is designed and how it is studied.

The strategies that instructional designers use to deploy colours, images, layout elements, icons, and other aesthetic tools are intended to increase the likelihood that students will not just read but also understand, analyze, reflect on, and synthesize the content. Aesthetics can create a certain pace and insert pauses, entice learners to complete activities, or invite them to read content deeply that they might otherwise skim. Indeed, the aesthetic choices that online instructional designers make mirror the mechanisms through which people learn: they create repetitions, patterns, and contrasts.

Consider how design aesthetics in Examples 3.1 and 3.2 change how you read and respond to the same content.

In Example 3.2, aesthetic elements such as the activity panel, the shading, the heading (with its implied repetition of a previously established pattern of activities), and the icon all work to prompt a pause in reading in order to think about the content more deeply.

Example 3.1: Example of Initial Content Submission

Modern Perspectives on Cats

While cats have been popular with humans for centuries, since the advent of the internet, cat-related content has grown exponentially. Albert Schweitzer once said: "There are two means of refuge from the miseries of life: music and cats."

While amusing, modern feline-related web content has also advanced several debates related to the ethics of cat ownership and care. Some of those questions include:

- Is it ethical to keep a pet cat indoors and prevent them from going outside?
- Is it ethical to declaw a pet cat?
- Is it ethical to spay or neuter a pet cat?

Take a few minutes to make an inventory of your own ethical positions on these topics. We will return to this at the end of the course to measure whether and how your perspectives have changed.

Aesthetics that are pleasing and functional in online courses are crucial to convincing the learner to engage fully in the learning process.

SANDY HUGHES

Aesthetic Links at a Program Level

Over the past few years, I was involved in the complete redesign of the horticulture diploma, a program consisting of approximately 20 courses. The study of horticulture is both

Example 3.2: Example of Content Designed for Online Learning

Modern Perspectives on Cats

While cats have been popular with humans for centuries, since the advent of the internet, cat-related content has grown exponentially.

> *There are two means of refuge from the miseries of life: music and cats.*
>
> *—Albert Schweitzer*

While amusing, modern feline-related web content has also advanced several debates related to the ethics of cat ownership and care.

Activity 2.2: Ethical Inventory

Take a few minutes to make an inventory of your own ethical positions on these topics. We will return to this at the end of the course to measure whether and how your perspectives have changed.

- Is it ethical to keep a pet cat indoors and prevent them from going outside?
- Is it ethical to declaw a pet cat?
- Is it ethical to spay or neuter a pet cat?

a science and an art. In fact, horticulture is often defined as the art or practice of garden cultivation and management. The study of this field involves a strong aesthetic component. When designing the online horticulture program, there was a need not only to design the course website aesthetics in a functional way but also to inspire students in the visual aspects of the subject matter.

With the program content in mind, I led the aesthetic development of the program, creating a malleable template and an approach for the courses. These courses include many images (how could this not be the case when discussing plants, flowers, and landscapes?), but consistent layouts kept the sites from feeling cluttered and presented images in thoughtful and effective ways. We also used icons and specific colours as identifiers for recurring types of activities to establish behavioural learning patterns. The consistency of these elements across courses within the program gave students a familiar, welcoming feeling with every course that they took.

Enrolments and student evaluations suggest that these efforts were a considerable success. Students loved the new look (and, of course, refreshed content), and enrolment nearly doubled the first year after relaunching and increased a further 30% the following year (Open Learning and Educational Support, 2021, "Continuing Education" section, and 2022, "Continuing Education" section). The aesthetics of the program helped to bring students "into" the world of horticulture as they learned. Aesthetics speak to more than just using a particular font or colour or making a course "look nice." Aesthetics comprise an active component of how students engage with the content and (hopefully) the transformative learning experience that they expect.

CYNTHIA EDEN

Maintaining Intentional Design: The Balancing Act of Course Maintenance

My role as an online learning quality assurance specialist involves reviewing and updating existing online courses with instructors who might or might not have been the course authors in the initial course development processes. It requires an ability to work with limited time and resources while balancing the need for existing quality standards to be upheld, the evolving needs of learners, and the need for course instructors to have agency.

The beauty and tension are that refining an existing course requires an understanding of how aesthetics contribute to quality course designs and quality learning experiences. As Parrish (2010, p. 204) outlines, "just as artworks can be designed to draw in readers or viewers to puzzle out a plot or to sympathize with characters, . . . or to have a vicarious somatic experience in watching a dance, learning experiences can be designed aesthetically to stimulate similar forms of engagement."

What I have found most helpful in working with course instructors to update existing courses is using the Quality Matters *Higher Education Rubric Standards, Sixth Edition* (Quality Matters, 2020), as an educational resource to begin a conversation on aesthetics and the quality standards that they serve. A common request from instructors is to update the images in courses that they have inherited. I often approach these conversations by creating spaces in which to discuss how image selection sets the stage for deeper learner engagement, deeper student learning, and learning-centred design. More specifically, we discuss how an image visually scaffolds core concepts, offers learners a space in which to engage with course content more deeply, and becomes the primary focus. From there, conversations on accessibility emerge. Part of the leadership that I provide is to guide the merging of aesthetics and accessibility standards, and I have found that the most effective approach is to begin by asking questions. Doing so allows me to understand better the instructor's aims and the context in which students will be able to understand and access the requested media. Although these conversation cycles take time, they result in a process of course revision that naturally situates aesthetics within quality standards for course design.

Conclusion

This chapter has brought together the perspectives of five women who work in distance education course development at a Canadian university. Our narratives call attention to the understated and undervalued area of aesthetic leadership in online education and demonstrate that visual design elements such as colour, font, and white space do not just make an online course pretty but also improve its overall quality. While acknowledging that we are writing from within a single institutional context, we nevertheless believe that our observations and experiences add value to the fields of instructional design and distance education. Campbell (2015, p. 235) notes that instructional designers exercise agency "quietly, invisibly, subversively, without status," yet as our narratives show our work affects teaching and learning across our institution. By highlighting the significance of our aesthetic design practices at course, program, and institutional levels, we reject the trivialization of feminized instructional design aesthetic work and call for its recognition as a form of leadership in the creation of high-quality online learning experiences.

References

Al-Mahmood, R. (2012). LMS encounters: Promises and realities: (e) Learning for sustainable futures? In M. Brown, M. Hartnett, & T. Stewart (Eds.), *Future challenges, sustainable futures: Proceedings of the Australian Society for Computers in Learning in Tertiary Education, Wellington 2012* (pp. 21–35). https://www.ascilite.org/conferences/Wellington12/2012/images/custom/al-mahmood%2c_reem_-_lms.pdf

Campbell, K. (2015). The feminist instructional designer: An autoethnography. In B. Hokanson, G. Clinton, & M. Tracey (Eds.), *The design of learning experience, educational communications and technology: Issues and innovations* (pp. 231–249). Springer. https://doi.org/10.1007/978-3-319-16504-2_16

Carroll, F., & Kop, R. (2016). Colouring the gaps in learning design: Aesthetics and the visual in learning. *International Journal of Distance Education Technologies, 14*(1), 92–103. https://doi.org/10.4018/IJDET.2016010106

David, A., & Glore, P. (2010). The impact of design and aesthetics on usability, credibility, and learning in an online environment. *Online Journal of Distance Learning Administration, 13*(4). https://ojdla.com/archive/winter134/david_glore134.pdf

Intentional Futures. (2016, April). *Instructional design in higher education: A report on the role, workflow, and experience of instructional designers*. https://uploads-ssl.webflow.com/61bb092a5c21437cb3a10798/624241a510e63d6f7eee6cd0_Instructional-Design-in-Higher-Education-Report.pdf

Open Learning and Educational Support. (2021). *2020 annual report*. University of Guelph. https://opened.uoguelph.ca/annual-report-2020

Open Learning and Educational Support. (2022). *2021 annual report*. University of Guelph. https://opened.uoguelph.ca/continuing-education-2021

Parrish, P. E. (2005). Embracing the aesthetics of instructional design. *Educational Technology, 45*(2), 16–25. https://www.jstor.org/stable/44429197

Parrish, P. (2010). Aesthetic decisions of instructors and instructional designers. In T. Volkan Yuzer & G. Kurubacak (Eds.), *Transformative learning and online education: Aesthetics, dimensions and concepts* (pp. 201–217). Information Science Reference.

Quality Matters. (2020). *QM higher education rubric standards, sixth edition*.

Rose, G. (2001). *Visual methodologies*. Sage.

Schor, N. (1987). *Reading in detail: Aesthetics and the feminine*. Methuen.

Shen, W., & Joseph, D. L. (2021). Gender and leadership: A criterion-focused review and research agenda. *Human Resource Management Review, 31*(2), 1–16. https://doi.org/10.1016/j.hrmr.2020.100765

Zippia. (2022, September 6). Instructional designer demographics and statistics in the US. https://www.zippia.com/instructional-designer-jobs/demographics/

4 Leading Distance Learning in Canadian Higher Education

The Three Cs

Jennifer Lock, Patti Dyjur, and Michelle Mitchell

Distance learning in Canada has quickly evolved and grown over the past three decades. This has been the result specifically of rapidly changing digital technologies and infrastructures, purposeful instructional design integrating innovative pedagogies (e.g., connectionism, game-based learning) in support of robust technology-enabled learning environments, and growing expectations by students and society (e.g., accessibility, flexibility) for quality online learning experiences. With the recent shift to emergency online learning, distance learning has experienced growth.

We are women who have various leadership roles in our higher education institutions. Over our personal and professional lives, we have been distance learners, instructors, and administrators who have not only observed but also engaged in this ever-changing field. We have played major roles in leading work that has affected teaching and learning in our institutions. As leaders, in leadership roles, we continue to be agents of change in both our institutions and the Canadian distance learning landscape.

We begin by positioning the current state of Canadian distance learning to provide context for the chapter. We reflect on our experiences by sharing our narratives as women leaders in distance learning. Each narrative provides an example of the implementation of the three Cs in leading distance learning: connection, communication, and catalyst. From the analysis of our stories, we identify and discuss key elements per each of the Cs and share recommendations for practice in leading distance learning today and for the future.

Distance Learning in Canadian Higher Education

Distance learning technologies have changed from paper-based correspondence to teleconference, to audio and video communication, and now to multimedia desktop delivery, including synchronous and asynchronous communication through high-speed connections (Ives & Walsh, 2021; Simonson et al., 2009). Along with the change in technologies, there has been growth in enrolment in distance learning, particularly with hybrid and online learning. In 2019, the Canadian Digital Learning Research Association reported that "online course registrations grew by around 10% between 2016–17 to 2017–18" (Johnson, 2019, p. 10). With the COVID-19 pandemic, the shift to online learning had a major impact on modes of course delivery. In 2021, findings showed that 93% of institutions expected growth in hybrid learning, and 78% expected growth in online learning (Johnson, 2021). About 90% of postsecondary institutions anticipated greater use of digital teaching materials, and 88% anticipated increased use of technology (Johnson, 2021). Supporting this ongoing evolution requires leadership attentive to the complexity in providing quality distance learning.

Narratives of Three Women Leaders

We use reflection-in-action and reflection-on-action (Schön, 1983) to examine and analyze our leadership practices. By engaging in reflection-in-action, we begin by sharing our experiences with distance learning, and then we examine our actions with regard to a salient moment in leading a distance learning initiative. In the discussion section, we use reflection-on-action to discuss the three Cs that emerge from our narratives and offer recommendations for practice.

Leading Technology Implementation

As a student and an instructor, I have engaged with various modes of distance learning. As a faculty member, I have developed and taught online courses and been involved in creating a student orientation for online learning from our institution using online videoconferencing software along with a learning management system (LMS). Reflecting on the changes in modes of delivery leads me to look to the future to explore the possibilities for immersive learning (augmented to immersive virtual reality) and other forms of technology-enabled learning.

A salient moment for me as a leader was in my former role as associate dean of teaching and learning, with two technology transition decisions. The first was when the university decided to transition to a new LMS. The second was when the faculty decided to change online videoconferencing software. At that time, the faculty was delivering a large online program. A technical issue presented a major challenge for course delivery and required a timely solution. Given our online program, this decision was a priority for the faculty, but it was not a priority for others. Without central support, we needed greater internal leadership and support. From decision to implementation, it required students and instructors to develop understanding of the new technology as well as confidence and competence in using it to support distance learning.

The leadership issues included the variety and nature of communication and the fostering of connection in support of stakeholders from the time of the announcement of the decision to the implementation of the technology for student learning. Careful and purposeful communication was needed to support everyone learning about the new technology and how to use it. For example, what I learned from the transition to the new LMS helped me to develop a plan to support students and instructors so that they had the needed knowledge and skills to use the technology at the start of the new semester. It was imperative to listen carefully and be responsive to the needs of instructors and students for such a transition to be successful and less stressful for end users.

Another characteristic supporting the leadership of these technology transitions was that of being a catalyst or an advocate of change. With the decision for new online videoconferencing software, advocating for a faculty solution was critical and challenging when the institution was not ready for it. Part of the advocacy required investigating possible solutions to see what would work within the current infrastructure and then promoting it for a faculty decision. Being a catalyst required not only helping to lead the decision process but also working with various groups (e.g., IT) to ensure that adequate and relevant educational development would meet the needs of all users.

Leading Educational Development

My first experience with distance education was in the 1990s. I registered for an independent study course consisting of modules with readings and written assignments delivered through the mail. Ten years later I took my first distance education course online. Since then I have instructed several higher education courses and facilitated hundreds of professional development sessions online. Recently, I also led a team of people responsible for supporting faculty members who teach online for a large university campus.

When the COVID-19 pandemic hit in March 2020, my team and I had little time to prepare for the sudden intense need to help instructors move their face-to-face courses online. We had about three days in person in which we held drop-in support sessions, created an emergency remote teaching website, scheduled online professional development and support sessions, and identified topics that required resource development. After that, we abruptly shifted to an online support model. As the team leader, I had to make many decisions quickly, such as which programs and initiatives to pause, where to spend our limited time and energy in order to support thousands of instructors, and how to meet the most pressing needs. It was a stressful, busy, productive, and memorable time.

I generally prefer a consultative leadership style in which I discuss decisions with my team. I learned that it was essential in the short term to adopt a more authoritative approach when circumstances required rapid decisions. During this time, we had to branch out quickly into topics and activities not previously within our portfolio, causing some uncertainty for team members. My role as leader was to encourage them to take up these challenges and to support them as they stretched into their new roles. I acted as a catalyst in supporting them to identify topics for new online workshops and develop their online facilitation and support skills.

Another significant aspect of leadership during that time was connection both with each other and with the campus community. Some activities required us to work together with a high degree of collaboration; it was also critical that we did not duplicate efforts. I scheduled frequent team meetings so that we could coordinate our efforts. In meetings, we shared what we had heard from the campus community about challenges that they were facing and areas where increased support was needed. I learned that sometimes my own team members needed flexibility and understanding as their home lives changed dramatically, such as home-schooling their children while working or losing their child care arrangements. We also connected through Microsoft Teams, keeping track of projects, consulting with each other, and sharing resources.

Most importantly, through this experience, I realized that I could trust my team to do high-quality work, even when there was no direct daily oversight of their activities. This allowed team members to have autonomy in their work. Since most of the team had specialized areas of expertise, they played informal leadership roles in those areas. This resulted in a stronger team.

Supporting Distance Learning

My first experience with distance education was as an instructor teaching in an online program in a college in rural Canada. After years teaching in the K–12 system, I was eager to move into adult education but had no frame of reference for online teaching. In the 16 years since then, I have completed two graduate degrees online and facilitated many online workshops, and currently I lead a team responsible for providing professional development, curriculum development, and instructional design within my distance education institution.

My institution uses a Supported Distance Learning (SDL) model, which involves online instruction in a supportive environment, also offered entirely by distance education. When the COVID-19 pandemic began, there was little change in terms of program and course delivery. Students were already taking their courses online, and many faculty members worked from a home office, so there was little notable change. Because the college had campuses in remote communities that provided technology and internet connectivity to students attending their online classes, it became a challenge for some students to access their online courses. This meant figuring out how to provide internet access when campus doors were closed to the college community. This hurdle was overcome by offering "drive-up" internet access by which students could drive to the parking lot of any campus to access their synchronous classes or course content. In rare instances, course materials were downloaded to external drives and sent to students who had no means to access internet connectivity.

Many staff who worked on campus found the transition to working from home difficult. My team, also dispersed, had to find creative ways to remain connected with peers and to ensure that they were adequately supported so that in turn they could support their students. This was a noteworthy moment for me, the importance of maintaining connections with our faculty members so that they were supported and able to support their students. Weekly virtual coffee breaks were scheduled in an effort to maintain personal connections.

My team had been in the process of transitioning to a new LMS. Upon reflection, though the transition occurred fairly smoothly from a technical perspective, it added to the anxiety of faculty members and students during an already stressful time. The synchronous teaching platform also had to change, which caused further stress for faculty members and students. Because faculty members were experienced online educators, we were able to move forward positively with minimal disruption to students.

My leadership style is centred on connections. When I was a high school teacher, relationships with my peers and students were a priority, and they remain a priority for me as a leader in higher education. During the pandemic, finding ways to maintain connections with my team and the broader college community was essential and had to be strategic. I found myself in constant meetings and had little time to work on new initiatives. Although it was challenging at times, I learned many lessons that have since become part of my post-pandemic practice and support greater connections among all members of the college community.

Discussion and Recommendations for Practice

Each narrative above provides an example of the integral role and the interweaving of the three Cs needed in leading distance education: connection, communication, and catalyst. Underpinning these three Cs is flexibility. As leaders, we need to be flexible in our practice and create and support flexibility in how we work with various stakeholders.

Connection

Evident from each narrative above is the intentional building and sustaining of relationships that support the work of distance education. Intentionality is critical in fostering connections with various stakeholders and forging relationships with each other within the campus community. Developing relationships requires getting to know the people with whom we work on such initiatives. Relationship building requires empathy for and understanding of our colleagues and their circumstances and the needs of the campus community. Such work requires a sustained approach and a commitment to soliciting other people's perspectives and feedback.

As leaders, it is important that we create and foster connections with colleagues given their various roles and expertise as well as with others within the institution given the scope of the initiatives. The nature of the connections might be two people working together for a limited time or large groups working together for a sustained period. The length and vitality of the connection are grounded in a reciprocal relationship. As leaders, we acknowledge a continuum of connection in which one end might have limited but timely interactions with people and at the other end there are prolonged and sustained relationships. The nature of these connections is continuous but not constant over time based on the needs of the work and the people involved.

Our first recommendation for practice is the commitment to develop and foster relationships with various stakeholders when leading distance learning initiatives. Identifying and fostering connections and developing relationships require finding time and being open to listening carefully to the needs in order to support the work moving forward.

Communication

Ongoing communication is critical in leading distance learning initiatives. It is important for everyone on the team to know the expectations and goals. Effective communication plays a critical role in the development of trust, connection, and collaboration. As leaders, we need to develop trust among members of the team as well as trust the team in doing the work. When leading initiatives, there is a high degree of collaboration. What becomes imperative is that the collaboration occurs without duplication. As leaders, we need to know who has the expertise and skills so that we can consult with them, ask them questions, and/or invite them to lead particular components of the work. We need to understand what people are working on and how we can best support them in their work.

Communication is critical to the transparency of leadership. Through our selected communication channels, we strive to be open about our practice as well as demonstrate the integrity of our leadership. We use communication to inform and engage colleagues and stakeholders. When managing change, "communicating directly about what you know and what you do not know and how it affects employees shows your transparent nature and that you are also sharing the same feelings of uncertainty" (Leekang, 2020, p. 55).

Our second recommendation for practice is that leaders require humility and a strong sense of trust in the people with whom they work each day. Leading initiatives can be stressful and challenging. As leaders, we need to listen carefully and communicate effectively to foster transparency and trust.

Catalyst

Leaders play an important role in sparking initiatives to create change. In some cases, we created the conditions for change to occur; in others, we led the process of change. Evident from our experience is the need to recognize the expertise of various people in their roles and of the teams and create opportunities for them to lead the process of change. As noted in their study of online learning, Ives and Walsh (2021, p. 37) stated that "leaders at all levels must facilitate the conditions for change by enabling conversations throughout the institution about the value of online teaching and learning. Those with knowledge, skills, and competencies in distance education and experience in online learning are essential to effective implementation." As catalysts of change, we need to encourage the agency and autonomy of others and to support them as leaders in their work.

Our third recommendation for practice is to act as a catalyst to develop the expertise and skills of others on the team, thereby empowering them. Leadership is not a solo task. By creating the conditions that empower others to take on tasks and develop their leadership skills, they can contribute to leading the process of change.

Conclusion

Reflecting on our leadership, we acknowledge and appreciate the importance and the interconnectedness of the three Cs—connection, communication, and catalyst—when leading the process of change. With the steady increase in hybrid and online learning in Canadian higher education, leaders should also be mindful of the need for flexibility because of rapid change. Through our narratives, we have highlighted different scenarios in which the three Cs were effective leadership strategies in distance education. Our recommendations for practice involve a commitment to develop and foster relationships, communicate effectively, and act as a catalyst to empower your team, and they should guide others in leadership roles in distance learning in higher education.

References

Ives, C., & Walsh, P. (2021). Perspectives of Canadian distance educators on the move to online learning. *Canadian Journal of Higher Education, 51*(1), 28–40. https://journals.sfu.ca/cjhe/index.php/cjhe/article/view/188971

Johnson, N. (2019). *Tracking online and distance education in Canadian universities and colleges: National survey of online and digital learning 2019 national report*. Canadian Digital Learning Research Association. http://www.cdlra-acrfl.ca/wp-content/uploads/2020/07/2019_national_en.pdf

Johnson, N. (2021). *2021 national report: Lessons from the COVID-19 pandemic*. Canadian Digital Learning Research Association. http://www.cdlra-acrfl.ca/wp-content/uploads/2022/05/2021_national_report_en.pdf

Leekang, M. (2020). Keeping the machine and culture in sync: Creative management of technology-enhanced teams. In J. Vivolo (Ed.), *Managing online learning: The life-cycle of successful programs* (pp. 44–55). Routledge.

Schön, D. A. (1983). *The reflective practitioner: How professionals think in action*. Basic Books.

Simonson, M., Smaldino, S., Albright, M., & Zvacek, S. (2009). *Teaching and learning at a distance: Foundations of distance education* (4th ed.). Pearson.

5 Leadership in Distance Education

Vision Is Vital

Kim Myrick and Denise Stockley

Distance education in Canadian higher education emerged as a formal option in the second half of the 20th century. University leadership at the time often positioned distance education as an extension service, meaning that it was recognized largely as something outside the main structure of academic units, instructors, and on-campus learning. With a focus on technology, one option was to establish separate units or departments responsible for the design, development, and delivery of credit courses and degree programs via distance education. A distance education unit engaged or contracted instructors to design and develop courses and programs, and it made offerings to students through educational technologies. Because of this distinct separation, instructors and students in distance education were displaced from the traditional university teaching and learning experience.

Now, in the 21st century, Canadian universities have had to shift at times to being virtual campuses, particularly in times of crisis or disruption, when everyone involved in the learning process has had to participate remotely and thus adapt to approaches of distance education. Centres for teaching and learning (CTLs) have assumed a lead role to support sudden transitions between traditional on-campus classes and remote learning. This has been largely because of their functions in supporting online learning and on-campus courses and the teaching of faculty and instructional staff. These functions are separate within CTLs, with online learning evolving from distance education as a function distinct from on-campus education. However, shifts between modes of delivery are blurring the functions of CTLs and the roles of their instructional designers, educational developers, and technology and multimedia experts.

Reflecting on our own role as women leaders in the field of higher education, in particular distance education and CTLs, we recognize that there have been significant changes in our 30-plus years in the field. When we started in the field, we operated in a space where the traditional correspondence models of distance education were prevalent, and leadership was dominated by men. However, as the field shifted to more online learning offered through CTLs, women-oriented leadership began to prevail at our institutions.

Many CTLs in Canada today are led by women able to leverage talent quickly to develop creative solutions, especially in disruptive and unstable environments. A crisis is a strong driver of creativity, innovation, and change (Zenger & Folkman, 2020). Women leaders are a driving force behind this creativity. The leadership style of women has been described as creative, democratic, caring, ethical, and collaborative (Acker, 2012; Kloot, 2004; Offermann & Foley, 2020). These characteristics have empowered effective and sustainable innovation and will be vital in the future of distance education. The *Harvard Business Review* argued that women are more effective leaders in times of crisis because of their ability to pivot, build relationships, and communicate while developing new skills (Zenger & Folkman, 2020). These characteristics and skills are needed at universities in new environments in which distance education merges with the broader function of teaching and learning.

With movement between delivery models of education, we see that the lines have shifted dramatically, and past differences between learning environments have become blurred. Distance education is more relevant to teaching and learning, and there is thus an opportunity to embrace these times and the new-found relevance and place of distance education in higher education.

A strong institutional vision is vital to shift the position of distance education within a university. We believe that having a clear vision is critical for people to continue to engage with teaching and learning.

As women leaders in teaching and learning in higher education, we take a systems approach to institutional vision by applying six essential elements of vision: performance, purpose, people, place, product, and period (of time). Research by Myrick and Kelloway (2018) suggests that these "six Ps" lead to a vision that will allow universities to effectively integrate distance education into the orthodox system of academic offerings.

In this chapter, we apply the six Ps as a conceptual framework to changes within distance education. We draw from our research in system approaches and leadership, our experience in teaching and learning, as well as our common knowledge of one Canadian CTL that evolved from a distance education unit with a legacy of leadership in the field. We share this knowledge through earlier research involving its history as a distance education unit and leadership experience through its transition to a CTL (Stockley, 2002, 2004). The CTL began as a distance education unit in the late 1960s and was responsible for the design, development, and delivery of credit courses and degree programs via distance learning. As a CTL, it has been recognized internationally for its approach to supporting teaching and learning.

By taking this approach, we recognize that the work of distance education is not isolated within the institution. Using the six Ps of vision, we articulate the key elements of repositioning distance education from being on the periphery to having a more integrated role in teaching and learning and how this shift has allowed for a smoother transition to remote learning during times of disruption. The six Ps of vision are evolving for distance education from a focus on it as an extension service of a university to an integration into the teaching and learning function of higher education. CTLs are the conduit for this integration. Articulating this evolution in this manner is a meaningful contribution to a leadership vision for the future of distance education in higher education.

Performance

The first P is how an institution is seen to exist in terms of its level of performance. A vision conveys an ideal state of performance, such as portraying an institution as being a leader in its industry or sector now and in the future. A traditional distance education unit has a legacy of leadership providing students with flexibility in time and location to complete courses and programs at a distance. This leadership has been separate from that of academic disciplines, and thus instructors and students have been outside the traditional university teaching and learning experience.

CTLs evolved distance education to deliver online courses to a broader range of students (online and on campus). However, students learning at a distance have continued to receive the same experience of distance education, and they can pay an extra fee to study at a distance. Universities do not deliver the experience of the greater student population in terms of on-campus supports and services. In this way, universities are not performing at the highest level.

Performance is often highlighted during times of crisis that require a shift to remote instruction. On-campus students deprived of what they have known as the "university experience" can question paying full tuition for what is perceived as a diminished experience. This can have an impact on university enrolment. The challenge is not just to deliver classes remotely but also to deliver an experience that has significant value, thereby attracting and retaining students.

During times of disruption or crisis, we have led our teams to act as first responders for the continuation of effective teaching and student success. Our role as women leaders has been to ensure a high level of performance by nurturing instructor-student relationships and ensuring that all voices have been heard and acted upon as appropriate. A key priority has been to advise on planning for remote courses and to connect instructors to CTLs' support services for instructional and technological solutions. We have initiated new support services, assigning senior instructional designers and educational developers to academic units. We have also collaborated with non-academic units to adjust on-campus services for online delivery.

As women leaders, we see that our performance ensures the successful future of distance education programs. Leading organizations with diverse team members, we leverage individuals' talents and are more likely to succeed (Offermann & Foley, 2020). The ability to develop creative solutions, multitask, and work collaboratively is critical to delivering higher-quality programs and services.

Purpose

The second P is why an institution exists in terms of its operational focus (e.g., to develop, deliver, or support a program or service). A vision states a purpose to give direction on what an institution can do to achieve a desired performance. Purpose guides decisions and actions to achieve outcomes intended to enhance performance.

Student participation in university courses and programs and faculty-student interactions are aspects of a university that define its purpose. In traditional distance education, student participation and interaction with other students and faculty are limited. Since these interactions operate in a different space, faculty members and students relate differently to the purpose of a university.

CTLs have evolved over time to contribute more to the mission of educators and the success of students. Through continuous adaptation to the academic community and its needs, our core activities have grown to include not only online course/program development and delivery but also administration of the university's learning management system, use of educational media and technologies in classrooms, and professional development programming and training for educators.

We have observed that the reasons a university exists operate in different spaces for all educators, staff, and students during times of crisis or change, displacing a university's purpose. Universities face seismic shifts in how they do things when they shift to fully remote instruction. All faculty members, students, and staff alike are disrupted in their sense of why their universities exist.

As leaders of teaching and learning, we have found ourselves at the centre of disruption. We have recognized the gap in the teaching and learning experience at a distance and been forced to fill it. We have organized staff immediately to create an unprecedented number of resources and webinars on remote learning, communication, student support, community building, feedback, and so on.

Universities benefit when they are seen as leaders in innovation. Innovation is needed to grow and develop the purpose of universities in new directions at a distance. Women have proven to be effective leaders in this area through times of disruption and crisis. As the field of distance education changes, we feel well positioned to lead innovation to re-establish the purpose of our institutions.

People

The third P refers to the who of an institution, both internal and external stakeholders. A vision references key stakeholders who contribute to or benefit from the purpose of an institution. References to stakeholders can help them to identify with an institution and influence them to interact in a purposeful manner.

The primary stakeholders of a university are its students and faculty members, detached from the physical environment and the greater institution in distance education. Instructors have a responsibility outside their academic units and programs, implying a separation between their on-campus teaching and their teaching at a distance. Students interact with the CTL and can be classified as a group of "other" students under an extension service.

During times of instructional disruption or crisis, all students and faculty members can be compelled to teach and learn at a distance with no sense of how to transition and engage with each other. They have no time or plan to detach from one environment and immerse themselves in another. As caring, supportive leaders, we have kicked into action during these times to provide resources and supports critical for students stressed by disruptions to how they learn and for faculty and staff distraught from unknown and unfamiliar teaching methods and tools.

We have recognized the importance of developing strong relationships not only in times of disruption but also in distance education. As women leaders, we have seen the need to provide warm and comforting support to remote instructors and students, alone and displaced from their environments and interactions. This human connection is an ethical and caring solution that provides people with a sense of unity (Kloot, 2004). As a result, it is important to the ongoing offering of distance education.

Place

The fourth P is where an institution exists (i.e., in which environments, e.g., geographic, workplace, infrastructural, or technological). Stakeholders receive direction on the environments in which they perform and fulfill their purpose.

Distance education is delivered through various technologies. They provide instructors and students with a sense of place unique from the geographic location of a physical campus. The traditional services and supports are not replicated for distance students or instructors.

A major disruption to instruction significantly affects a university's sense of place as defined by geographic location. Creating a sense of place is a challenge with everyone learning in different locations. Moreover, distinguishing a unique sense of place within a common virtual space with other universities requires significant investments in service delivery.

As women leaders, we have fostered a sense of community at a distance through online forums, webinars, and gatherings of instructors and students, providing a sense of place to come together. We have supported instructors to develop online spaces and discussions for students in courses. We have also provided the online ability and support to bring student life services to students. Overall, we have been creative with the resources that we have available.

Product

The fifth P is the what of an institution, what it develops, delivers, or supports. This information can differentiate an institution from similar institutions.

A major product of a university is its teaching and learning experience for faculty members and students. The delivery of this product through technology alters the format of the content and the learning experience since it is not delivered in the same way by instructors or experienced in the same way by students.

Since universities' main "product" offerings are courses and programs as well as faculty-student interactions, they are largely adapted during times of disruption or crisis when in-person classes can be cancelled and moved to remote environments. With different time zones and technologies for students, universities need creative and flexible options for faculty teaching and for students to complete programs remotely. Universities have had to invest in technologies and ways to make remote teaching as accessible as possible.

CTLs have evolved to support university product offerings with a growing number of campus students taking online courses, an increasing demand for educational technology in classrooms and online teaching, and an emerging role in enhanced programming and pedagogical support for academic units and educators. Overall, CTLs are now more collaborative partners and play a central role in the academic community for teaching and learning excellence.

Additionally, CTLs have engaged with stakeholders in research through collaboration with faculty members, facilitating engagement in the scholarship of teaching and learning. Staff expertise in areas of curriculum and assessment development, educator and instructional development, and educational technology application and integration supports faculty research on new approaches to teaching and learning for dissemination to internal and external academic communities. Staff have collaborated on topics related to teaching with technology, online and alternative assessments, active learning, blended learning, academic integrity, and more recently hybrid learning.

As universities develop more CTL services to enhance their "products," women leaders can ensure that these services are reflective of the needs of both educators and learners at a distance. Through periods of disruption and crisis, we have been able to grow and adapt the services of our CTLs that support the greater teaching and learning product of the university and integrate it into distance education.

Period (of Time)

The sixth P is when an institution realizes its vision, orienting people in time to achieve that vision. Reference to time might be intended to inspire people in the institution. People are oriented to a time frame in order to fulfill their purpose and achieve the desired performance.

In distance education, students have always had the flexibility to learn in a self-directed schedule rather than a set schedule of classes. Instructors follow a schedule of course delivery but have flexibility in when and how they interact with students. During times of disruption, instructors and students continue to participate in education on a semester basis. However, there are greater expectations that students learn on a self-directed schedule rather than a set class schedule. There are also greater expectations that instructors will support students and allow flexibility in course assignments and when and how they interact with students.

CTLs adapt quickly to times of disruption, and the resilience and creativity of women leaders help to meet the challenges of flexibility and continued interaction. It has been argued that women leaders are preferred in times of change (Offermann & Foley, 2020), and this was evident in how well women leaders adapted during sudden instructional disruption as a result of the COVID-19 pandemic (Zenger & Folkman, 2020). These characteristics allow us to realize a vision in both the short term and the long term.

An Institutional Vision for the Future of Distance Education

CTLs have evolved from or with distance education in higher education. The response of CTLs to the needs of their academic communities during a crisis has been such that nimble cross-functional collaborations can provide an integrated approach to addressing the challenges of a fully remote or virtual university environment. By leveraging the resources and capabilities of a CTL, staff can be brought together to collaborate across the university and support academic units, faculty members, and students in transitioning into distance education.

An integrated and aligned vision is vital within postsecondary environments for CTLs and distance education. We can no longer separate distance education or online learning within or from the function of teaching and learning at a university. This vision is critical for the advancement of teaching and learning within higher education, and using the six Ps creates a path toward alignment.

We will continue to require a vision of innovation. Indeed, during times of disruption or crisis, universities are naturally focused on the short term. However, institutions that focus on the long term and a clear vision will experience renewed energy for new ideas as individuals feel inspired to collaborate in securing their future. At our institutions, we advocate to ensure that on-campus, online, and distance education come closer together, that their separation pragmatically and structurally does not hamper student learning.

As women leaders experienced in the field, we hope that we have demonstrated through our approach that the vision of distance education needs to be reimagined since the field has evolved. The six Ps help us to articulate the vision by identifying performance, purpose, people, place, product, and period (of time) required by our responses to disruption and crisis. Otherwise, we might run the risk of stagnating or shifting back to old ways.

References

Acker, S. (2012). Chairing and caring: Gendered dimensions of leadership in academe. *Gender and Education, 24*(4), 411–428. https://doi.org/10.1080/09540253.2011.628927

Kloot, L. (2004). Women and leadership in universities: A case study of women academic managers. *International Journal of Public Sector Management, 17*(6), 470–485. https://doi.org/10.1108/09513550410554760

Myrick, K., & Kelloway, E. K. (2018). Reconceptualizing organizational vision at the intersection of leadership and strategic management. Academy of Management Annual Meeting *Proceedings, 2018*(1). https://journals.aom.org/doi/10.5465/AMBPP.2018.15054abstract

Offermann, L. R., & Foley, K. (2020). Is there a female leadership advantage? In L. R. Offermann & K. Foley (Eds.), *Oxford Research Encyclopedia of Business and Management*. Oxford University Press. https://doi.org/10.1093/acrefore/9780190224851.013.61

Stockley, D. (2002). *Canadian strategic planning, infrastructure, and professional development for technological innovation in post-secondary education*. [Unpublished doctoral dissertation]. Simon Fraser University.

Stockley, D. (2004). Strategic planning for technological innovation in Canadian post-secondary education. *Canadian Journal of Learning Technology, 30*(2), 113–124. https://doi.org/10.21432/T2002R

Zenger, J., & Folkman, J. (2020, December 30). Research: Women are better leaders during a crisis. *Harvard Business Review*. https://hbr.org/2020/12/research-women-are-better-leaders-during-a-crisis

6 Building Alternative Futures

Co-Creating an Online Asynchronous Degree Program for Early Childhood Educators

Sherry L. Rose and Kim Stewart

In this chapter, we explore the implementation of the University of New Brunswick (UNB) Bachelor of Education in Early Childhood Education (BEd in ECE) online asynchronous degree for early childhood educators (ECEs). Completion of the degree awards a New Brunswick Teacher's Certificate 4. In designing this degree, we thought and acted with Sara Ahmed's (2021, p. xi) question in mind: "How to open universities up, to dismantle existing structures, [to] build alternative futures?" As program designers and first-generation university graduates, we embrace our leadership responsibilities. We explore navigating leadership responses to the tensions that arise as we design and implement an online degree. What do we need to challenge in the name of distance education? We draw from lessons learned and critical insights to make practical recommendations to current and future leaders in the field of distance education.

Designing a degree is both exciting and challenging. Initially, we designed a four-year degree that had to be redesigned to five years and then to a two-plus-two degree by government request. It is important to contextualize this degree initiative with prior government-university partnerships aimed at supporting ECEs. As school leaders in 2007, we were seconded to the Early Childhood Research Team, co-writing a New Brunswick Curriculum Framework for Early Learning and Child Care—Anglophone (2008) and seven support documents. These documents were intentionally values based, grounded in the belief that early education is a space of social justice and transformation disrupting the hegemony of developmentalism, racism, classism, ableism, and sexism.

The creation of a values-based curriculum framework allowed room for contextualized and relational co-learning of ECEs and children, shaped by places, diversities, and the undoing of colonial histories. Our educational leadership is grounded in values of co-authorship, co-supervision, co-teaching, collaborative practices, and the teaming processes and strategies that enact a commitment to forge communal solutions and possibilities through uncomfortable truths (Braidotti, 2022). We embedded these values in the degree. As educational leaders, we co-created a program of professional learning for ECEs in New Brunswick. During development of this program, we challenged systemic inequities between schoolteachers and ECEs, bringing together professionals who supported children, including those in public schools, ECE centres, and non-profit organizations for book studies, research projects, and conferences. This bridging between ECEs in child care, family services, and public schooling is also modelled in the degree.

Designing the Degree: Building Alternative Futures

In March 2020, the COVID-19 lockdown made visible the lived inequities of many children and their families. We experienced this inequity first hand when our UNB Children's Centre, which had operated for 43 years, was forced to close, leaving 35 families without child care and five educators without employment. Low pay, inadequate basic and continuing education, financial instability, loss of income, and high turnover have long been cruel features of ECEs' teaching experience. The designations of "child-care workers," "registered ECEs," and "teachers" reiterate hierarchies restricting our capacity to resolve educational inequities. Researchers have found that ECEs with a bachelor's degree are more likely to remain in the profession (Akbari & McCuaig, 2014; Anderson et al., 2020; McLachlan, 2011; Urban et al., 2011, as cited in Berger et al., 2020). However, a bachelor's degree insufficiently addresses the pay and work inequities that exist across Canadian educational landscapes. There is a pressing need to think deeply about pay equity and the provision of educational opportunities across inequitable worlds (Butler, 2022) to support children, families, and ECEs.

Within this complex landscape, we started an online asynchronous two-plus-two degree for ECEs, teaching our first cohort during the COVID-19 lockdown. To date, all degree applicants except two have been people who identify as women, non-binary, or trans persons. Many need to maintain an income to support children or care for extended family members. We intentionally designed an asynchronous degree to serve ECEs who cannot or do not want to participate in face-to-face teaching (Holmberg, 2003). As a social justice action, this degree opens a pathway for ECEs to enter or re-enter the university house (Ahmed, 2021), for many have always dreamed of obtaining a degree. It is thrilling to share that in 2025 we had 342 applicants, and in September 2025, 208 early childhood educators will be enrolled in the program. By fall 2025, we will have graduated 187 early childhood educators.

Our degree process began with an Atlantic Canada feasibility study funded by the Margaret and Wallace McCain

Family Foundation and the Jimmy Pratt Family Foundation and conducted by an ECE community partner, Lynda Homer (2013). Our dean, Dr. Ann Sherman, formed a committee of five ECEs to design the degree and select the courses. Each of us had extensive leadership experiences in school systems, professional learning communities, curriculum development, and initiating and participating in action research projects. Several factors shaped the design of the degree. Our aim was to minimize the cost of tuition in recognition of the level of pay that ECEs receive. The duration of the degree was determined by three factors: expectations of the government of a two-plus-two degree, expectations of the Maritime Provinces Higher Education Commission, and provision of required credits, including a nine-week practicum determined by New Brunswick Teacher Certification. We split a typical university term so that students could take two courses simultaneously, completing four courses in the term and fulfilling full-time student status. This made achieving a degree while working possible and allowed ECEs to access student loans.

In the early stages of degree planning, the leadership of Dr. Sherman was significant. She met with the certification branch to determine which level of certification ECE graduates would obtain. After several meetings, and varied reiterations of the degree, the Office of Teacher Certification with the New Brunswick Department of Education and Early Childhood Development and the UNB Faculty of Education signed an agreement confirming that graduates from the BEd program in ECE would be awarded a New Brunswick Teacher's Certification 4, qualifying them to teach in K–3 classrooms. Trusting the credibility of a distance education degree was a challenge for many as they questioned whether provincial certification bodies would recognize our online degree. Over time, this challenge dissipated as provincial certification was achieved.

Completing the program structure, we needed to determine the courses. The first factor was to meet the New Brunswick Teacher Certification requirements. Maintaining our role as pedagogical leaders (Beaudoin, 2003), we understood the need for additional literacy courses in our provincial context, so we created the following courses: Children's Literature, Singing, Poetry, and Performance; Multi-Modal Literacies in Early Childhood, Home, and School Literacies; and Digital Literacies in the Early Years to expand the one required literacy course, Literacy Learning in the Early Years. Recognizing that most of our learners would identify as women, non-binary, or trans persons charged with caring for and educating a diversity of children and families, we knew that a course about feminist theories was essential.

Engaging ECEs with early childhood research, we created the course Research in Early Childhood Studies. Challenging the "schoolification" (OECD, 2006) of the early years, the downward push of academic learning, we added the following courses: Observation and Pedagogical Documentation and Project Approach in the Early Years and Problem Solving with Young Children. Responding to the Truth and Reconciliation Commission (2015), we created an Indigenous Education course to be taught by an Indigenous scholar. Additionally, we led the team of instructors to include Indigenous scholars, artists, historians, activists, and writers in every course. Once the courses were selected, our program design team dissolved, and we were left to lead the design of course content.

Course Curricula

Our course curricula recognized that we are all beings of overlapping multiple worlds (Butler, 2022) in which many sexualized, racialized, and naturalized others do not benefit from the privilege and entitlement that support the flourishing of the few

(Braidotti, 2022). Course assignments needed to be contextualized, informed by many world views, and transformative for those learning together, adults and children, the human and more than human, and ECEs forging learning communities online. This ethic seems to be imperative in a current climate in which we witness the banning of books authored by BIPOC and LGBTQIA2S+ authors, resistance to non-white histories, challenges to anti-racist, anti-bias education, the overturning of *Roe v. Wade*, and the destruction of our shared planet. We recognize that educators can be positioned in a precarious role when encouraged to think and teach with a critical social justice ethic.

Within such a precarious climate of uneven childhoods and uneven worlds (Duhn et al., 2020), it becomes critical to support the responsibilities for living, teaching, and learning together by foregrounding education as a commitment to equity, well-being, and social justice. Likewise, the call for cross-disciplinary education that cultivates ECEs' intellectual curiosity, while deepening their engagement with the responsibilities of living, teaching, and learning in an increasingly complex, endangered, and inequitable world (Berger et al., 2020), reinforces the continual need to curate course content that foregrounds "own voice texts" amplifying positive representations of diversity (Robertson, 2022). As Ahmed (2021, p. 104) writes, a "syllabus can tell you who is being valued, what is valued, who comes first, who has priority." Course content needs to value the scholarship of diverse voices, including critical early childhood researchers, Indigenous scholars, class-conscious pedagogues, critical disability activists, radical and ecological feminists, anti-racists, and queer/trans scholars.

Pedagogical Practices

As leaders developing the online degree, we were committed to pedagogical practices that foreground the complexities of diverse world views intentionally to disrupt the hegemony of white Western content. Committed to education as social justice, we believe that learning needs to confront colonialism, white privilege, ableism, and classism, and we question many of our embodied educational practices and beliefs. Unlearning (Cochran-Smith, 2003), questioning long-held ideas, beliefs, and practices, and learning are entangled, complex, heart-and-soul processes. In a distance education online learning community, well-being needs to be foregrounded and articulated aloud frequently (in the syllabus, during Microsoft Teams meetings, and in responding to individual ECEs' emails and texts). We need to recognize that learners' contexts are parts of their educational spaces (Gibson 1998, cited in Gunawardena, 2013). Learners know their contextual responsibilities better than instructors do. Learners are trusted: we do not request doctors' slips; we understand that they might have to triage their course and life/relational responsibilities. We trust them to take the time that they need to read, dialogue, and construct learning artifacts in modes of their choice.

Initially, we eliminated due dates, recognizing that learners could set their own dates in response to life's demands, but this became an oppressive experience for some learners and instructors. We provided flexible due dates as guides, accepting assignments upon completion. We realized that university processes of extensions and grade change forms could maximize temporal flexibility. In our efforts to be ethically responsive to a wide range of subjectivities, we recognize that there are learners and learning communities that might benefit from a hybrid degree—those who experience inequitable internet access or those who might benefit from a balance of face-to-face human connection in combination with online learning choices. This can be especially true for international and Indigenous students embedded in a cultural context that cannot be understood by instructors (Gunawardena, 2013). However, as Gunawardena

(2013) and Gunawardena and colleagues (2006) theorize, a wisdom community instructional design model can amplify cultural inclusivity that values the diversities that each learner brings to the course content.

As in wisdom communities, in education there are no single answers but a need to consider multiple perspectives, solve problems, negotiate meaning, and socially construct knowledge within the emerging culture of each online learning community. We recognize that within each course, each cohort, a unique learning culture is unfolding as learners dialogue, negotiate meanings and perspectives, share contextual experiences, and co-construct knowledge. The online space creates a learning community in which each learner's voice is heard or read, amplifying diverse perspectives and experiences (Gunawardena, 2013). Our commitments are to support learning while keeping the institutional doors open to many who might have been marginalized by prior educational experiences or gendered life demands.

As Morrison (2020) states, there is a need for "a teaching praxis rooted in universal design—a teaching focused on a much broader kind of accessibility and inclusion for all rather than accommodations for individuals." This means that course descriptions, processes, contents, and assignments are modified prior to and during the online course in response to learners. As leaders, meeting with a team of instructors, we intentionally present alternative perspectives, challenging the hegemonic constructions of learners and learning, striving to enact online pedagogies and a focus on social justice. We also do this intellectual, affective, and reflective labour for each other, disrupting embodied dominant discourses such as the deficit, individualizing constructions of learners, and loosening rigid practices. Pedagogies and assessment practices are anchored in learning the strengths and passions of each learner. Assessment practices are formative, providing learners with specific conversational comments, questions, and suggestions that feed forward into learning, just as we hope that ECEs will enact with children.

As leaders of this degree, we commit ourselves to sharing course contents, assignments, the learning management course shell, and each syllabus as we co-design or co-teach with new instructors. In turn, instructors adapt and share additions or modifications to courses. We model and encourage co-teaching to support well-being since we recognize that the provision of individualized feedback to classes of 30 or 60 ECEs is a necessary but demanding part of teaching online (Holmberg, 2003). In designing the online course content, we invited ECEs to choose from a list of activities that might have the same learning goals as we enact and cultivate a social obligation to call in and support each other (Gunawardena, 2013) through sacred problem solving (Richardson, 1997). Morrison (2022) invites online instructors to share responsibility for course curricula with learners. Shared responsibility frees instructors to engage more in meaning making with learners through social connection, individualized feedback, and problem solving. Reflecting on collective meaning making between learners and instructors, and attempting more co-construction of course content, we created two modest discussion areas within the course shell, one where learners could choose to contribute content and another where they could share completed assignments with each other, providing another feedback loop for them. We recognize that there is room for growth here.

Dis-Ease and Discomfort

So much of what we have achieved conflicts with university timelines, grading policies, and workload responsibilities. As women faculty members, we struggle and often feel silenced in our attempts to discuss the complexities and unsupported commitments beyond our own team. Raising questions to university leaders and in faculty meetings, we experienced dis-ease and discomfort since our words seemed to be inadequate. With the failure of our words, we are left with difficult lived experiences, such as an email sent to our dean questioning the abuse of two new faculty members, defences of intellectual freedom rather than discussions of online pedagogies, and a challenge to the provision of our cell phone numbers on course syllabi for immediate responses to students' course and assignment questions. Other struggles included answering questions directed at who is qualified to teach in this online degree and addressing faculty resistance to discussing workload using traditional criteria (e.g., number of students served, number of programs, development of new course content, consideration of face-to-face and online courses, and so on).

We hoped for a critical discussion of how class size might be unique to various programs and how the absence of transparent university budgeting constructs walls against difficult collaborative conversations in which we might collectively "stay with the trouble" (Haraway, 2016) to imagine universities otherwise. Within these moments, the implications of our gender and classed histories are most felt, provoking a retreat, back to our team. Retreating does little to trouble the inequities of university policies, practices, and gendered inequalities of teaching and learning in online spaces. How can we engage in conversations that open doors within this institution rather than shaming, silencing, and individualizing uncomfortable truths?

Lessons Learned and Critical Insights

We recommend that degree initiatives that respond to societal needs and the goals of women and children need to be supported through recognition that centres our collective well-being (Morrison, 2022) while dismantling existing structures or modifying existing sets of arrangements (Ahmed, 2021) to invite many others through the university doors. Lessons learned in designing and implementing an online asynchronous degree might support both online designs and pedagogies as well as opening the doors of the university to many more people by creating spaces for sacred problem solving to forge communal solutions and possibilities through uncomfortable truths across programs. Such a space could focus on learning about online pedagogies and how learners and instructors co-construct online wisdom communities.

Prioritize faculty learning about the uniqueness of each online program and reflect on how created structures and processes unique to the program might be necessary to support the learning of specific communities of learners. Examine how leaders and colleagues call in and support every faculty member. Examine processes to hear the diverse voices and perspectives of instructors and learners in online programs. Can universities invest in supporting new program initiatives with university funding rather than deans and faculty members having to seek funding? Explore how we might support the early days of intellectual, affective, and reflective labours of designing and implementing an online degree especially for new faculty members. Consider university practices, such as graduation, which might need to change in support and recognition so that learners who choose online programs are just as valued as those who attend face-to-face programs. Consider consulting learners in online programs when designing online degrees. Finally, ask which communities in our province might we as a faculty serve or invite through the university doors.

References

Ahmed, S. (2021). *Complaint!* Duke University Press.

Akbari, E., & McCuaig, K. (2014). *Early childhood education report 2014.* Ontario Institute for Studies in Education. https://www.academia.edu/17129603/Early_Childhood_Education_Report_2014

Anderson, L., Sing, M., & Haber, R. (2020). *Next step: A competitive, publicly funded provincial wage grid is the solution to BC's ECE shortage*. Coalition of Child Care Advocates of BC and Early Childhood Educators of BC. https://childcarecanada.org/documents/research-policy-practice/20/06/next-step-competitive-publicly-funded-provincial-wage-grid

Beaudoin, M. (2003). Distance education leadership: An appraisal of research and practice. In M. G. Moore & W. G. Anderson (Eds.), *Handbook of distance education* (pp. 519–530). Lawrence Erlbaum Associates.

Berger, I., van Groll, N., & Vericat Rocha, Á. (2020). Thinking with/in/through binaries and boundaries: Sparking necessary and ongoing conversations in early childhood education. *Journal of Childhood Studies, 45*(4), 1–3. https://journals.uvic.ca/index.php/jcs/article/view/19932

Braidotti, R. (2022). *Posthumanism Feminism*. Polity.

Butler, J. (2022). *What world is this? A pandemic phenomenology*. Columbia University Press.

Cochran-Smith, M. (2003). Learning and unlearning: The education of teacher educators. *Teaching and Teacher Education, 19*(1), 5–28. https://www.sciencedirect.com/science/article/abs/pii/S0742051X02000914?via%3Dihub

Duhn, I., Malone, K., & Tesar, M. (2020). *Urban nature and childhoods*. Routledge.

Gunawardena, C. N. (2013). Culture and online distance learning. In M. G. Moore (Ed.), *Handbook of distance education* (3rd ed.) (pp. 185–200). Routledge. https://digitalrepository.unm.edu/cgi/viewcontent.cgi?article=1170&context=ulls_fsp

Gunawardena, C., Layne, L., Carabajal, K., Frechette, C., Lindemann, K., & Jennings, B. (2006). New model, new strategies: Instructional design for building online wisdom communities. *Distance Education, 27*(2), 217–232.

Haraway, D. (2016). *Staying with the trouble: Making kin in the Chthulucene*. Duke University Press.

Holmberg, B. (2003). A theory of distance education based on empathy. In M. G. Moore & W. G. Anderson (Eds.), *Handbook of distance education* (pp. 79–86). Lawrence Erlbaum Associates. https://scholar

.google.ca/scholar?q=Holmberg,+B.+(2003).+A+theory+of+distance+education+based+on+empathy.+Handbook+of+distance+education,+79-86.&hl=en&as_sdt=0&as_vis=1&oi=scholart

Homer, L. A. (2013). *Feasibility study for a 4-year online Bachelor of Early Childhood Education degree for the Atlantic region.* University of New Brunswick.

McLachlan, C. (2011). An analysis of New Zealand's changing history, policies and approaches to early childhood education. *Australasian Journal of Early Childhood, 36*(3), 36–44. https://doi.org/10.1177/183693911103600306

Morrison, A. (2022, August 9–10). *Crossing the rubricon.* Keynote address, 8th Digital Pedagogy Institute Conference. University of Waterloo.

Morrison, A. (2020, December 9). Resilient pedagogy for fragile times. *Hook & Eye Blog.* https://hookandeye.ca/author/aimeemorrison/

OECD (Organization for Economic Cooperation and Development). (2006). *Starting strong II: Early childhood education and care.* OECD.

Richardson, L. (1997). *Fields of play: Constructing an academic life.* Rutgers University Press.

Robertson, D. (2022, November 30). *Creating change today and tomorrow.* The Sherman Early Childhood Learning Series Literacies across a Lifetime: Celebrating Canadian Authors. University of New Brunswick.

TRC (Truth and Reconciliation Commission of Canada). (2015). *94 Calls to Action.* http://www.trc.ca/

UNB Early Childhood Centre Research and Development Team. (2008). *The New Brunswick curriculum framework for early learning and child care (English).* Department of Social Development, University of New Brunswick.

Section II
Communicating and Collaborating

7 Through a Glass Darkly
Middle-Level Leadership in an Era of Online Education

Amy Burns

To see through a glass darkly is to have interruptions to sight and understanding, to see an incomplete picture. In the pages that follow, I chronicle my leadership experiences as the associate dean of a large, complex Bachelor of Education degree program as I looked through a glass darkly during those uncertain days now known as *the pandemic*. Although our program had included both online and in-person learning for many years, for me this was an educational crisis that resulted in online education becoming the only option.

This crisis was "an urgent situation that requires immediate and decisive action by an organization and, in particular, by the leaders of the organization" (Smith & Riley, 2012, p. 58), and it was hallmarked by perceptions of unpredictability, increased time pressures, and the feeling of a distinct threat to the well-being of the organization and those within it (Elliott et al., 2005). I faced the unpredictability, often accompanied by fear, that leaders face in times of crisis. We encountered new complexities, including the lightning-fast movement between teaching modalities required as we responded to the many changes created by COVID-19 and its impacts on public health. As of the time of writing, a return to some semblance of normality has occurred, but many lessons have been learned, and I, as a leader, have certainly changed.

One question that could be asked of me, and rightly so, is why I have chosen to focus on the moment in time hallmarked by the crisis. I was a leader of online education before it and will continue to be in the future. The reasons for this focus are the impact and the resultant unique leadership context effected by the situation, resulting in the need for immediate decision making and the lack of choices regarding online modalities for learning. Prior to March 2020, our students, for the most part, had choices in how they engaged with their learning. They chose an on-campus program with carefully selected online opportunities with which they could engage as they saw fit. Or perhaps they selected a program with increased opportunities for online learning. Whatever their choices, they had some agency in how they engaged with their education and were confident that their choices would be honoured. Additionally, as a leader in postsecondary education, I had choices too. I chose to maintain strong programs both on campus and online. I had the time to plan for course modality based on sound pedagogical practices, ensuring that students knew well in advance whether they would be learning online or in person. All of this is to say that we had choices and the time to make them, and it was the sudden lack of both precipitated by the pandemic that resulted in my engagement in crisis leadership from a distance.

Crisis Leadership from a Distance

Gigliotti (2020, p. 2) defined the word *crisis* from a leadership perspective as "disorienting and unwieldy events for an organization and its leaders. These often senseless and complicated moments become crucible experiences for those with leadership responsibility." The extended period of health crisis, which could certainly be described as "disorienting and unwieldy," provided a unique opportunity to consider how educational leaders at all levels lead students, faculty, and staff through and beyond a lengthy, life-altering event. When discussing crises that affect educational institutions, it is often violent and sudden acts that permeate the public discourse (see, e.g., Beabout, 2010; Connelly, 2013; Geis, 2019; Stanley, 2018), but COVID-19 presented us with an extended timeline. Much like a storm on the prairie, we in education at all levels watched the danger roll in before those fateful days in March 2020 when K–12 school systems and many post-secondary institutions closed their doors and made the switch to full-scale online delivery.

Smith and Riley (2012) highlighted the critical attributes that allow leaders in crisis situations to take in large amounts of information quickly and make informed, collaborative, and efficient decisions, all while ensuring the continued well-being and support of those experiencing the emergency. The three leadership lessons presented in this chapter are framed within these three overarching themes of information gathering and synthesis, leadership opacity versus transparency, and support of people with particular attention to the role of the online environment in providing this leadership. Drawing from my personal leadership journal started in 2018, as well as data collected in a funded study on women in middle-level postsecondary leadership, I will consider the following questions. How does one lead alongside others over a long period of time marked by continual upheaval, change, and threat? What have I learned about leading a large undergraduate education program through a shift to ubiquitous online learning?

Information Gathering and Synthesis: Information Overload

> *I think I had better just accept that the changes and the shifts will be my new reality for a long time. The K–12 system has closed the doors, and we have 500 students who were slated to start practicum today. I met with my team today to get everyone set up for working from home. Everyone is on edge. I have had meetings today on Zoom with just about everyone who has anything at all to do with preservice teacher education from community to K–12 to postsecondary and beyond. We have to create a practicum experience that doesn't involve any K–12 students. How does that happen?! There are so many decisions to be made, and they need to be made now but in a really informed way. Everyone has a need, everyone wants answers and reassurances, but I have the same information as everyone else. (personal leadership journal, March 2020)*

This crisis leadership situation required me to become infinitely more embroiled in both the academic and the administrative aspects of the program that would normally have been delegated to others given the incredible rate of change and the volume of information accompanying the changes. As a leader, I was required to step into this work much more fully. I was faced with uncertainty regarding the most elemental of policies, such as the impacts on teacher certification of the pandemic and interrupted teacher education practicums (see Burns et al., 2020). Conflicting philosophical views emerged on whether particular courses were even able to be taught online and in particular whether it was possible to do a teaching practicum well in the online environment using peer teaching. Coupled with short course development turnaround times for successful student learning, adaptation to the online environment, fear of the future, and uncertainty in the present, all of these decisions required the gathering and synthesis of information in a significantly shortened timeline while working in isolation.

Although the timeline at the beginning was short, the virus resulted in a long-game predicament also hallmarked by increased levels of information, leading to information overload in many cases. This was evident in some of the more administrative elements of my work as a leader because of the continual change resulting from the extended timeline. Although the movement to exclusively online program delivery, save for the practicum, for the 2020–2021 academic year was additional work, it was familiar to us. We had a long history of online programming, and the courses that our students would have taken on campus were transferred to the online environment without too much distress. The exception, again, was the practicum since it had returned to an in-school format, and the levels of information that resulted were unimaginable as we began to track student and teacher absences because of illness, school shutdowns and moves to online courses, mentor teacher absences, and so on. On a daily basis, the practicum team, and by extension I as leader, navigated the shifting realities of life in K–12 schools, all from a distance as we did this work from our home offices.

Lesson Learned upon Reflection

Although one might expect the most important lesson to come from the quick changes and information overload to be flexibility, for me it was a reminder to look for the opportunities that can come from a crisis situation (see Danyluk et al., 2022). Particularly in the area of the practicum, a once untouchable aspect of teacher education, the requirement to utilize the online space resulted in ongoing innovations. Burns et al. (2020, p. 19) noted that the pandemic "ignited a historical moment in education to reimagine the possibilities for practicum," but the reimagining must not stop there. As a leader in online education, I have had the opportunity to look where we might engage differently in a myriad of spaces from experiential learning to mentorship.

Opacity versus Transparency: The Realities of Time

> *I did something today that I swore I would never do. I had to make a decision without really consulting those I would normally consult, and then I had to simply ask them to trust me. It got me wondering, if I was them, would I trust me? Without knowing all of the information, would I be willing to trust me? But there is just so much information that I can't possibly share it all. I used to consider myself a transparent leader, but right now I don't know. I'm not hiding anything, but I'm not sharing it all either. I'm lucky to have the relationship with them that I have, or this could have been painful. (personal leadership journal, September 2020)*

The example provided above, upon reflection, speaks clearly to the impact of the online environment on my work as a leader. Previously, when a difficult decision had to be made and time was of the essence, I prided myself on seeking all those affected and going from office to office to ensure understanding and consultation, even if little could be changed. Doing so created community. As a leader in an online environment, I sent out multiple emails to set up numerous Zoom calls, the time required simply not feasible for the situation, resulting in a sense of isolation and a reliance on my pre-existing relationships with my colleagues. A key factor in successfully navigating this more isolated working environment was attention to leadership integrity.

The criticality of leadership integrity was highlighted by Lucas and Katz (2011, p. 93) when they stated that those in both the educational community and the wider community "want to trust that you are doing all that you can on their behalf during a crisis." This was especially important to my leadership practice as the pandemic continued. Although decision making needed to be instantaneous at first, many of the decisions made were outside our immediate control, and therefore there was a lessened expectation that all information would be shared. However, as the timeline extended, there remained a need to filter and synthesize the vast amounts of information in order to make decisions quickly, thereby causing me to rely on what I truly hope others saw as leadership integrity. Leadership decisions sometimes became opaque where they might otherwise have been transparent.

The issues stemming from the time that it took to connect and remain transparent from a distance were also discussed by several participants in a study that I conducted on women in middle-level postsecondary leadership. When asked how COVID-19 and working remotely affected their leadership, participants spoke of increased meetings and the time that it took to arrange them by email, resulting in an inability to be as collaborative or consultative as normally would have been the case. "It's easier to turn around and ask a question than actually do an email. . . . [I]t takes forever" (Elizabeth, March 2022). Others described it as a feeling of disconnection and isolation exacerbated when important decisions had to be made, making them feel like they either had no choice other than to make them alone or had no choice in making them at all since decisions were made at other levels, and their job was to implement them. But others also saw the mandated move to online communication as an opportunity to "just see how we might do things differently, efficiently, but let's not lose the human touch" (Sam, March 2022). Given the ubiquitous nature of online communication now with platforms such as FaceTime, Teams, and Zoom, one does wonder not if but how the pandemic has altered the opacity or transparency of leadership and the time that it takes to consult with others.

Lesson Learned upon Reflection

Strangely, the lesson that I took from reflecting on my experiences with opacity versus transparency in a time of crisis had less to do with the time that it took to aim for transparency and more to do with my own confidence in instances of leadership opacity. Not only in challenging times, but perhaps especially in times of crisis, leaders must trust themselves as well as others. Cairns and Stephenson (2009, p. 9), speaking of professionalism, referred to the ability to take "appropriate and effective action" in unfamiliar contexts, but that could easily apply to leadership. I had to trust that what I was doing was appropriate for the circumstances, even when I was unsure.

The Support of Others: Heart-Led Leadership

> *It's been a week with a lot of uncertainty about what the future looks like. I have been meeting almost non-stop with various people who just want to talk through what they think it will all be like. And they want to know what I think. I'm not even sure I know what I think, but I believe it helps just to listen. Not only for them but for me too. It brings me back to my work on heart-led leadership, and I am surprised at how important this has been over the past few weeks. People are wondering if we will ever get back to normal. I wonder that, too, but as a heart-led leader I know my role here is to be reassuring and to listen. (personal leadership journal, February 2021)*

Perhaps at no other time in my leadership history was heart-led leadership more important than during the COVID-19 crisis. Several prominent authors, both directly and indirectly, argue for meaningful, robust models of leadership that honour collective wellness, mindfulness, vision, and sustainability (e.g.,

Brown & Olson, 2015; Burns, 2020; Hargreaves, 2009; Hawkins, 2017; Kouzes & Posner, 2017; Novak, 2009; Starratt, 2009). For example, Hawkins (2017, p. 154) noted that "we are very much in need of positive, wise and sympathetic models of leadership—people who can demonstrate a balance of cleverness with wisdom, analytical skills with compassion, head with heart." This, I believe, is one of the greatest capacities that we can hold as leaders, perhaps particularly when those with whom we work are at a distance and we do not have the benefit of facial cues or subtle gestures that show care.

Lesson Learned upon Reflection

The lesson learned as I reflect on my leadership during that time is that perhaps it was not so much everyone else who needed me to be heart-led. I needed that for myself. Not only during times of crisis but perhaps more so during those times, we need to learn to support ourselves in the same way that we support others or risk an unsustainable leadership life. And, when coupled with the potential isolation that comes as a risk in the online world, yet again this is more important for leaders of online educational communities. Hargreaves (2009) describes sustainable leadership as a path to enduring educational change, and it requires leaders also able to endure. The airline instructions for mothers to don their own masks first comes to mind. If we as online leaders in a time of crisis are to endure, then we need to look after ourselves as ardently as we do others.

Conclusion

The act of reflecting on our leadership is what helps us to grow. For me, this meant an examination of my experiences in a time of crisis that saw me go from leader of both in-person and online education characterized by relative stability and calm to a leader housed entirely in the online world in a time of upheaval and fear. In this reflection, I grappled with information overload, the realities of information sharing and time, and the need to engage both my heart and my head in my work as a leader. That I have been changed by my experiences as the leader of a wholly online program during a time of great uncertainty is undeniable, and I can only hope that I never forget the lessons that I learned in spending that time as a leader looking through a glass darkly.

References

Beabout, B. R. (2010). Leadership for change in the educational wild west of post-Katrina, New Orleans. *Journal of Educational Change, 11*, 403–424. https://doi.org/10.1007/s10833-010-9136-8

Brown, V., & Olson, K. (2015). *The mindful school leader: Practices to transform your leadership and school.* Corwin Press.

Burns, A. (2020). Living with heart: Self-care, collective care, and justice. In A. Burns & M. A. Mitchell-Pellett (Eds.), *Leading with heart* (pp. 133–140). Word and Deed Publishing.

Burns, A., Danyluk, P., Kapoyannis, T., & Kendrick, A. (2020). Leading the pandemic practicum: One teacher education response to the COVID-19 crisis. *International Journal of E-Learning and Distance Education, 35*(2), 1–25. http://www.ijede.ca/index.php/jde/article/view/1173

Cairns, L., & Stephenson, J. (2009). *Capable workplace learning.* Sense Publishers.

Connelly, S. (2013). Inside out—Reflections from Newtown. *Reclaiming Children and Youth, 22*(3), 12–13.

Danyluk, P., Burns, A., Hill, S. L., & Crawford, K. (Eds.). (2022). *Crisis and opportunity: How Canadian Bachelor of Education programs responded to the pandemic.* Canadian Research in Teacher Education: A Polygraph Series (Vol. 2) [eBook edition]. Canadian Association for Teacher Education. http://dx.doi.org/10.11575/PRISM/39534

Elliott, D., Harris, K., & Baron, S. (2005). Crisis management and service marketing. *Journal of Services Marketing, 19*(5), 336–345.

Geis, P. J. (2019). Has student voice been eliminated? A consideration of student activism post-Parkland. *Philosophical Studies in Education, 50*, 82–93.

Gigliotti, R. A. (2020). *Crisis leadership in higher education: Theory and practice*. Rutgers University Press.

Hargreaves, A. (2009). Sustainable leadership. In B. Davies (Ed.), *The essentials of school leadership* (2nd ed.) (pp. 183–202). Sage.

Hawkins, K. (2017). *Mindful teacher, mindful school: Improving wellbeing in teaching and learning*. Sage.

Kouzes, J. M., & Posner, B. Z. (2017). *The leadership challenge: How to make extraordinary things happen in organizations* (6th ed.). John Wiley and Sons.

Lucas, F., & Katz, B. (2011). Gone with the wind? Integrity and Hurricane Katrina. *New Directions for Student Services, 135*, 89–96 . https://doi.org/10.1002/ss.407

Novak, J. M. (2009). Invitational leadership. In B. Davies (Ed.), *The essentials of school leadership* (2nd ed.) (pp. 53–73). Sage.

Smith, L., & Riley, D. (2012). School leadership in times of crisis. *School Leadership & Management, 32*(1), 57–71. https://doi.org/10.1080/13632434.2011.614941

Stanley, E. (2018). . . . And a child shall lead them. . . . *Journal of Language and Literacy Education, 14*(1), 1–11.

Starratt, R. J. (2009). Ethical leadership. In B. Davies (Ed.), *The essentials of school leadership* (2nd ed.) (pp. 74–90). Sage.

[illegible] (20[illegible]). Does leadership [illegible] ethical [illegible]

[illegible] (20[illegible]). [illegible] University Press.

H[illegible] (2000). Sustainable leadership. In [illegible] (Ed.), [illegible]

[illegible] (20[illegible]). [illegible] Sage.

[illegible] (20[illegible]). *[illegible]* (2nd ed.). John Wiley and Sons.

Lucas, [illegible], & K[illegible], R. (2001). Gone with the wind: Integrity and the [illegible]. *New Directions for Student Services*, [illegible] https://doi.org/10.1002/ss.107

[illegible] (20[illegible]). [illegible] leadership. In [illegible] (Ed.), *The essentials of school leadership* (2nd ed.) (pp. [illegible]). Sage.

Smith, [illegible] (20[illegible]). School leadership [illegible] *School Leadership & Management*, [illegible] https://doi.org/[illegible]

Stanley, [illegible]

[illegible] (20[illegible]). Ethical leadership. In B. Davies (Ed.), *The essentials of school leadership* (pp. [illegible]). Sage.

8 Leading In, Through, and Beyond a Crisis

Lynn Corcoran and Margaret Edwards

Leadership is an essential element of the development and success of students, faculty members, and administrative staff in higher education. During a crisis, strong and capable leadership is critical. The commitment and expertise of leaders enable the university community to navigate through a crisis to a new context beyond the crisis. This is especially true for distance education in the setting of a virtual university consisting of distributed learners and a distributed workforce. Adding to the complexity of this distance education context is that our practice is situated in Faculty of Health Discipline in which our learners, faculty and staff, and leaders are primarily women.

In this chapter, we will outline the background and setting, including details of our faculty within our university, ourselves as leaders, and the challenges that we have faced during crises. We will also describe leadership strategies and illuminate them using examples from our experiences. Finally, we will suggest broad lessons for leaders and leadership teams to be considered beyond crises.

Background and Setting

The University and the Faculty

The distance education context for this narrative is our Faculty of Health Disciplines (FHD) at a Canadian university focused on removing barriers to access and facilitating success in university studies for adult learners on a global basis. Our faculty is composed of approximately 43 academic faculty, 18 administrative staff, 10 undergraduate tutors, and 75 graduate sessional instructors. We have over 7,000 students from across Canada and around the world enrolled in theory courses and over 350 students in various types of clinical practicums in the health disciplines, including nursing and counselling psychology.

There will always be a crisis at some point. Previous crises—including the SARS epidemic and climate disasters such as wildfires and floods—provided opportunities to refine our leadership strategies. The contexts and details of crises will always be different. Our challenge as leaders is to learn how to respond to them and build upon our learning by scaffolding the lessons learned from the current crisis to the next crisis and the time between crises.

The Leaders

The leadership context for this narrative involves two seasoned women faculty members. Dr. Edwards was the dean of the FHD at the onset of the coronavirus pandemic, and Dr. Corcoran was a program director with responsibilities related to curricular, clinical, and day-to-day operations in the Bachelor of Nursing (BN) programs. Combined, we have 40 years of experience working within a Canadian distance education university. Our leadership strategies developed over decades as we took on increasingly senior academic roles. Because our leadership approaches were already applied to a largely remote and virtual workforce, no massive changes were required to address the move to online learning during a crisis such as the recent pandemic. We relied on the leadership strategies that we had been implementing for years during and between previous crises. We applied the same strategies much more visibly, intentionally, and consistently during the recent crisis as principles to address faculty concern and anxiety in a rapidly unfolding context.

DR. EDWARDS

As the dean of the faculty, I focused on providing strong, stable, and visible leadership. As a faculty, we had faced and overcome previous crises. We built upon those experiences. As a nurse, my practice had been in a cardiovascular surgery ICU where a patient rupturing a coronary artery graft and bleeding out through the chest tubes was an emergency. In my leadership practice in postsecondary education, there has never been that level of emergency. Rather, there has always been a way to address a crisis in an educational setting. I situate my educational leadership against this backdrop. My leadership approach has been consultative, measured, and decisive.

DR. CORCORAN

Overwhelmingly, my leadership, time, and energy were focused on pragmatic aspects of clinical affairs, including ongoing, unfolding issues expressed by students, faculty members, and stakeholders in the health system (e.g., nurse preceptors and managers). I developed leadership experience making collaborative decisions related to students and day-to-day operations in clinical settings during a local flood in which a state of emergency was declared in 2013. This initial experience with a local crisis facilitated my reflection on leadership regardless of the type of crisis faced.

The Challenge

Leading through previous disasters, we have always focused on meeting the needs of our learners and colleagues. Faculty members have demonstrated agility in their teaching practices. Support staff have provided guidance to learners based on their circumstances and while working within academic policies and procedures. New crises provide us with the opportunity and requirement to sharpen and advance these practices based on rapidly changing and unpredictable circumstances.

Leadership Strategies

Leadership strategies can be general or specific, well established or innovative. Whatever the strategy, the leader must be intentional regarding its implementation. We offer four general leadership strategies: personal and institutional values alignment, communication, support, and provision of structure. We discuss the specifics of how they were implemented in our leadership practices.

Personal and Institutional Values Alignment

Leadership strategies need to be based on the individual values of the leader ideally in combination and alignment with the organizational values of the distance education institution. The values of leaders matter (Bookey-Bassett et al., 2020; Streeton et al., 2021). Strategies need to be placed carefully atop a foundation of values. Crises tend to upend individuals and organizations. After an initial upending, values provide a landing pad: they are a place to reset and begin again. If values remain foundational despite initial and periodic imbalances, then they will provide both an anchor and stability. Our distance education institution has five main "I care values" as part of the strategic plan: integrity (actions are guided by ethics, honesty, and fairness), community (embracing collaboration and connectivity among diverse individuals), adaptability (flexible and responsive to the changing needs of learners), respect (every individual is valued), and excellence (enhancing the quality of all that we do) (Athabasca University, n.d.).

DR. EDWARDS

In various exercises, I have identified my key values as integrity, authenticity, and compassion. I align directly with the institutional values noted above and enact them by leading within a culture of collegiality. People are always my priority. I delight in encouraging others to reach their full potential and in supporting them as they take calculated risks to grow.

DR. CORCORAN

In my practice as a nurse educator or leader, my values reside firmly in relational practice from a humanistic perspective. I value relationships with people; understanding and empathy are important to me. I look at power imbalances—individually or structurally in systems—and I place value on working to even out power differentials. The "I care values" of integrity, community, adaptability, respect, and excellence align with my own values.

Communication

Although communication is accepted as one of the keys to effective leadership, during a crisis its importance is amplified. Frequent and decisive communication helps to build trust and subsequently the credibility of a leader (Hartney et al., 2021). Communicating clearly, consistently, and frequently while being intentional and slowing down to ensure that there is consistent messaging are vital (Raderstorf et al., 2020).

DR. EDWARDS

When the World Health Organization characterized the global outbreak of the coronavirus as a pandemic on March 11, 2020, communication began immediately with our existing leadership group in the FHD, the Dean's Advisory Group (DAG). As with any crisis, my goal was to send clear and frequent messages to all stakeholders: students, faculty members, and administrative staff. On March 12, 2020, a message was posted on the student learning management system (LMS) acknowledging the impact of the pandemic on students, indicating that additional information would be posted on the LMS, and linking to university services (e.g., counselling). Within four days, we had cancelled all practicums (in nursing and counselling), and the term was considered completed for all graduate theory courses. These decisions were communicated to students through email and the LMS. A town hall was held both to listen to students and to communicate our decisions.

My first message to all faculty and staff on March 13, 2020, noted that the crisis of the pandemic was unfolding and that I would let them know everything as soon as I came to know it. I also asked that people email me if they came to know information before I did, particularly in relation to clinical practicums. Links were included to Health Canada sites to provide credible information. I organized weekly TGIF sessions on the Zoom videoconferencing platform so that faculty and staff could share what was happening in their city and province. These virtual face-to-face meetings were vital to group communication and even more to providing support to one another. They were also an opportunity for me to be visible to the faculty and to give assurance that there was a plan, however evolving.

DR. CORCORAN

I believe that part of clear communication is active listening. While I listen to the content of a verbal message from an individual student or faculty member in the midst of a crisis, I also listen to the tone of voice and cadence of speaking. I believe that active listening paves the path toward empathy and reduces the possibility of a leader making assumptions. Listening to multiple and diverse perspectives helps people to feel heard and supported (Keselman & Saxe-Braithwaite, 2021).

Support

When a crisis occurs, whether it is personal and individual (e.g., the illness or death of a family member) or widespread and collective (e.g., a communicable disease outbreak), people need support. Students need lenience related to due dates for assignments in theory courses. Learners in face-to-face practicums need the choice to continue as scheduled or take a pause and defer the practicum to a time when they are mentally and physically ready. These are not easy decisions for our adult learners with competing priorities and responsibilities. During the pandemic, some students chose to take time away from their nursing work (in which they were very likely needed) to continue to pursue their educational goals. Other students occupied multiple roles (e.g., nursing student, mother, daughter) and were caregivers of immuno-suppressed children or elders in their families. These students often chose to defer their face-to-face clinical practicums. Their choices were pragmatic but also posed moral dilemmas; support from leaders such as faculty members or clinical instructors was essential.

Faculty members also need ongoing support. They, too, are confronted with individual and collective crises during their work lives. Their fitness to maintain their practice is of paramount importance. A leader must provide support through active listening and problem solving.

In the FHD, the majority of faculty members, administrative staff, tutors, and sessional instructors are women. Although women are acknowledged to take on major roles in domestic labour, there is also a matrifocal tilt related to kin keeping, such as caring for elderly parents and maintaining communication among family members (Brown & DeRycke, 2010). We suggest that a crisis tends to amplify this burden on women. It is with these underpinnings that support such as negotiating and renegotiating workloads in the FHD was offered.

DR. EDWARDS

Regardless of whether the FHD is in a crisis or not, as a leader I speak about supporting our learners and each other. Occasionally, I offer my own frustrating experiences, which encourage others to share theirs. I focus my support on the DAG so that in turn they can support faculty members in their issues and concerns. In DAG meetings, during crises, our associate dean, a psychologist, provided short, action-focused coping strategies that engendered discussions and collegial support. One of my mantras, illustrating my intentional focus on support, is "people before paper."

DR. CORCORAN

As a leader, it is important that I encourage and support faculty members so that they can support our learners flexibly, non-judgmentally, and empathically. In undergraduate nursing programs, the curriculum is fairly rigid. Nursing is a regulated profession, and patient safety is of paramount importance. We must follow the rules of our regulatory college of nursing. However, a crisis calls for some degree of flexibility. Unfortunately, a crisis is when some educators feel the need to cling more tightly to rules, seemingly for the sake of stability. Exercising flexibility and divergent thinking related to students' learning is easier for some faculty members than others. In my role as a leader, support was intertwined with communication (the initial strategy articulated in this narrative). I actively listened to what a faculty member was communicating and engaged in problem solving toward a student-centred solution. Although initially time consuming, this type of support built individual faculty member capacity and, as time unfolded, functioned as role-modelling to other faculty members. For example, I often shared the saying "no fast moves" with my colleagues. It related to being intentional about decisions and setting priorities for decision making. Over time, both trust and capacity were enhanced. Faculty members would contact me even if they did not have a problem to solve, just wanting to check in and catch up in a gesture of mutual support that I appreciated. In addition, I would hear colleagues say "no fast moves" during a discussion, and this showed me that, as a group, we were being intentional with decisions.

Providing Structure

Structure is an antidote to chaos. In times of crisis, people are anxious because of the uncertainty of an ambiguous threat (Klann, 2003). For some, this can be paralyzing. Providing structure enables people to rely on a framework, a way of being and doing to guide them to take the first step and then the next step and then a few more steps—until they are walking maybe not quite with confidence but with some sense of purpose and direction.

DR. EDWARDS

The ultimate responsibility for providing structure was that of the dean. Our faculty had a well-established DAG that met monthly. Having this organizational structure in place, with a clear chain of command through program directors, was a strong determinant of making decisions rapidly based on principles and a broad understanding and then communicating decisions back to students, faculty, and staff. I position myself as having a sound way forward. I use the analogy of walking at night with a flashlight; you have only a small circle of light in front of you, and that is where you take the next step. The principles that we followed were simple (e.g., keep our processes consistent) and one step at a time (e.g., as deliberately as possible, make today's decisions today, and then tomorrow, when the circle of light moves, make tomorrow's decisions tomorrow). I was also clear in my communication and with the DAG that we would make mistakes because decisions had to be made with incomplete information, but when they came to light we would remedy them.

Insights for Crisis Leadership and Beyond

These lessons in leadership are applicable to both future crises (e.g., emerging communicable diseases, climate events) and periods of stability. They highlight the importance of consistent, principle-based leadership situated in seemingly simple but ultimately complex strategies when unpacked in detail within a distance education context, as we have demonstrated in this chapter. We have developed the following insights while leading in, through, and beyond a crisis.

Values alignment. The leaders' personal values must align with those of the institution. Dissonance not only will make it exceedingly difficult to provide authentic leadership but also, over time, likely result in moral distress. Conversely, when these values align, the foundation upon which leadership is built is solid. Values alignment horizontally among all faculties and vertically among all levels of leaders creates a stable structure.

Communication. Communicate early, often, and authentically to build trust and credibility. The importance of clear, frequent, consistent, and intentional communication cannot be overstated. The visibility of leaders provides confidence to students and colleagues that we are present and managing the situation as well as possible.

Support. Providing ongoing support as demonstrated by connecting with students and colleagues while showing concern for both their personal and their professional lives is essential. Do not underestimate the multiple roles that people occupy or the additional load for women.

Structure. Although structure is important during a crisis, the establishment of structures and processes before crises occur is foundational. Well-established networks for gathering input to make decisions and support programs and people help to mitigate the effects of unanticipated crises.

Conclusion

During a crisis, leadership is stripped to the basics with a focus on facilitating the most positive outcome for all students and colleagues (Chen-Nielsen et al., 2020). By grounding ourselves in our fundamental values, and by adopting simple practices applied visibly, intentionally, and consistently, we were able to support our students and colleagues during and beyond a recent crisis. Regardless of circumstances, leadership is challenging. It takes courage and requires an ongoing openness to raw vulnerability.

References

Athabasca University. (n.d.). *Imagine plan: Transforming lives, transforming communities.* https://imagine.athabascau.ca/

Bookey-Bassett, S., Purdy, N., & van Deursen, A. (2020). Safeguarding and inspiring: In-patient nurse managers' dual roles during COVID-19. *Nursing Leadership, 33*(4), 20–28. https://doi.org/10.12927/cjnl.2021.26424

Brown, L. H., & DeRycke, S. B. (2010). The kinkeeping connection: Continuity, crisis and consensus. *Journal of Intergenerational Relationships, 8*(4), 338–353. https://doi.org/10.1080/15350770.2010.520616

Chen-Nielsen, N., D'Auria, G., & Zolley, S. (2020). *Tuning in, turning outward: Cultivating compassionate leadership in a crisis.* McKinsey & Company. Cultivating compassionate leadership during Covid-19 | McKinsey

Hartney, E., Melis, E., Taylor, D., Dickson, G., Tholl, B., Grimes, K., Chan, M., Van Aerde, J., & Horsley, T. (2021). Leading through the first wave of COVID: A Canadian action research study. *Leadership in Health Services, 35*(1), 30–45. https://doi.org/10.1108/LHS-05-2021-0042

Keselman, D., & Saxe-Braithwaite, M. (2021). Authentic and ethical leadership during a crisis. *Healthcare Management Forum, 34*(3), 54–157. https://doi.org/10.1177/0840470420973051

Klann, G. (2003). *Crisis leadership: Using military lessons, organizational experiences, and the power of influence to lessen the impact of chaos on the people you lead* (2nd ed.). Center for Creative Leadership.

Raderstorf, T., Barr, T. L., Ackerman, M., & Melnyk, B. M. (2020). A guide to empowering frontline nurses and healthcare clinicians through evidence-based innovation leadership during COVID-19 and beyond. *Worldviews on Evidence-Based Nursing, 17*(4), 254–257. https://doi.org/10.1111/wvn.12451

Streeton, A. M., Kitsell, F., Gambles, N., & McCarthy, R. (2021). A qualitative analysis of vertical leadership development amongst NHS health-care workers in low to middle income country settings. *Leadership in Health Services, 34*(3), 296–312. https://doi.org/10.1108/LHS-11-2020-0089

9 Interpersonal Communication

A Critical Reflection Tool

Sarah MacRae

> *If you get people to pause and reflect, they might decide that the very notion of applying group stereotypes to individuals is absurd.*
>
> (Grant, 2021, p. 139)

My experience in postsecondary education, as both a student and an educator, is rooted in the practice of critical reflection. I believe that this component of experiential learning is needed across disciplines for learners to grasp fully new concepts and absorb new knowledge. As a university instructor in the discipline of communication delivering both online and on-location offerings, a student enrolled in an online graduate program, a small business owner delivering services virtually, and a mother of three young children, I have used reflective practices in sustaining, improving, and strengthening my offerings and leadership skills.

In this chapter, I explore the importance of reflective practices, effective communication, and inclusive language in educational spaces. Inclusive language is respectful and sensitive to diversity while promoting equality and equity (COSWL, 2016). The language expected from, used to speak to, and used about women in society is fundamental to the perceived qualities and levels of leadership that they can attain. As I refer to "leadership" throughout this chapter, it does not refer only to one's professional trajectory, and I encourage you to apply the term synonymously with "educator" in your various teaching and learning spaces.

A reflective practice is a powerful tool for learning and connection; online education can be too. Online opportunities for both educators and students are fundamental in achieving more equitable spaces and places, as well as increased accessibility, for women (Vandenbosch, 2022). Other barriers that both traditional and non-traditional online education address through accessibility are the limited reach, exposure, and access to services that ruralism can entail. Through online spaces, women can increase their interpersonal network exposure that geographical location once limited, allowing further opportunities to learn from, connect with, and contribute to a broader community and disciplinary scholarship.

While reflecting on my own experiences, I wondered about those of my female peers elsewhere in academia and education. Did we share similar sentiments regarding leadership opportunities? Did we engage in comparable language that affected our self-concepts and interests in pursuing leadership opportunities? Were we aware of our own language use in our teaching and learning spaces? With their permission, these women's varied experiences and stories have been interwoven anonymously throughout the chapter.

From this work, I hope to encourage exploration of how critical reflective tools in interpersonal communication can help to strengthen connections, expand an understanding of others, encourage a community in teaching and learning spaces, challenge common misconceptions of effective leadership styles, and reposition traditionally feminine qualities as strengths.

A Critical Communication Approach

Communication has long been considered a "soft skill." I challenge that misconception here and explain why that very term undervalues the skill from the start, how it affects one's behaviour and effectiveness, and why many find it quite hard.

In her book *Atlas of the Heart: Mapping Meaningful Connection and the Language of Human Experience*, Dr. Brené Brown (2021) encapsulates George Lowenstein's (1994) work, explaining that "we have to have some level of knowledge or awareness before we can become curious, [for] we aren't curious about something we are unaware of or know nothing about" (p. 64). Therefore, I believe that reflecting on our everyday use of language, particularly the gendered use of language and the implications for education, is important and necessary. Too often "soft skills" are overlooked and considered as inherent instead of acquirable (Martin, 2019), and I suggest that changing the term "soft" to describe such skills would change the connotations surrounding them and increase their value.

In various contexts, "soft" is synonymous with "weakness" and therefore often undervalued in professional environments such as academia. Through my professional roles, I have shared many conversations with industry leaders who describe the need for improved effectiveness of interpersonal communication and acknowledge that this skill set is not always innate. Could it be that the importance of communication skills was overlooked in the pursuit of more academically rigorous and unique capabilities? Has the skill set been undervalued because of its relational positioning (Corbin & White, 2009) and traditionally feminine connotations? Has the accelerated rise of communication technologies affected our interpersonal interactions? Has communication been taken for granted as inherently natural and therefore unteachable? Perhaps.

Luckily, the research shows that communication effectiveness can be learned (Corbin & White, 2009), and as I share with my students it is one thing to have a good idea, but it is another thing to be able to communicate that idea effectively. Communication does not always come easily and should be fundamentally valued in leadership. Language is important. If we reconsider the socio-cultural value of our lexicon and its implications for our perceptions, we will start to understand the roots of everyday terminology and how a simple turn of phrase is often far more complex than we realize.

This re-evaluation of terms and perceptions is the same process that I invite my students to engage in each semester. I encourage them to be "deconstructionists," challenging the messages that they see in their everyday lives, including the readings and texts used in my courses. Learning the practice of deconstruction improves an understanding of the motive behind the message and the considerable impact that the message can have on our opinions. As philosopher Ludwig Wittgenstein (2010, p. 74) wrote, "the *limits of my language* mean the limits of my world," and to expand on schools of thought and acquired knowledge we must first encourage a learning, and an unlearning, of language.

How We Speak

As educators, we have a responsibility to understand the implications of our language choices and the weight of our words. What we do or do not say matters. We can motivate, persuade, encourage, undermine, exclude, invite, and limit our students' experiences through our language. A simple illustration of the power of language is the following. With a colleague's encouragement, I stopped asking my students "do you have any questions?" Instead, I started asking them "what are your questions?" I was pleasantly surprised at how this simple change in phrasing elicited an increased student response. To demonstrate further the complexity and power of language, its impacts on women in leadership, and the importance of critically reflective practices, I share the following narratives from my peers.

When reflecting on her experiences in leadership and education, a middle-school teacher in the private school system lamented her initial approach to leadership. At her first opportunity to lead in an educational space, she emulated leaders with whom she had experience, but her behaviour was met with resistance and failed. From her self-reflective process, she figured out why this position felt so unnatural to her. She realized that the discomfort stemmed from the behaviour that she thought was *expected* of leaders: authoritarian, tough, and unilateral, qualities traditionally seen as masculine. Interestingly, she described a positive shift in the workplace climate, and personal confidence, when a woman stepped into her school's senior leadership position and led with kindness, empathy, and collaboration. Suddenly, the middle-school teacher saw herself represented in leadership and felt more confident to pursue future opportunities to lead. When we see ourselves represented in leadership positions, we believe that we can become leaders too.

Relationships are positioned on a continuum of confirmation and disconfirmation (Corbin & White, 2009). To create a climate of confirmation, we demonstrate recognition, acknowledgement, and endorsement. When teaching this to students, I ask them to consider important relationships in their lives, determine where they would be placed on the continuum, and reflect on why they would be placed there. Next I encourage students to include their relationships with themselves on the continuum and to consider that how we feel about ourselves affects how we communicate with others. One way to understand the power of language is to reflect on how we speak to ourselves about ourselves.

As educators, we have a responsibility to ensure diverse representation across our materials, readings, and contents and to encourage and amplify various voices through course forums, discussion posts, and group work. As a leader, are you providing an online climate in which students feel safe, brave, recognized, and supported to participate in their learning? Do your online spaces allow students to connect in a positive climate of trust and build community?

How We Are Spoken About

A professor teaching in an online environment referred to recent course evaluations to illustrate the language used to describe her work, contributions, and skills. She prefaced the example with an impressive list of descriptors often received when summarizing her leadership qualities and teaching style. The words were again (unsurprisingly) common for the women with whom I spoke and mostly centred on traditionally "feminine" qualities that we are socialized to admire, or expect, in working women. Words used in the course evaluations and professional reviews included *empathetic*, *enthusiastic*, *attention* (to detail), *organized*, *passionate*, *accommodating*, *collaborative*, *encouraging*, and *curious*. Although admirable qualities, they are often undervalued when juxtaposed with the commendable qualities of their male counterparts.

The specific example shared from her course evaluations was "she is a really nice, friendly, and adorable professor. I like her a lot." Although it was complimentary, the professor wondered whether her male colleagues were described in the same way. I was curious too. So, for the sake of comparison, I shared her question with a male colleague. Positive comments for him included phrases such as "the professor is smart" and "well dressed"; although subjective, these terms connote professionalism, unlike "adorable," and are examples of the juxtaposition mentioned above.

This language pattern affects women disproportionately in the workplace. Although intended positively, it lacks the professionalism and functional reasoning from an important stakeholder group that one would highlight in an application for a promotion, potentially limiting opportunities for advancement.

Caretaking Leadership

Women have a long-standing reputation as the "primary" caregivers in their family structures, especially women in the "'sandwich' generation" (Miller, 1981), those who care for both their aging parents and their children. These caretaking duties come with time and financial stressors and demand a high level of energy, thought, and attention that can be difficult to utilize in market-driven systems. Because these duties tend to fall disproportionately to women, it can be difficult for them to maintain educational and professional aspirations. Opportunities might be limited; the expectations, and assumed limitations, are different. Remaining reasonably flexible in timelines and deadlines in our online educational spaces would be an equitable consideration regarding our students.

I believe that caretaking leaves should be considered intrinsic to the culture of a workplace, not detrimental to individuals' long-term success, financially and positionally. I argue that this type of resumé gap should be equitably valued as the switching of professional roles, highlighting the acquired skills of time management, prioritization, active listening, and problem solving. Two benefits of online educational spaces in this context are providing women educators with flexibility and balance while limiting barriers for women who want access to education.

I would not be able to maintain any semblance of a "life-work balance" if not for the intricate support network, relationships, and connections (see Capra, 2010) that share child-rearing responsibilities for my three young children. I rely heavily on my husband, early childhood educators, grandparents, siblings, friends, and colleagues, various nested systems, flows, and cycles to sustain a dynamic balance needed to survive, and I hope thrive, in my roles as a mother and an educator.

Learning in Critical Reflection

Through the discipline of interpersonal communication, I invite students to examine their relationships with themselves, their families, their new and old friends, the media, their environments, and how what they know and have experienced have been influenced by and through these connections. I am continuously exploring creative ways in which to deliver material and drive student engagement for "buy in" to the critically reflective, and sometimes uncomfortable, process in which I ask students to participate.

Critical reflection and critical self-reflection can be differentiated by understanding a person's particular focus of thought. Gray (2007, p. 497) explains the former as "assessment of the validity of one's assumptions, examining both sources and consequences," whereas the latter is "reassigning the way one has posed problems and one's orientation to perceiving, believing, and acting." Gray continues to reference Mezirow's (1990) work to explain how "reflecting critically in these ways encourages learning at a deeper, transformative level" (p. 497).

Tools, by definition, help us to perform more efficiently (Gray, 2007), so it makes sense that incorporating critical reflective tools into our teaching and learning spaces can be effective in fostering and promoting the process of reflection among students. I believe that, as students move through their professional and personal lives, these are the types of tools that will be continually applied, referenced, and remembered long after the disciplinary material is relevant.

My online distance education students often span the globe and its time zones, and they have varying cultural upbringings and value and belief systems, so the chance to communicate peer to peer in a supportive, encouraging, and reflective environment gives them space in which to learn, and unlearn, a lot about themselves. I see this most at play inside my communication labs—a mandatory experiential learning component of our introductory courses. I provide opportunities, asynchronously, for my online students to break out into small groups to share their thoughts, opinions, and experiences in relation to the weekly reading material. I monitor these groups but encourage students to be leaders in their learning by sharing their own impressions and moving the conversations forward through peer-to-peer feedback. A portion of their grades is based on these components of participation. This space for critical self-reflection, story sharing, and intercultural learning has proven to be effective and credited for their deepest learning of course material.

I hope that the learning experience looks something like this: engage, learn, question, apply, reflect, share, repeat. The process includes assigning activities that allow students to apply theory to experience, testing their initial reactions/understandings in their real-life scenarios, learn (and unlearn) the impacts of the various concepts on their interpersonal relationships, and consider how these relationships influence their perceptions of the world around them. Our rural location should no longer be a barrier to pursuing educational and professional goals and expanding our understanding of the world and our relationship with it.

Many of my university students over the past decade have been first-generation students from small, post-industrial communities, and having the opportunity to network and learn with people from neighbouring provinces, countries, and continents offers them a global experience. I work hard to make the asynchronous learning environment feel as connected and community based as possible, a supportive space in which to reflect, deconstruct, and explore. I recognize that coming from a discipline that studies the communicative behaviour of people allows for ease regarding these methods of teaching and learning, but I believe that there is a benefit in this type of engagement across disciplines.

A peer and professor of archaeology recently highlighted the importance of telling stories in her classrooms to facilitate learning, and this practice makes her an effective educator both from her own perspective and from her students' perspectives.

Through my graduate studies, I found myself studying areas of knowledge familiar from my previous educational experiences, at least at first glance. However, I have easily pulled threads from sustainability scholarship and tied them to communication theory, especially in the context of educational spaces and well-being. My opportunities to reflect and connect have been plenty, and I have benefited from the spaces created to learn from classmates, many of whom have a stronger scientific background.

I have not yet experienced anything that requires more mental flexibility than parenting, especially while being a working parent. I had to explore flexible systems upon my return to work to be successful. Gaining an understanding of the importance of ecological cycles and systems, feedback loops, and networks through application to my personal experience was twofold: it allowed me to break down and understand the disciplinary jargon as well as the complexity and importance of reciprocity between person and planet more effectively. This not only advanced my understanding of specific course content but also strengthened my hypothesis that an element of critical reflection should be present across disciplines to help students learn most effectively.

Considerations

Interpersonal communication is cyclical. There is no real beginning or end. How we interpret messages is influenced by communication before the interaction, and that interaction can influence how we perceive what comes next. What will students take from your online educational environments? Will lessons transcend academic or professional pursuits? How can you plant seeds of thought to grow and have impacts on their future thought processes? We can lead by example, encourage learning and unlearning, and facilitate reflective practices through our intentional communication. We can encourage students to understand their places in and relationships with the disciplines.

In addition to rethinking how we share disciplinary knowledge, I encourage critical reflection on our long-standing, culturally reflexive, value-driven impressions of what it means to be masculine or feminine. We can create a world of opportunity for all of us by reimagining how to express emotions effectively, communicate thoughts and ideas clearly, enforce rules and regulations equitably, educate students inclusively, and identify and demonstrate leadership qualities continuously.

Before you continue on to the next chapter, I will leave you with another quotation from Adam Grant (2021, p. 203): "I believe that good teachers introduce new thoughts, but great teachers introduce new ways of thinking."

References

Brown, B. (2021). *Atlas of the heart: Mapping meaningful connection and the language of human experience*. Random House.

Capra, F., Center for Ecoliteracy. (2010). *Ecological literacy—Parts 1–3* [Video]. YouTube. https://www.youtube.com/watch?time_continue=3&v=vohcled-kto

Corbin, C., & White, D. (2009). *Interpersonal communication: A cultural approach* (5th ed.). Cape Breton University Press.

COSWL (Committee on the Status of Women in Linguistics). (2016). *Guidelines for inclusive language*. Linguistic Society of America. https://www.linguisticsociety.org/resource/guidelines-inclusive-language

Grant, A. M. (2021). *Think again: The power of knowing what you don't know*. Viking.

Gray, D. E. (2007). Facilitating management learning: Developing critical reflection through reflective tools. *Management Learning, 38*(5), 495–517. https://doi.org/10.1177/1350507607083204

Loewenstein, G. (1994). The psychology of curiosity: A review and reinterpretation. *Psychological Bulletin, 116*(1), 75–98. https://doi.org/10.1037/0033-2909.116.1.75

Martin, B. H. (2019). The artistry of innovation: Increasing teachers' artistic quotient for innovative efficacy. *Canadian Journal of Education, 42*(2), 576–604. https://journals.sfu.ca/cje/index.php/cje-rce/article/view/3755

Mezirow, J. (1990). How critical reflection triggers transformative learning. In J. Mezirow (Ed.), *Fostering critical reflection in adulthood: A guide to transformative and emancipatory learning* (pp. 1–20). Jossey-Bass.

Miller, D. A. (1981). The "sandwich" generation: Adult children of the aging. *Social Work, 26*(5), 419–423. https://doi.org/10.1093/sw/26.5.419

Vandenbosch, B. (2022, July 20). *3 ways online learning can narrow the higher education and workforce gender gap*. World Economic Forum. https://www.weforum.org/agenda/2022/07/online-learning-workforce-gender-gap/

Wittgenstein, L. (2010). *Tractatus logico-philosophicus* [eBook edition]. Project Gutenberg. https://www.gutenberg.org/files/5740/5740-pdf

10 First Year by Distance Education and Campus Manitoba

A Manitoba Women's Story

Kathleen Matheos

Is distance education women's work? When distance and correspondence study existed at the margins, it certainly was, and the students served were predominantly women. What was unique about these women that made things work? Did their work build foundations for a distance, blended, and online agenda now central to universities? My answer is yes. I would like to acknowledge Lori Wallace, Bonnie Luterbach, Cheryl McLean, Darlene Frederickson, Carol Girling, Donna Carriere, and Christine Marles—all wonderful colleagues whose commitment and collaboration made good things happen. I am honoured to be a part of this group. All of us worked at the margins, and for me there was not another place that I would have wanted to be. I have always worked in extension/continuing education, the borderland between university and community. Working in this place, I learned much about community needs, and I believe that we had a chance to make that boundary more permeable so that those excluded could participate in study toward obtaining a degree. In this chapter, I provide the opportunity to share my reflections and experiences working in the borderland.

Although a part of higher education in Manitoba for over 70 years, distance education has been situated at the margins of universities for most of its lifespan, housed primarily in continuing education or extension units. Despite its location, small budgets, and limited recognition, distance education provided degree courses first through print-based correspondence and then through other iterations (Anderson & Dron, 2011). Moreover, all distance education units in Manitoba universities were led by women, who themselves had accessed their post-secondary education through non-traditional means, whether undergraduate or graduate. I was one of those women, joining Brandon University in 1990 as a director of extension with a newly minted graduate degree (completed via intensive and distance study). I believe that our commitment and advocacy provided much upon which to build early distance education agendas, paving the way for subsequent exponential growth in the early 2000s.

Moving to the present and, optimistically, post-pandemic world, we observe hybrid and flexible learning in a new position of strength in the academy. The Academica "Top Ten Year in Review 2022" (Abramoff & Janzen, 2023) speaks to the normalization of flexible and online learning, which will permanently change the landscape of higher education. Forms of delivery that existed at the margins for over 40 years leapfrogged to the centre, associated with senior leadership portfolios. For me, one of the women administrators who worked at the margins, there is cautious optimism as these modes of delivery have become normalized, though we still need reassurance that students at the margins are being served.

Setting the Context

The University of Manitoba (UM) offered its first degree credit correspondence course in 1950 through the Continuing Education Division, and Brandon University (BU) by the early 1980s was offering several print-based courses through its Extension Division. The UM correspondence offerings grew significantly post-1950 and by the 1980s included a BA degree with several majors and courses from other faculties. The UM Distance Education Area was staffed and led by female faculty members. All of these women joined the department holding graduate degrees and completed doctoral studies while working, focusing their research on distance and online learning in higher education.

Graduate work was completed at American institutions and the Open University in the United Kingdom using academic leaves for research and writing. As the University of Winnipeg (UW) and Brandon University became involved in distance education, their units mirrored that at the University of Manitoba, led by women concurrently studying and completing graduate degrees. I joined Brandon University with a non-traditional MSc from the University of Guelph, where course work was completed over a three-week period in the spring, complemented by an online course, a comprehensive examination, and a thesis. My graduate work required me to balance multiple priorities: family, work, community service, and study, and living in a rural area I found internet access a challenge. Fortunately, my workplace provided me with much-needed access. I travelled to Guelph for three summers to complete the MSc course work and then finally took time off work to complete my thesis; this was a luxury that many women do not have. This experience in both my MSc and my PhD (which I eventually completed at a distance from a UK university) made me familiar with the challenges faced by those studying at the margins. Moreover, I was fortunate to do my graduate research first with rural female students and then with Indigenous female learners accessing education in a northern Indigenous community. Learning from these women was a humbling experience for me and guided my academic practice.

Early Days: First Year by Distance Education Program and Inter-Universities North

By the mid-1980s, politicians in Manitoba spoke about increasing access to higher education and serving students in rural and remote areas. Concurrently, new technologies were emerging, and courses began to include teleconferencing sessions augmented by print, with one-way video soon available. In 1989, the provincial government directed the three universities to work together to provide a first year of study at five rural northern settings to reduce relocation expenses for students. The program was known as the First Year by Distance Education (FYDE), launched in the fall of 1990.

Fortunately, the government already had an operating agency in which to situate the administrative arm and an agreement that would streamline the academic operations. The FYDE utilized the Inter-Universities North (IUN) agreement and placed administration of the program in the existing IUN office in Thompson. The IUN agreement—a special arrangement made in 1971 by the Committee of Presidents of Universities of Manitoba—allowed students living north of the 53rd parallel taking courses through IUN to use these courses for both credit and residency at the Manitoba university where they wished to graduate. The impetus for the IUN agreement was the growth of industry in northern Manitoba and the provision of education for transported southerners (primarily female partners of individuals moving north for employment) who wished to complete their education. Many teachers with only one year of Normal School completed their degrees by participating in the forward-thinking IUN agreement. Although transfer credit is always important, the residency component made the agreement exceptional, and students in this region did benefit. The first woman who utilized IUN to graduate was Emily Sawicki, who graduated in 1979 (archival documents, Brandon University).

The IUN office in Thompson was led by a female administrator, an internationally trained physiotherapist who, after coming to Canada, began her university study at night school, completing both her undergraduate and her graduate degrees. The FYDE was assigned to an IUN coordinator—a woman who had utilized the IUN agreement to complete her degree and went on to further education through non-traditional programming. These two women, Shirley Lyon and Carol Girling, made the FYDE happen within a one-year window, laying the foundation for further initiatives.

It was an intensely busy year. The FYDE directed funds to all of the universities to develop and deliver courses. Each course was offered in a three-hour block over 13 weeks, utilizing one hour of video and two hours of audio-conferencing, along with print materials. This mirrored the three-hour-per-week lecture model within face-to-face delivery. Sites were established in dedicated spaces at high schools in five centres in the province: Dauphin, Russell (south of the 53rd parallel), Thompson, The Pas, and Flin Flon (north of the 53rd parallel). Coordinators were hired to manage the centres. A range of courses offered in the social sciences, humanities, and natural sciences recognized the need to equip students with foundational courses to enter into second-year programs.

Although initially the politicians intended to build distance education capacity equally across institutions, doing so was not practical. We had three very different institutions. The University of Manitoba was the oldest and largest institution, with the only professional faculties and medical and doctoral studies. The University of Winnipeg was primarily an undergraduate school and had not ventured into distance education prior to the FYDE. Brandon University was a small institution outside Winnipeg with a handful of correspondence courses, a strong access mission, and the northern teacher education program for the province. When determining which university would take on development and delivery of an FYDE course, respective academic departments had to agree to offer a course and identify and contract an instructor prepared to teach the course in the FYDE format.

Despite the willingness of designated distance units within the respective institutions, the challenge came when seeking agreement from departments and finding an instructor willing to teach the course. Therefore, the University of Manitoba offered most of the courses, in English, psychology, sociology, philosophy, economics, calculus, and linear algebra. The University of Winnipeg, which had never offered distance education, agreed to offer courses in chemistry, biology, and history. Although Brandon University was only able to offer six credit hours in computer science, it became involved in other ways. While the FYDE supported an already established distance education program at the University of Manitoba, for the University of Winnipeg it provided a foray into remote learning (a catalyst for further televised credit education in Winnipeg). Services and supports were also divided among the partner universities. Even with these challenges, within one year and by the fall of 1990, the group of women administrators (of which I was not yet a part) demonstrated their commitment to access to education by getting the work done. The FYDE was up and running.

Although responsibility for operationalization and delivery of the FYDE rested with IUN, the academic home of and responsibility for the courses rested with the three southern universities. I was the newest member, having joined Brandon University when the first FYDE courses became available. I was fortunate to have female colleagues at the University of Manitoba and the University of Winnipeg who answered questions and provided advice, often outside work hours. Courses were delivered by faculty members from one of the three universities using first video- and teleconferencing and then computer conferencing as technologies evolved. Compensation for course development and delivery and other associated costs was provided to the respective universities, but tuition flowed to IUN as per the agreement. At the outset, packages of print material were sent to each location. All of us remember delivering boxes of textbooks and materials regularly to bus depots for subsequent delivery to students. Similarly, the face-to-face IUN course offerings that continued alongside the FYDE and involved fly-in professors also required logistical support (e.g., flight arrangements, airport pickup, and transport to the off-site classroom). In the 1970s and 1980s and into the 1990s, IUN and FYDE course delivery was labour intensive and completed by a committed group of women in both faculty and support positions. It is now hard to imagine how things got done in the absence of email and digital materials. Today phone and fax are seldom used, and Greyhound, our main bus carrier, is no longer in business.

Identifying and contracting instructors for IUN courses remained a challenge, but the group of women administrators formed a network, calling on each other for assistance when an instructor was needed or a problem emerged. We built relationships that remain intact today. Moreover, we were all still completing graduate programs alongside our work.

Evolution of the FYDE and IUN

The year 1990 saw changes for IUN, including the hiring of a new executive director, a man with a doctorate in science but a career in community-based and distance learning. With his arrival, the staff grew to include another female coordinator and new positions in student support. The IUN agreement and offerings initially supported transported southerners in northern urban areas, but Indigenous communities called for on-site programming. A third female coordinator, an Indigenous woman, was hired, and she also completed her graduate education while working. In consultations with communities, IUN initiated formalized, community-based, full-degree programming for a cohort of learners in First Nations communities. Local coordinators were hired in communities to provide student support and services. These new ventures were not without challenges, but committed staff made things work. It is interesting to note that almost 100% of the learners involved in postsecondary community-based studies were women; only a few Indigenous men entered postsecondary studies, and in most cases they withdrew from them (Matheos, 2000). University College of the North (UCN, n.d.) data reflect this trend today, with Indigenous women participating in studies toward a degree in greater numbers than Indigenous men.

As technologies emerged, it became possible to offer IUN courses via audio-conferencing or courses in a hybrid model in which instructors made some face-to-face visits supplemented by audio-conferencing. With the affordances of technology, along with exponential growth in demand, the pressure on university distance education units increased, often with no increases in resources; in spite of such challenges, though, offerings increased.

Northern communities had long articulated the need for a regional university. Although students could complete two years of study at a local college, most needed to travel to Winnipeg or Brandon to complete their degrees. With the plan to establish a university, IUN was moved to Keewatin Community College in 1996. This was justified since the college was the higher education institution in the North, soon to become a university college with degree-granting status. The FYDE was not so easy to move since students were not all located in the North. As well, rural communities throughout Manitoba voiced the need for local degree credit courses. Moreover, though offering a first year of university credits was helpful, some individuals throughout Manitoba had completed some postsecondary studies and wanted a means to complete their degrees. Most importantly, the residency and transfer credit features of the IUN agreement were essential to student success throughout the province.

In 1998, the FYDE disbanded and was replaced by Campus Manitoba (COPUM, 1998). Its administration relocated to the Brandon University Extension Division, where I became the director. The Campus Manitoba mandate expanded the FYDE introduction of courses beyond the first-year level and the establishment of sites throughout Manitoba. I saw this as a very positive change; many students, particularly women who stopped their postsecondary education before its completion, needed courses to obtain a credential. As programming grew and colleges joined the partnership, the IUN transfer credit agreement was no longer used.

By 2002, 21 new courses were added. By 2006, all seven public institutions became members of Campus Manitoba. By 2008, 15 regional centres were established, to be phased out by 2013. Campus Manitoba became a fully online course provider, including degree, diploma certificate, and professional learning courses. It now maintains an online catalogue of e-courses, including transfer credit information as well as a streamlined process by which letter of permission fees are waived. To support the development and delivery of online offerings, the Flexible Learning Hub, accessible to faculty and staff from all partner institutions, was launched in cooperation with the UM Centre for the Advancement of Teaching and Learning. Currently led by a woman, Campus Manitoba is also a strong advocate of open educational resources, launching and funding such resources and open textbook initiatives. What began in 1990 as the FYDE in five Manitoba centres offering 60 credit hours of first-year programming from three universities has grown exponentially to provide access to e-courses at multiple levels to individuals across Manitoba (Britton, 2006).

With the establishment of University College of the North in 2004 as the successor to Keewatin Community College, IUN became Inter-Universities Services—a consortium of four universities (UCN, UM, UW, and BU), now led by an Indigenous female administrator, Lavina Fecteau. After moving to the University of Manitoba as the associate dean of extended education, I was fortunate to join the Inter-Universities Services committee and to see the excellent work being done to provide courses in northern communities.

Concluding Comments

I have seen enormous growth and transformation in distance education. Technology has provided new affordances to teach and learn, and the pandemic pushed us in much-needed directions. In the three original FYDE and IUN partner institutions, there are no longer distance education units in extension divisions with responsibility for distance and online learning. These modes of delivery are offered by faculties alongside hybrid and face-to-face offerings. As I think back to 1990, it is important to acknowledge the women leaders whose commitment and collaboration created the firm foundation for the present online and hybrid learning.

References

Abramoff, K., & Janzen, R. (2023, January 3). The top ten year in review 2022. Academica Forum. https://forum.academica.ca/forum/a-review-of-2022-the-top-ten-year-in-review

Anderson, T., & Dron, J. (2011). Three generations of distance education pedagogy. *International Review of Research in Open and Distributed Learning, 12*(3), 80–97. https://doi.org/10.19173/irrodl.v12i3.890

Britton, A. J. (2006). *A historical listing of significant events in Manitoba's elementary–secondary education, post-secondary education and training systems 1989–2006* [Unpublished manuscript]. Campus Manitoba.

Committee of Presidents of Universities of Manitoba. (1998). *Towards a virtual learning environment* [Unpublished manuscript]. Campus Manitoba.

Government of Manitoba. (1994, June). *Doing things differently: Response of the government of Manitoba to the report of the University Education Review Commission.* https://news.gov.mb.ca/news/archives/1994/06/1994-06-23-doing_things_differently_response_of_the_government_of_manitoba_to_the_report_of_the_university_education_re~1.pdf

Matheos, K. (2000). *Community-controlled education: Putting education back into the culture* [Unpublished doctoral dissertation]. University of Kent at Canterbury.

UCN (University College of the North). (n.d.). *Graduate satisfaction and employment report.* https://soar.ucn.ca/ICS/icsfs/2016-2017_GSES_2017-2018_SEP.pdf?target=230606c3-08ea-442d-adfa-56bea40bc666

11 A Strategic Response to the Demands of the Pandemic

A Black Woman's Leadership Story

Sophia Palahicky

The COVID-19 pandemic brought in a tsunami of change that resulted in 100% of courses and programs delivered online within a two-year period. This created shock waves for teaching and learning centres that support learning development, learning design, faculty development, and faculty support. This narrative features my voice, that of a Black woman leader, sharing a personal account of how the demands of the pandemic compelled a strategic response within a teaching and learning centre. The centre is situated within a publicly funded university in western Canada that offers mostly graduate-level programming. The centre comprises three teams that work collaboratively: the learning technologies team, the media services team, and the learning design team. This is my leadership story that focuses on my work as an associate director responsible for learning design services, including the following three areas: instructional design, faculty development, and faculty support. The learning design team serves approximately 80 core faculty members and from 200 to 500 associate faculty members.

"Centres for teaching and learning in postsecondary educational institutions in Canada seek to serve the professional development needs of faculty members throughout the college or university" (Mooney, 2018, p. 39). These centres are critical resources and were instrumental in providing faculty members with just-in-time supports when the pandemic demanded a pivot to fully online delivery within tight time constraints. Along with my team of 10 instructional designers and two faculty support staff, I responded strategically, addressing the dramatic increase in demands for learning design services. This response embodied an opportunity to demonstrate how leadership in distance education demands a diverse knowledge base that requires intersections among pedagogy, design, technology, research, systems thinking, and more. In this narrative, I highlight the strategies used to enhance faculty development programming and the strategies used to support my team of instructional designers.

Strategic Expansion of Faculty Development Programming

"*Faculty development* is the process of providing professional development training and coaching to faculty members to help them improve their work performance, particularly in specific areas such as teaching and research" (Devran & Elçi, 2020, p.124). *Faculty training* is a subset of faculty development. *Faculty support* includes "strategies employed to provide faculty with the knowledge, skills, abilities and infrastructure to effectively facilitate student success" (Hastings & Rasmussen, 2017, p. 437), and this includes just-in-time supports to solve problems and make improvements to teaching.

Before the arrival of the pandemic, my team of learning designers offered a forecast of faculty development sessions that addressed technical skill development, pedagogical elements, and values-based approaches. We also had a mechanism for faculty support in the form of a helpdesk called Studio that provided quick turnaround times from Monday to Friday for faculty members who had live courses running. When the pandemic hit, it became clear to me that, though the infrastructure for faculty development and faculty support existed, only about a third of the faculty community engaged with our services regularly. Also, the emergence of a digital community versus the on-campus community revealed that faculty engagement in a digital community was lagging. Major (2010, p. 2160), who studied faculty members' experiences in higher education, pointed out that even before the pandemic some faculty members "agreed that a general lack of knowledge about what works well in a distance setting and a lack of training in the use of technology could be disadvantages of online learning."

As the pandemic took root, we saw a dramatic increase in requests for instructional design supports and synchronous tools, and as was expected all face-to-face courses, including two-week residencies, needed to be moved online. We faced a significant increase in demands for supports that had to be addressed within exceedingly tight timelines. The number of offerings for faculty development workshops had to be doubled and, in some cases, tripled. If I had scheduled one offering of facilitating learning online in June, for example, instead of running only one section of this offering, I would arrange for two or three additional sections to accommodate the increase in demand. Faculty development workshop participation rates increased from 50% to 85%, and this meant that my team was super engaged and challenged with workload issues. To provide extra support, casual instructional designers already trained were granted more hours to facilitate additional faculty development offerings and assigned "low touch" instructional design projects. I had already established the importance of having a small team of two to three casual instructional designers on staff. This gave me more capacity to take on the additional workload and was an effective succession planning tactic since a few of the instructional designers in full-time roles had started out in casual roles.

Strategic planning. I prepared a report on faculty development and faculty support for the academic leadership team to initiate conversations on strategic planning. As a result of the report, three areas of improvement were identified as critical to implementing a strategic plan to ensure that faculty development programming met the emergent needs of faculty members and that they could access workshops and offerings provided by our team of learning designers. These areas of improvement included the following.

- *Diversify offerings* to ensure that faculty development covered a comprehensive list of workshops, including technical (synchronous and asynchronous), pedagogical, values based, team based, and research based.
- *Enhance relevance* to ensure that learning outcomes, contents, and resources were "value adding" and relevant to meet the needs of faculty members.
- *Enable application* to ensure that workshop activities and assessments provided opportunities for authentic learning since faculty members were guarding their time and only wanted to engage in activities that they could transfer directly to their teaching.

Community building was the common thread in each of the areas of improvement and, as Mooney (2018) points out, is essential to effective engagement in faculty development programming.

Changes implemented. First, to enhance relevance, I worked closely with my team of instructional designers to revise the course called "Facilitating Learning Online." This popular course saw an increase in participation of up to 85%. The changes included revising learning activities and formative assessments to make them authentic: for example, modelling online activities that could be applied to teaching across disciplines. Second, to diversify offerings, my team and I promoted the Pedagogical Values Series to highlight successful teaching strategies that reflect care, social justice, equity, diversity, decolonization, and inclusion. I facilitated a session focused on the pedagogy of care. Third, to enable application, I supervised the development of three new courses for teaching with Zoom (beginner, intermediate, and advanced). Additionally, all faculty development courses designed for face-to-face delivery were converted to an online format. It is important to keep in mind that these changes were accomplished without any increase in full-time staffing. Effective leadership and strategic planning skills enabled the team to achieve efficiency. Mslia, who studies Black women leaders in education, argues that "effective leadership depends more on the relevant qualities of leaders and . . . that qualities such as motherhood, flexibility, loyalty, mentoring, and collaborative leadership were among the qualities that were common among women leaders" (2022, p. 16). In hindsight, I drew from the skills of my mother as she raised 15 children, "mothering" that enabled me to be successful. I led the team in daily, hour-long, digital meetings, and we HUDDLED: H—helped each other, U—understood that we had to do things together as a team, D—dedicated time for planning, D—divided the work equitably, L—limited distractions, E—embraced opportunities to do things differently, and D—deepened relationships by listening and demonstrating empathy.

Critical reflection. Santamaria and colleagues, who study BIPOC women leaders, point out that "leadership is carried out by women of color who have transcended psychological, emotional, or societal barriers including experiences with racism, discrimination, and/or oppression; these powerful understandings inform their expression of leadership in qualitatively different ways" (2022, pp. 185–186). My personal experiences with racism and discrimination as a Black woman leader have helped me to develop important skills for recourse and resilience—being able to bounce back from challenges and negative experiences with a deep desire to create change, growth, and personal strength. The key learning for me is that the demands of the pandemic created a ripened climate for change, improvement, growth, and innovation. The crisis underscored the critical role that centres of teaching and learning play in postsecondary environments. With the support of my team of instructional designers, we were able to respond adequately to the increase in demand for services. I also attribute our success to the instructional designers who took on informal leadership responsibilities as they utilized effective change management skills, increased opportunities for dialogue, listened, and took action to ensure that faculty members were supported.

Power, who conducted case studies of instructional design work, argued that instructional designers can be torn "between faculty needs and limits and the exigencies of their profession, [and] instructional designers must find a middle ground wherein they can effectively assist faculty in developing quality, online learning environments" (2007, p. 65). The following discussions focus on strategies that I utilized to strengthen our team of instructional designers.

Strategic Supports for Instructional Designers

Any instructional design team requires onboarding supports to ensure that, when new members join, they are fully supported and have opportunities to develop the skills and knowledge to be able to perform their duties effectively. A process of creating supports for new instructional designers served a double purpose since it was also a tool to engage long-serving and recent hires in a process of rebooting. I was focused on building capacities and providing opportunities for instructional designers to develop their leadership skills. One of the strategies was to implement a robust orientation. The orientation focused on building mentorship capacity and providing information about how the learning design team provided support to faculty and staff and how the team supported each other. The orientation included an introduction to institutional mission, vision, values, and practices critical to consider when examining faculty needs and provided critical reflection on the following questions. Which values guide my work? How can I build relationships and networks? How can I develop leadership skills? How do I contribute meaningfully? What do I need to know about this institution to be effective in my role? How do I plan, manage, and ensure that my work reflects sustainable practices? The orientation allowed every instructional designer to take time with the new person coming in to discuss the questions posed above. It also gave long-serving and recent hires time to reflect on these questions as they provided support for the new team member.

Although the orientation provided reflective opportunity and leadership development for me and the instructional design team, it was lacking in terms of preparing instructional designers to implement the institutional learning design processes. Hence, I collaborated with my team to create a new online training course that would take 10 to 12 hours for new instructional designers to complete. Although it was not required for current instructional designers, they did need to review it and participate in feedback loops to improve it. Three new casual instructional designers completed the new training course and following are some of the anecdotal comments that they shared. "I feel so well supported in my new role." "The course really helped me understand the institution and how I fit in." "This is an outstanding resource for me, and I will be using it as a guide and tool for my work." Generally, the new online training was well received. Time was indeed the most important consideration, and new instructional designers were not assigned any projects in the first four to six weeks to give them time to complete all training required to perform their duties. This was another effective strategy that helped to ensure that instructional designers were well prepared for their role and understood the tasks, challenges, demands, and responsibilities before diving in. The one drawback for me was the investment of my time during the new instructional designer's probationary period. A case in which the instructional designer did not successfully complete the probationary period could be noted as the one drawback of this strategy. Probationary periods are times when two sides must be aligned (i.e., is this work a good fit for me? and am I a good fit for this work?).

Strategies to foster informal leadership. Eddy, who studies leadership in higher education, argued that "building an equity framework for leadership development requires questioning underlying assumptions about who can lead and what leadership should look like, which requires fundamental organizational change" (2018, p. 9). I am inclined to support an approach that values both informal leadership and formal leadership. Yet the former type is often understated and cannot thrive within a hierarchical organizational structure. I was happy to share some of my leadership tasks with my team and made space for instructional designers to chair team meetings and lead professional development microsessions for our team. Some of the instructional designers organized a book club that I attended, and we committed to collaboration on scholarly writing and research projects (done from the sides of our desks).

Critical reflection. The pandemic quickly affirmed what some scholars have known for decades: effective distance education must be rooted in systems methodology acknowledging that leadership roles are necessary for many subsystems of a *suprasystem*, including administrative functions, teaching responsibilities, research, instructional systems design, curriculum design, program design, learning technologies, faculty support, student support, and more. To get the job done well demanded sacrifice of personal time and required strategies to maintain health and well-being. Davinson, a leadership scholar, noted that "being a leader requires the constant balancing of dissonance: balancing the vision of the institution with the daily workload, balancing the professional elements of the job with the personal aspects of one's life" (2012, p. 17). Exercise, healthy eating habits, and resilience had instrumental roles to play in keeping me focused amid tensions. I was able to draw from personal resilience that embodies many elements: flexibility, strength, buoyancy, and spirituality. A key learning for me is that effective leadership must be rooted in relationship building that promotes collaboration, teamwork, and a human-centred approach that makes space for an appreciation of differences.

Recommendations for Leadership in Distance Education

All of us have the potential to lead. When we have developed the skills and knowledge within a discipline, subject, field, or art that can be labelled as a form of expertise, it is critical to take up informal or formal leadership as the circumstances demand. When working within a team environment, every member is accountable to take on leadership in different ways and at different times. Women have demonstrated strategic leadership and are capable and competent when carrying formal and informal leadership responsibilities (Mslia, 2022). I argue that women can rise to the challenge and perform well in leadership positions, bringing to the fore a desire to nurture the leadership development of members within their team. However, it is important that we shift the focus from qualities of women leaders to qualities of effective leadership.

When educational leadership fails, students, local communities, and the global community are affected. Therefore, it is important for individuals in formal leadership positions, as well as those who perform leadership responsibilities without formal titles, to spend some time reflecting on the "ingredients" of effective leadership in higher education (Palahicky, 2020, p. 185).

The following effective leadership "ingredients" will be useful for any woman (or other individual) taking up or continuing a formal or informal leadership role in distance education: (1) practise critical self-reflection, (2) commit to people first, (3) practise shared decision making, (4) build community, (5) express gratitude, (6) prioritize self-care, and (7) model inclusive practices. I am grateful to have had the opportunity to serve in my formal leadership role as a Black woman who recognizes that not all women across the globe will have such privileges, particularly women of minority groups.

References

Davinson, P. L. (2012). The 24/7 public possession: Understanding the dissonance and grace of being a post-secondary leader. *Canadian Journal of Higher Education, 42*(2), 13–33. https://journals.sfu.ca/cjhe/index.php/cjhe/article/view/183580

Devran, B. Ç., & Elçi, A. (2020). Traditional versus digital assessment methods: Faculty development. In E. Railean (Ed.), *Assessment, testing, and measurement strategies in global higher education* (pp. 20–34). IGI Global. https://doi.org/10.4018/978-1-7998-2314-8.ch002

Eddy, P. L. (2018). Expanding the leadership pipeline in community colleges: Fostering racial equity. *Teachers' College Record, 120*(4), 1–18. https://doi.org/10.1177/016146811812001404

Hastings, N. B., & Rasmussen, K. L. (2017). Designing and developing competency-based education courses using standards. In K. Rasmussen, P. Northrup, & R. Colson (Eds.), *Handbook of research on competency-based education in university settings* (pp. 232–249). IGI Global. https://doi.org/10.4018/978-1-5225-0932-5.ch012

Major, C. H. (2010). Do virtual professors dream of electric students? University faculty experiences with online distance education. *Teachers' College Record, 112*(8), 2154–2208. https://doi.org/10.1177/016146811011200802

Mooney, J. A. (2018). Emergent professional learning communities in higher education: Integrating faculty development, educational innovation, and organizational change at a Canadian college. *The Journal of Teaching and Learning, 12*(2), 38–53. https://jtl.uwindsor.ca/index.php/jtl/article/view/5526

Mslia, V. (2022). Black women school leaders: Building effective schools against the odds. *Multidisciplinary Journal of Gender Studies, 11*(1), 1–23. https://hipatiapress.com/hpjournals/index.php/generos/article/view/8925

Palahicky, S. (2020). Innovative leadership: The higher educational context. In S. Palahicky (Ed.), *Enhancing learning design for innovative teaching in higher education* (pp. 183–206). IGI Global.

Power, M. (2007). From distance education to e-learning: A multiple case study on instructional design problems. *E-learning, 4*(1), 64–78. https://journals.sagepub.com/doi/10.2304/elea.2007.4.1.64

Santamaria, L. J., Manriquez, L., Diego, A., Salazar, D. A., Lozano, C., & Aguilar, S. G. (2022). Black, African American, and migrant Indigenous women in leadership: Voices and practices informing critical HRD. *Advances in Developing Human Resources, 24*(3), 173–992. https://doi.org/10.1177/15234223221100847

Section III
Reflecting on Experiences

12 Hurry Slowly
A Conversation about Leadership in Distance Education through Multiple Roles

Michelle Harrison, Christina Hendricks, Tannis Morgan, Anne-Marie Scott, and Elizabeth Childs

One of the gifts of working in higher education is that it requires constant curiosity and an openness to possibilities. It is not surprising, then, that collectively we wondered why there is not more written about what it means to be a leader in distance education, particularly given the global recognition of Canada as a leader in this area. At the intersection of distance education, online learning, open educational pedagogy (OEP), and digital technologies (Axe et al., 2020), we wondered about the contribution of women in decision making in these areas and the absence of women's stories in the field and the literature. Perhaps this can be accounted for by the historical misconception that distance education is less rigorous (Paul, 2023). Or the rapid pace of change in higher education coupled with rapid advances in technology. Or perhaps those doing the work are so busy with *doing it* that there is no time to write about, share, or examine lessons learned and ways forward. As identified by Latchem and Hanna (2001, p. xvii), "such [an] uncharted environment calls for leaders of change [in open and distance learning] at all levels to energise and empower others to share their vision of what can be accomplished through open learning, to change work cultures and to create systems that are built to last but constantly adaptable."

We observed that distance education leadership, framed in this manner, is less accessible to women given the current scarcity of women with the transdisciplinary skill set that it requires (Castro Benavides et al., 2020). However, the calls for transformation in higher education and for resilient leadership in the open and distance learning spaces are strong (Johnson, 2020: Paul, 2023). We thought that these calls might be well supported by a feminist approach to leadership that we resonate with, which Batliwala (2010, p. 14) highlights is based on a social justice perspective, from which the aim is to use "inclusive structures and processes" to lead with a focus on "transformation for equality and the realization of human rights for all."

Although we recognize, as white women with significant privileges, that our perspectives are by no means reflective of those of women with other intersecting identities, we hope that our various perspectives can provide insights as the field of distance education itself iterates and evolves. We approached the writing of this chapter using an asynchronous dialogic process and a self-study approach (Hamilton & Pinnegar, 2014) so that we could take time to reflect on our leadership journeys. Through previous projects, we have an established sense of trust, and each of us recognizes the value and benefit of the peer support, community, and connection that we have experienced in working collaboratively—elements also essential in successful distance education initiatives (Childs & Crichton, 2018; van Oostveen et al., 2017). Our process reflects the realities of being a leader today, namely the difficulties in finding time to connect with peers to learn given the multiple crises encountered and the rapidity, both perceived and actual, of responses required. We hope that others can learn from our conversations, just as we have learned from and with each other.

Getting Grounded

Our opening writing prompt for our conversation was an invitation to *examine and reflect on how we got into this work.*

CHRISTINA

I started as a faculty member in philosophy. I have always been eager to learn more about teaching and learning and continually improving my practice. I have been particularly interested in and affected by the work of the Centre for Teaching, Learning, and Technology at the University of British Columbia in Vancouver related to Indigenous engagement, equity, diversity, inclusion, accessibility, and open education. I have learned a great deal from staff in our centre on these and other topics, and I was excited to be able to contribute to and lead a unit that upholds values that I hold deeply by becoming the academic director.

ANNE-MARIE

I started working in IT project leadership roles in education and grew into being a learning technologist. I describe educational technology now as both my discipline and my profession. I enjoy getting things done and using knowledge for practical purposes, so I have actively pursued administrative roles rather than academic ones; however, I have always tried to be scholarly in my approach and my work and take opportunities to research and publish since I think that they are a way to reflect on and improve my work. I have deliberately pushed myself into senior management roles because I think that you can either shout from below or roll up your sleeves and try to do better yourself. I am a very values-driven person, so if I have career ambition then it is about doing work that I believe aligns with those values and has the impacts that I think are important. Ultimately, I think that my values and wanting to have a certain impact comprise my leadership practice, and reaching for leadership roles has been the mechanism by which I can put those things into action.

MICHELLE

For me, geography and distance have often created barriers to accessing education, so my initial student experiences with distance education highlighted how structures and policies of most traditional institutions of higher education are embedded in inflexible and often unreasonable frameworks that reflect organizational or process requirements rather than the needs of students. A focus on removing barriers to access has led to leadership roles in which I can try to find the nooks and crannies within institutional structures. My leadership has been primarily in a chairperson role, working with colleagues and teams to focus on finding spaces and people where pockets of innovation can be found. Networking and building relationships with others with shared values have helped me to push for change in policies, practices, and processes.

ELIZABETH

Growing up in a rural tourism setting taught me much about the value of cultivating relationships, building community, and demonstrating care for others across all ages and stages of life. It also instilled in me an entrepreneurial mindset and a deep respect for the various ways in which people come to know what they know, an acute awareness of the inequities inherent in systems, and the power of possibility in working creatively to address them. Transitioning from K–12 educator to corporate training and learning designer to consulting on online and blended learning, I have had the privilege to work on several local, national, and international projects focused on increasing flexibility and access to education and building capacity within systems for alternative approaches to teaching and learning. Reflecting on my professional journey thus far, I believe that relationships, collaboration, care, and curiosity have guided my work and enabled me to influence change at practical and systems levels.

TANNIS

I started as an instructional designer in a distance education unit, largely motivated by the experiences of family members who benefited, in life-changing ways, from open universities and distance education. This role allowed me to focus on technology as a means to remove barriers to access to education, leading me to technology-supported design and delivery. When I changed institutions, I was motivated to occupy more of a leadership role to have some degree of influence over the direction of technology-supported teaching and learning. I was eventually responsible for an institute-wide strategy that included openness as part of a plan for technology-supported teaching and learning. This helped to guide the activities and focus of the centre, and it was motivating and rewarding to see the tangible impacts made in those areas. In my current role, my focus is on helping to make significant shifts in institutional practices. If I reflect on this trajectory, then I find a common thread and set of values that guide how I approach the role: greater access to education as a goal, openness as a means to do the work, and leveraging technology in thoughtful ways to create meaningful experiences for students.

Taken together, our professional journeys provide insights into a set of shared values and beliefs consistent with the time-proven practices of distance education itself: access, equity, community, relationships, and care as highlighted in the introduction of this book.

Exploring the Size and Scope of Leadership

Our second writing prompt was an invitation to *examine and reflect on "big L versus small l" leadership and to discuss how we navigate the possibilities and challenges that this distinction exposes as well as the difference between the two in terms of affecting our work.*

Bottom-Up or Top-Down?

TANNIS

I think of leadership as big L and small l. This has been defined in various ways in different disciplines, but in the context of the work that I do big L leadership includes large and visible efforts often associated with the position, whereas small l leadership comprises the less visible and tangible efforts often associated with care and capacity building. For me, the two types are in constant negotiation. I do not know whether this is a gendered experience, but I have never been in a role in which only big L leadership was required, and I think that it would be a lot easier if that was the case. Small l leadership can be more hidden, time consuming, and less rewarding, but the impact can be equally important.

MICHELLE

I have been pondering the question "do you need small l (and perhaps more distributive models of leadership) and big L leadership to make transformative change?" Recent research on the institutional implementation of open education (Morgan et al., 2021) highlights the importance of both senior leadership and grassroots distributed networks as essential.

CHRISTINA

A policy or initiative promoted only from the big L level likely will not go very far if it is not supported at the grassroots level. Connecting those levels seems to be critical. This also makes me think about how in my role I am in a middle space that can be powerful.

ANNE-MARIE

I am thinking about the leadership role that one plays in an organization by being a connector of many others. We all know someone in our institutions who knows everyone else there. Often those people are not in positions of hierarchical power, but they have immense social and cultural power and are vital to things getting done. So the kinds of middle-level leadership roles (Latchem & Hanna, 2001) that a few of us hold are important in terms of a similar function: that is, knitting together the various parts of our institutions.

When considering the roles that big L leadership plays, Anne-Marie and Christina highlighted the challenges that can be faced when there is a level of distrust in more senior roles.

ANNE-MARIE

In some cases, being the connector in the middle is immensely political, and recently I have found myself on the receiving end of some pretty harsh vitriol ultimately targeted elsewhere, but I am right in the line of fire. It hits me hard because it absolutely hits me in my values.

CHRISTINA

That sounds really challenging! At times, I struggle with the vitriol aimed at senior leadership. I think that some of the distrust might come from a lack of transparency, which can be a complex issue. I have had the experience of wanting to say more about something that also hit me deep in my values, struggling a lot, and being quieter than I would have wanted. It was one of the most frustrating and difficult things of my career so far.

Navigating the tension between what can and cannot be made transparent, Elizabeth highlighted the role that an external consultant can play in supporting leadership at both levels.

ELIZABETH

You have certain liberties and operate within different power dynamics (as the external) that facilitate the ability to influence change and navigate big L and small l in different ways from someone embedded in the institution. At its core, the end users and their contexts are central to the overall approach taken, and the use of a participatory approach to the work of gathering, involving, and moving forward with multiple perspectives can be facilitated by working with someone from outside the organization.

Distance education leadership requires both big L and small l leadership, and in many respects navigating between the two is the leadership "dance" that we have experienced in our careers.

Defining Leadership in Distance Education

Our third writing prompt asked us to *examine what leadership looks like for us and where we find inherent value in doing this work.*

TANNIS

Leadership is about executing change systemically, provided that the rationale for the change is sitting on a foundation in which I believe. This is why it is easier for me to get behind initiatives that relate to open education, distance education, and access to higher education. A tension point for me is that I am working toward significant change, so small successes do not actually feel like successes, but maybe they should.

CHRISTINA

Large changes (usually) do not happen quickly. It is challenging for me to remember this and to try to celebrate the smaller changes.

ANNE-MARIE

Small steps are important because they are many people's first steps. I am reminded of adrienne marie brown's (2017) description of the repetitious/fractal nature of small changes. Lots of them add up to something much bigger.

MICHELLE

How do you manage when you need to support initiatives or spend your time on tasks on which your values or interests do not necessarily align?

CHRISTINA

This can be very challenging, though depending on the role one can have the ear, as it were, of some of the folks who make higher-level decisions. It is true that there might be times when leaders end up having to do things that do not fully align with their values, and that can feel like having an ethical rift inside oneself. Working toward change at the same time might help one to start to heal.

Leadership for me includes balancing priorities and working to put in place the structures, communication channels, and resources necessary for people in the unit that I lead to do their best work, to collaborate with other units, and to work with faculty members and students to support and improve teaching and learning. I think of myself in part as a facilitator and a champion for others, and I spend a lot of time working fairly quietly behind the scenes.

TANNIS

In my current role, I do not see myself as a facilitator and champion so much as helping to steer a ship, but facilitators and champions are very much needed.

CHRISTINA

I agree that a clear plan and direction are needed. Perhaps because my role is sort of a middle level, I need to steer our unit within broader roadmaps, such as strategic plans and priorities at the institution, while negotiating our own goals as well.

MICHELLE

To extend the ship metaphor, without this overt steering through the establishment of priorities/guidelines, and finding the resources to support them, I think that teams feel *rudderless* and *adrift.* I think that this also relates back to the discussion where the idea of transparency came up. I think that, if senior leaders can be as transparent as they can about the direction, rationale for change, and the why/how of priorities and outline how they align with both institutional and personal values (realizing of course that not everything can be shared), then change is more likely to be embraced.

ANNE-MARIE

It is incredibly important to be open and transparent when things are not going well. Leadership work is not composed of 100% successes; neither are we some kind of superhuman beings. I think that it is important to talk about what is not going well when we can, to talk about the things that are hard, and generally to be open to being a little vulnerable as a leader. That can be an incredibly difficult and sometimes risky thing to do as a woman in a digital leadership role, but I think that it is important in terms of making our roles accessible to women who might want to come after us. The confidence to accept a bit of failure as part of the job is key.

ALL

There is an inherent need to establish boundaries and priorities and not to compromise personal needs and wellness so that one can be effective in creating a thriving environment for others. At all levels, putting effort into participating in creative and fun projects is valuable, for they are personally and professionally fulfilling, and they foster relationships, networks, growth, and motivation.

Distance education leadership is about promoting change, systematically and incrementally, and providing direction as well as the structures, supports, and resources for people to do their work. It is also about providing support for the imperfect big L and small l leadership acts done each day.

Morals of the Stories

Each of our journeys reflects a set of shared values for creating more open and accessible educational spaces by considering how equitable uses of technology can help us to overcome barriers or generate innovative approaches. Common across our stories is a deep care for the work that we do and a commitment that it has an impact in supporting others. Justice and equity compel us in our work, and one of the big challenges that we have encountered is an ethical rift: that is, misalignment between what you might be asked to do as a leader and what your values tell you is the right thing to do.

Holding on to your values, being authentic, and being as open and transparent as possible, including talking about failures, can not only sustain your commitments but also model what leadership can be in this space. In higher education, in which the culture cultivates debate and rewards the persona of the public intellectual, being able to navigate the institutional structural requirements while being able to get things done is not for the faint of heart. Having trusting relationships with other women in leadership positions is critical, for both formal and informal mentorship and support are often lacking, particularly in senior leadership positions, in which hierarchical structures can create power imbalances.

The pathway into and through distance education leadership roles is best approached with an orientation to hurry slowly, recognizing that values-based leadership requires time to consult, reflect, and then act. In the digital learning space, there is time pressure built into the work partly because of the changing nature of the technology itself. The rush to be empathetic, help, and fix is great, and responding to every call has its costs. Making time to slow down and take up a values-based leadership approach can help us to go further, faster, together.

References

Axe, J., Childs, E., DeVries, I., & Webster, K. (2020). Student experiences of open educational practices: A systematic literature review. *Journal of e-Learning and Knowledge Society, 16*(4), 67–75. https://doi.org/10.20368/1971-8829/1135340

Batliwala, S. (2010, May 11). *Feminist leadership for social transformation: Clearing the conceptual cloud.* JASS: Just Power. https://justassociates.org/sites/justassociates.org/files/feminist-leadership-clearing-conceptual-cloud-srilatha-batliwala.pdf

brown, a. m. (2017). *Emergent strategy: Shaping change, changing worlds.* AK Press.

Castro Benavides, L. M., Tamayo Arias, J. A., Arango Serna, M. D., Branch Bedoya, J. W., & Burgos, D. (2020). Digital transformation in higher education institutions: A systematic literature review. *Sensors, 20*(11), 3291. https://doi.org/10.3390/s20113291

Childs, E., & Crichton, S. (2018). A consideration of the pressures impacting distance education in higher education and the use of a design-based instructional approach. In M. Moore (Ed.), *Handbook of distance education* (4th ed.). Routledge. https://doi.org/10.4324/9781315296135

Hamilton, M. L., & Pinnegar, S. (2014). Intimate scholarship in research: An example from self-study of teaching and teacher education practices methodology. *LEARNing Landscapes, 8*(1), 153–171. https://doi.org/10.36510/learnland.v8i1.680

Johnson, N. (2020). *Digital learning in Canadian higher education in 2020: Ontario report.* https://www.ecampusontario.ca/wp-content/uploads/2021/04/Digital-Learning-in-Canadian-Higher-Education-in-2020-The-Ontario-Report-EN.pdf

Latchem, C. & Hanna, D.E. (2001). *Leadership for 21st century learning: Global perspectives from international experts.* Routledge.

Morgan, T., Childs, E., Hendricks, C., Harrison, M., DeVries, I., & Jhangiani, R. (2021). How are we doing with open educational practice initiatives? Applying an institutional self-assessment tool in five higher education institutions. *The International Review of Research in Open and Distributed Learning, 22*(4), 125–140. https://doi.org/10.19173/irrodl.v22i4.5745

Paul, R. (2023). Introduction to organization, leadership, and change in ODDE. In O. Zawacki-Richter & I. Jung (Eds.), *Handbook of open, distance and digital education,* 463–474. Springer. https://doi.org/10.1007/978-981-19-2080-6_86

van Oostveen, R., DiGiuseppe, M., Barber, W., Blayone, T., & Childs, E. (2017). New conceptions for digital technology sandboxes: Developing a fully online learning communities (FOLC) model. In T. J. Bastiaens & G. Marks (Eds.), *Education and information technology annual 2017: A selection of AACE award papers,* 143–152. Association for the Advancement of Computing in Education.

13 What's up, Doc? The Impacts of Graduate Study for Women

Jenni Hayman

On October 30, 2018, starting at 3:30 p.m. EDT, I stepped up to a virtual microphone with my Arizona State University (ASU) dissertation supervisor and committee in attendance. My task was to present my research, answer questions about it, and defend my dissertation as the culmination of a three-year professional doctorate in education. The title of my openly published dissertation was *Open Is an Invitation: Exploring Use of Open Educational Resources with Ontario Post-Secondary Educators*. By 6 p.m., I had passed my defence, and from that point forward I had earned the right to call myself Dr. Jenni Hayman.

For a first-generation graduate facing many barriers to post-secondary achievement, the right to be called Dr. Hayman was an important milestone. My sister phoned me right after my graduation, and her greeting—"What's up, Doc?"—was a fantastic laugh-out-loud moment for us, having grown up in the 1970s in the Bugs Bunny era. It was at once a ridiculous oversimplification of the difficulty of doctoral study and a humorous culmination of our shared family journey of more than 50 years. This is my story of why becoming Dr. Jenni Hayman was a worthwhile endeavour for me and why I believe that similar experiences can be important for women seeking postsecondary open and distance education leadership roles.

The Short Story

To situate myself for this chapter, I was born in the United States and raised in a dysfunctional and relatively poor family. I graduated from high school at 16 and engaged in a typical first-generation student undergraduate journey at three different schools. At 26, I received from Indiana University a Bachelor of Music in jazz studies with a major in voice. I married, moved to Canada, had two sons, parented, was a professional classical musician, and was divorced in 2008. I began graduate studies that year, worked many interesting jobs, remarried, moved several times, completed a Graduate Certificate and Diploma in Instructional Design, and graduated in 2014 with a Master of Education in Distance Education from Athabasca University. I completed my Doctor of Education in Leadership and Innovation four years later. I am currently an online (distance) program administrator and chair at a college in Ontario. I am also a researcher, an associate professor, and an advocate of the use of open educational resources (OER) and open pedagogy as part of postsecondary teaching and learning in distance modalities.

In my role as a chair for online asynchronous course delivery, I have significant opportunities to advise and influence course design for open practice, including the use of OER, student co-creation of learning and resources, use of the United Nations Sustainable Development Goals for content and learning outcomes, and open research practices. As an associate professor, I teach a graduate course openly designed in WordPress, and I support each cohort of learners to explore and examine the value of open pedagogy in their studies and professional roles. Open education, as a common good for global success, is my primary value as a distance education leader.

Problematization and Assemblage

This chapter is an auto-ethnographic account relying on relevant elements of method as provided by Hughes and Pennington (2017). They introduced problematization as a strategy for self-collection of data and scaffolding an auto-ethnographic account. I developed a statement related to their questions (p. 59) as follows: graduate study for women in the field of open and distance learning leads to engaging and better-paid leadership opportunities. With this statement in mind, I share my responses below.

Who am I to be making this statement? I am a woman administrator in open and distance learning with a history of graduate study, research, and leadership in global postsecondary contexts. My experiences have resulted in improved finances and personal capacity as an instructional designer, educational technologist, researcher, and leader.

For whom am I making it? I am making my statement to benefit interested women who might be considering administrative or senior leadership careers in open and distance learning at postsecondary institutions.

Why am I making this statement here, now? The invitation to participate in writing this book was an opportunity for me to share a relevant story. Preparing this chapter has been a method of professional development through reflecting and learning.

Whom does my statement benefit? My statement can benefit women who are early to mid-career practitioners working in postsecondary open and distance education by considering the value of graduate study.

Whom does my statement harm? Not everyone can afford the time and financial burden of graduate study, and I have not explored alternative pathways to leadership success. My experience of graduate education is that of a cis-gendered white woman with economic privilege, and I have selected literature from that perspective. I believe that my privilege, my lack of exploration of professional development outside graduate study, and my limited gendered experience, though not necessarily harmful, could be limitations of this chapter.

Along with problematization, Hughes and Pennington's (2017) idea of "assemblage"—combining auto-ethnographic narrative and literature—was valuable to me and helped me to frame this chapter. I selected the following reflection questions to guide my writing.

- In what ways does graduate education for women in the field of open and distance learning lead to engaging and better-paid leadership opportunities?
- What are some of the challenges of graduate education for women?
- Which changes in practice might make it easier for women to engage in graduate education?
- In what ways does graduate education for women in the field of open and distance learning lead to engaging and better-paid leadership opportunities?

Several life factors can affect the decision to undertake graduate study. As Boneva et al. (2022) found, perceptions of the benefits of completing graduate study varied depending on the lives and undergraduate experiences of prospective learners. In my case, as an at-home parent for many years facing separation from my spouse, I needed an opportunity to examine my capacity to learn and earn. My motivations to pursue additional education at the time of my separation were financial security and mental health healing. I researched programs that my skills, interests, and values might fit and participated in career coaching. My work at the time, as an Apple Store creative employee (teaching customers how to use the full suite of photo, audio, and video tools on their computers), inspired my love of technology for education. I chose the Athabasca University Graduate Certificate in Instructional Design and the University of Toronto Certificate in Adult Education as my start. I have been engaged in rewarding open and distance learning and work ever since.

One of the primary benefits of my graduate education has been a rise in income. Since earning my first graduate credential in 2009, my annual income has increased from approximately $65,000 to over $160,000. Each graduate credential that I have earned has had a positive impact on my income, long-term family support capacity, and opportunities to influence the quality of distance education design and delivery at multiple institutions. The financial benefits of graduate-level attainment in my field, and especially in professional programs, are well documented in national statistics (Statistics Canada, 2020; Stevenson, 2016).

As described by Posselt and Grodsky (2017), the more intangible benefits of graduate study in terms of personal confidence, access to influential roles, and increased social capital are not well represented in the literature. Many first-generation students like me have experienced the social capital stemming from the completion of undergraduate work (Gardner & Holley, 2011) and want to continue these benefits through further education. The intangible benefits of completing graduate studies might comprise an important avenue for further research.

Based on interests gained from my graduate studies, I resigned from my full-time work as an online instructional designer in 2013 to pursue a research start-up. A unique outcome of this experience was learning about the power of emerging self-publishing and self-promotion paradigms such as WordPress and Twitter. The rise and value of social media and blogging in education over the past 15 years are well documented in the literature (Lauricella, 2020; Malik et al., 2019; Weller, 2020), and these practices contributed to my capacity to build a personal learning network and a reputation as a competent academic. In 2015, I experienced a reward for my entrepreneurial adventures with an offer of work at Arizona State University. I was hired as the lead instructional designer for an ASU-edX partnership called the Global Freshman Academy. While I was engaged in this work, building MOOCs for thousands of global learners, I began my doctoral studies. In my experience, the value of the design, learning outcomes, and professional practice of the ASU doctoral program cannot be overstated. I use the research, leadership, and innovation skills that I acquired and used as part of this study nearly every day in my current work.

The final benefit for me of graduate study has been my increased confidence as a woman with sought-after and increasing skills. Because of my education and experiences over the past 15 years, I am empowered now in every sense of the word. I can speak with authenticity in any forum about topics in my fields of expertise. I can support others, I can lead others, I can collaborate on and contribute to projects and research that have positive impacts. Although an introvert by nature, I have developed a nurturing and deep network of global colleagues.

What Are Some of the Challenges of Graduate Education for Women?

Decisions about graduate studies are complex. Canadian statistics show that approximately 80% of women in master's programs graduate but that only 50% of women in doctoral programs complete their journeys (Statistics Canada, 2022a, 2022b). A recent scan of gender in master's and doctoral programs at the University of British Columbia indicated significant gains in the number of women for both master's study (now up to 62.16% from 51.15% in 1991) and doctoral study (currently 50.50% up from 33.21% in 1991) (University of British Columbia Graduate School, n.d.). This is an encouraging trend. However, during graduate studies, women can still face gender- and race-based discrimination and harassment (Deem, 2018; Roos, 2008), which can make their journeys more difficult. In the realm of PhDs, tenured faculty positions at universities have been challenging for women (Roos, 2008). In my experience, it is good to consult with a career coach, examine your current work environment, and talk with your family members to determine which type of credential might have the best value for your goals.

A typical question to ask about any decision on education is can I afford to go to school? At the time of writing, the degrees that I earned would cost a 2022 entry-level learner $20,548 CAD for the 11 courses in the Master of Education in Open, Digital, and Distance Education in Canada (Athabasca University, 2022) and approximately $39,000 USD for a three-year Doctor of Education in Leadership and Innovation in the United States (Arizona State University, 2022). Examining all financial options to pay for graduate education is an important task. An additional set of self-doubt questions that I explored in my decision making included the following. Am I selfish to take this time and money? Am I smart enough to be successful in graduate study? Will this choice of program really help me to achieve my financial and mental health goals? What if I fail? The interior voice of doubt and imposter syndrome for high-achieving women and many graduate students is well documented (Wilson & Cutri, 2019) and has been one of my loud life companions. Ultimately, I ignored my self-doubt and persisted.

For those who experience imposter syndrome, graduate study can be imbued with feelings of inadequacy (Gardner & Holley, 2011; Wilson & Cutri, 2019). When I first began reading academic articles in graduate school, I kept a dictionary nearby, and it often took me hours to read and reflect. I was anxious about writing papers and thought that I would be found out at any moment. My worst fear was failing. As a lifelong honours-level student, I felt out of my depth for graduate work. This was a barrier that I had to overcome to persist and get through the heavy workload on a course-by-course basis. As Wilson and Cutri (2019) suggest, forming a community of practice around academic reading and writing might be an important activity for anyone beginning graduate study.

Although I benefited from employer support for some of my tuition and fees, I had to use significant personal funds. Most of the time that I was enrolled in master's and doctoral work I worked full time, which made distance education an ideal choice for me and my family. I would not have been able to complete my studies without exceptional time and dedication from my spouse and sons. I am still returning funds to my retirement savings (a privileged funding option in Canada). Post-graduation debt continues to be a reality for most people who undertake graduate study (Stevenson, 2016). It can be difficult to calculate if increased wages related to further education eventually offset the time commitments and financial costs (Posselt & Grodsky, 2017; Stevenson, 2016). Therefore, decision making about graduate study should include a wide lens on the potential challenges and benefits.

Which Changes in Practice Might Make It Easier and More Effective for Women to Engage in Graduate Education?

There are challenges to being a woman in postsecondary learning and work environments. Being a very naive and introverted young woman during my undergraduate years, I experienced multiple instances of sexual harassment and abuse. Unfortunately, this type of abuse persists in higher education (Bondestam & Lundqvist, 2020). I had not been raised as a confident self-advocate and therefore was vulnerable. I did not experience sexual harassment during my graduate studies (thankfully), possibly because I chose predominantly online asynchronous modes of study—and I was more mature and confident. Online asynchronous study as a potentially safer pathway for women in graduate programs might be worth exploring. I would be delighted to support such research.

Although my years of work as a support staff instructional designer (from 2009 to 2016) were largely positive, I did experience occasional derision and oppression from men (and even some women) in positions of academic power. Conflicts between faculty members and instructional designers are described in the literature (Halupa, 2019; Miller & Stein, 2016; Romero-Hall et al., 2018). Anecdotally, among my instructional design peers, there are many examples of negative experiences, especially for women. One of my goals in seeking graduate-level education was to enhance my gender-based power in academic settings by enhancing my knowledge of research and evidence-based practice. I believe that I have achieved this goal in many ways, but I was unable to find any relevant studies in the literature related to the empowerment of women through graduate education. This might be an opportunity for further research.

Postsecondary and distance education environments continue to be dominated by white male educators who earn more and are more likely to receive grants, publish research, and be rewarded with university tenure than equally qualified women and racialized educators (Deem, 2018; Statistics Canada, 2022b). Racial and gender-based inequity persists across faculty, staff, and administrative roles in postsecondary contexts, especially at the level of senior leadership. Information about gendered pay differences for my field (occupations in education, law, and social, community, and government services) showed women earning 82% of what men earned in 2017, with a one-point drop to 81% in 2022 (Statistics Canada, 2023). There are also persistent gender and racial differences in doctoral salaries (Webber & Canché, 2015). Like other work environments, postsecondary education settings should become more equitable, inclusive, caring, and collaborative ecosystems (Deem, 2018; Timmons, 2021). An intentional part of postsecondary distance education practice should be continuing efforts to hire, equitably compensate, and support women into middle and senior leadership roles while working to change the power culture of academia.

The final piece of the puzzle related to change in practice for women in graduate studies might be the support of time (Fakunmoju et al., 2016). Davis and colleagues' (2022) focus on the time disparity (and related barriers to academic success) among tenured and tenure-track women during the first two years of the COVID-19 pandemic were revealing and highlighted ongoing systemic inequity for women academics as daughters, parents, and spouses. When external care provision and schooling were significantly curtailed by COVID-19 closures and restrictions, women were most likely to give up their jobs (or take leaves from them) to do the work of managing home and family (Davis et al., 2022). Equal distribution of family care requires further work from all stakeholders so that women can pursue meaningful careers in which they receive equitable compensation. Employers should find ways to support women who want to pursue graduate degrees, such as weekly time for study and short-term leaves for research or dissertation writing.

Summary

Writing this chapter was a great opportunity for me to explore some of the literature related to my experiences as a first-generation graduate moving through the lifelong joys and challenges of work, education, and family life as a woman. As echoed in so much of the literature by women in my field, I feel lucky to have chosen open and distance education as my area of study and expertise. I am grateful for the rich network of colleagues whom I have met and for the evolution of open and distance learning as strategic mandates for so many postsecondary institutions. I feel valued and valuable. In my time as an open and distance education practitioner, the places where I have worked have come a long way in terms of support and access for women. However, most colleges and universities still have a long way to go to establish themselves as places of authentic equity. Postsecondary employers, who clearly know the value of graduate-level skills and espouse the value of lifelong learning, should be leaders in the empowerment of women through graduate studies. When these changes begin to be enacted meaningfully, it will be easier for women to be successful in graduate studies and their subsequent careers. I hope that my ideas about the value of graduate studies for women are useful, and I look forward to continuing my support for women to achieve their goals through education, research, and leadership.

References

Arizona State University. (2022). Online Doctor of Leadership and Innovation. https://asuonline.asu.edu/online-degree-programs/graduate/edd-leadership-and-innovation/

Athabasca University. (2022). Master of Education in Open, Digital, and Distance Education. https://www.athabascau.ca/calendar/graduate/fhss/master-of-education-in-open-digital-and-distance-education.html#fees

Bondestam, F., & Lundqvist, M. (2020). Sexual harassment in higher education: A system review. *European Journal of Higher Education, 10*(4), 397–419. https://doi.org/10.1080/21568235.2020.1729833

Boneva, T., Golin, M., & Rauh, C. (2022). Can perceived returns explain enrollment gaps in postgraduate education? *Labour Economics, 77*. https://doi.org/10.1016/j.labeco.2021.101998

Davis, J. C., Li, E. P., Butterfield, M. S., DiLabio, G. A., Santhagunam, N., & Marcolin, B. (2022). Are we failing female and racialized academics? A Canadian national survey examining the impacts of the COVID-19 pandemic on tenure and tenure-track faculty. *Gender, Work, and Organization, 29*(3), 703–722. https://onlinelibrary.wiley.com/doi/full/10.1111/gwao.12811

Deem, R. (2018). The gender politics of higher education. In B. Cantwell, S. Coats, & R. King (Eds.), *Handbook on the politics of higher education* (pp. 431–448). https://doi.org/10.4337/9781786435026

Fakunmoju, S., Donahue, G. R., McCoy, S., & Mengel, A. S. (2016). Life satisfaction and perceived meaningfulness of learning experience among first-year traditional graduate social work students. *Journal of Education and Practice, 7*(6), 49–62.

Gardner, S. K., & Holley, K. A. (2011). "Those invisible barriers are real": The progression of first-generation students through doctoral education. *Equity & Excellence in Education, 44*(1), 77–92. https://doi.org/10.1080/10665684.2011.529791

Halupa, C. (2019). Differentiation of roles: Instructional designers and faculty in the creation of online courses. *International Journal of Higher Education, 1*(8), 55–68.

Hughes, S. A., & Pennington, J. L. (2017). *Autoethnography: Process, product, and possibility for critical social research.* Sage. https://dx.doi.org/10.4135/9781483398594

Lauricella, S. (2020). A feminist autoethnography of academic performance on Twitter: Community, creativity, and comedy. In T. Moeke-Pickering, S. Cote-Meek, & A. Pegoraro (Eds.), *Critical reflections and politics on advancing women in the academy* (pp. 33–51). IGI Global.

Malik, A., Heyman-Schrum, C., & Johri, A. (2019). Use of Twitter across educational settings: A review of the literature. *International Journal of Educational Technology in Higher Education, 16*(36). https://doi.org/10.1186/s41239-019-0166-x

Miller, S., & Stein, G. (2016, February 8). Finding our voice: Instructional designers in higher education. *Educause Review.* https://er.educause.edu/articles/2016/2/finding-our-voice-instructional-designers-in-higher-education

Posselt, J. R., & Grodsky, E. (2017). Graduate education and social stratification [Public access author manuscript]. National Library of Medicine. https://www.ncbi.nlm.nih.gov/pmc/articles/PMC6335048/

Romero-Hall, E., Aldemir, T., Colorado-Resa, J., Dickson-Dean, C., Watson, G. S., & Sadaf, A. (2018). Undisclosed stories of instructional design female scholars in academia. *Women's Studies International Forum, 71,* 19–28. https://doi.org/10.1016/j.wsif.2018.09.004

Roos, P. A. (2008). Together but unequal: Combating gender inequity in the academy. *Journal of Workplace Rights, 13*(2), 185–199.

Statistics Canada. (2020). Which doctoral degree programs were associated with the highest pay prior to the COVID-19 pandemic? A focus on very detailed fields of study. https://www150.statcan.gc.ca/n1/pub/11-626-x/11-626-x2020020-eng.htm

Statistics Canada. (2022a). Graduation of master's degree students, within Canada, by student characteristics. https://www150.statcan.gc.ca/t1/tbl1/en/tv.action?pid=3710013604

Statistics Canada. (2022b). Persistence and graduation of doctoral degree students, within Canada, by student characteristics. https://www150.statcan.gc.ca/t1/tbl1/en/tv.action?pid=3710013605

Statistics Canada. (2023). Average and mean gender wage ratio, annual. https://www150.statcan.gc.ca/t1/tbl1/en/tv.action?pid=1410034002

Stevenson, A. (2016). The returns to quality in graduate education. *Education Economics, 24*(5), 445–464.

Timmons, V. (2021). I didn't expect YOU to be the university president: A critical reflection on three decades of women's leadership in Canadian academia. In I. Management Association (Ed.), *Research anthology on challenges for women in leadership roles* (pp. 318–326). IGI Global. https://doi.org/10.4018/978-1-7998-8592-4.ch018

University of British Columbia Graduate School. (n.d.). Demographics—Gender [Web page]. https://www.grad.ubc.ca/about-us/graduate-education-analysis-research/demographics-gender

Webber, K. L., & Canché, M. G. (2015). Not equal for all: Gender and race differences in salary for doctoral degree recipients. *Research in Higher Education, 56*(7), 645–672. https://doi.org/10.1007/s11162-015-9369-8

Weller, M. (2020). *25 years of ed tech.* Athabasca University Press. https://www.aupress.ca/books/120290-25-years-of-ed-tech/

Wilson, S., & Cutri, J. (2019). Negating isolation and imposter syndrome through writing as product and as process: The impact of collegiate writing networks during a doctoral programme. In L. Pretorius, L. Macaulay, & B. Cahusac de Caux (Eds.), *Wellbeing in doctoral education* (pp. 59–76). Springer. https://doi.org/10.1007/978-981-13-9302-0_7

14 (Re-)Envisioning Instructor Leadership Strengthened through a Decolonizing and Culturally Responsive Lens

Erin Keith

There is a strengthening view of adjunct instructors' ongoing learning in higher education, specifically in their professional capacities as knowledge keepers and course facilitators, by which educators are encouraged to take the step forward to self-determine what they need for their own growth and learning (Donohoo & Katz, 2020). It is a decolonizing and culturally responsive view by which higher education administration and tenured faculty members see adjuncts for their strengths, capacities, and value. No longer should instructors be considered empty vessels to be filled or passive recipients of knowledge; rather, they are "analysts and synthesizers" (Blaschke & Hase, 2015, as cited in Akyildiz, 2019, p. 164) of their own learning through a variety of different modes, often beyond colonial institutional walls. However, obstacles to learning and growth still exist for many instructors, particularly distance education adjunct faculty like me, especially those who identify as women (Smith-Carrier et al., 2021). Adjunct instructor precarity and inequity have long been noted in research from the early 2000s (Dawson et al., 2019), yet hiring trends are increasing (Eidinger, 2021), leaving adjuncts without a sense of community, belonging, or leadership.

Leading with Capacity and Critical Consciousness

In education and other social science related fields, a focus on decolonizing and decentring whiteness tied to infusing culturally responsive and relevant contents and epistemologies into distance education courses is now evolving rapidly in teaching and learning (Khalifa, 2018; Lopez, 2022). Faculties now expect instructors to be leaders in diverse and critical ways of knowing and to include this knowledge in their course syllabuses, facilitations, and interactions with students, colleagues, and administrative staff (Hudley & Mallinson, 2017). However, much of this learning falls to the instructors to seek out, with little support or financial contribution from the very institutions demanding it (Rose, 2020). Within this chapter, grounded in critical race theory, instructor leadership is centred on a continuum of learning that views instructors' learning leadership as a *strength*—an ever-growing strength reinforced by colleagues who share their cultures and lived experiences, offering constructive feedback, storytelling/counternarratives, and equity-literate, compassionate dialogue.

My Journey of Instructional Leadership

Guided and heartened by Ladson-Billings' (1995) transformative article "But That's Just Good Teaching! The Case for Culturally-Relevant Pedagogy," I have sought to embed culturally relevant teaching into my pedagogical praxis since the onset of my K–12 teaching career in 1995. This article was a course reading during my Master of Education degree, and it changed my teaching trajectory. After years in the Canadian school system in various teaching capacities, and then becoming a university adjunct instructor in 2016, with most of my experience in distance education, I have witnessed firsthand the power of student learning when instructors embody Ladson-Billings' epistemology of "critical consciousness" (p. 162). As a white cis-gender woman and settler, I aim to deepen my critical consciousness while learning and unlearning about the ever-present oppressive hegemony and injustice in education that harm and retraumatize Indigenous, Black, and racialized students.

I continually endeavour to create opportunities for students to engage critically with content, invite multiple perspectives and cultural understandings, and become community problem solvers and social advocates, and I always expect high achievement outcomes (Ladson-Billings, 2021a). I recognize that not all instructors have had a learning path similar to mine; I also acknowledge the privilege of my intersectionality in being harboured and guided by willing tenured colleagues with access to rich professional learning and library resources. In reality, though, most adjunct instructors are pressured to work in a "system that is ready to get rid of [them] as soon as the working contract has finished, offering nothing other than 'unemployed excellence'—including stress, isolation, invisibility, constant movement, and mental health issues" (Stoica et al., 2019, p. 79). I have experienced this innumerable times throughout my sessional career. There is a culture of devaluing adjunct instructors that needs to change. Institutions must acknowledge that their adjunct scholars matter and begin to disrupt the second-class status that they have long held compared with their faculty colleagues.

The Erosion of Academic Humanity

Unfortunately, the number of adjunct instructors in higher education continues to rise, particularly in distance education (Rose, 2020). According to the Canadian Union of Public Employees (2018), 54% of faculty appointments in Canadian universities are short-term adjunct stints rather than permanent positions. At the college level, this statistic rises to over 70% (Zitko & Schultz, 2020) with women, who are often minoritized and racialized, making up more than two-thirds of the academic profession. The reason for this high rate of adjunct workers is primarily cost savings along with an increase in casualized labour (Mason & Megoran, 2021). Casual, contract staff are easy to forget about once they have fulfilled their contractual duties. They are mistreated because of their invisibility and rarely seen as equal academics by faculty colleagues (Mason & Megoran, 2021).

Racialized and minority adjuncts such as women also face more vulnerabilities than their male counterparts because of work exploitation, unfair demands to work beyond their contract obligations (e.g., grant writing, creating conference materials without being invited to present), and debriefing meetings to keep faculty administrators up to date on course progression (Caretta et al., 2018). This pink-collar workforce faces much dehumanization that slowly extinguishes the adjunct's flame of creativity, teaching, and scholarship. This results in a faculty's casualized workforce as mere empty shells of their former selves (Eidinger, 2021). I have felt this dehumanization as I became what felt like a cog on a wheel that could not slow down, and I could not say no to a course offering for fear that I might be sidelined in future terms. It is a long, painful, and debilitating erosion perpetuated by an unending lineup of new PhD and EdD graduates hopeful for a rewarding teaching career in higher education.

Culturally Responsive Instructional Leadership

As I return to Ladson-Billings' (1995, p. 159) urging that being culturally responsive in praxis is "just good teaching," I wonder whether its framework could disrupt the cog-on-a-wheel reality of adjunct teaching in higher education. According to Shah (n.d., para. 3), "culturally responsive and relevant leaders acknowledge and disrupt oppressive systems" by engaging in social activism that upholds equity and emphasizes that leaders unlearn as a part of their learning, centre self-agency and action, and create sustainable spaces of support and sustenance for themselves (Lopez, 2016). Since higher education institutions are predestined as "white spaces" (Joseph-Salisbury, 2018), I wonder whether adopting knowledge principles of culturally responsive instructional leadership that spotlight whiteness could help in restructuring the disparities and inequities of the adjunct system.

These instructional leaders are pervasive in higher education yet invisible because of their adjunct status. In addition, trends in cultural representation indicate that under-represented minorities who are racialized are eight times more likely to be sessional instructors versus white colleagues (Flaherty, 2016). Could this long-standing advice from Ladson-Billings grounded in critical race theory, among many other racialized scholars (Khalifa, 2018; Lopez, 2016, 2022; Shah, n.d.), disrupt the enduring hegemony in distance education that both white and racialized adjunct instructors face and shift their leadership dial toward liberation and freedom (Shah, 2018)? By leveraging culturally responsive principles of reflexive practice, counternarratives, and high expectations, adjuncts could collectively and relationally unite to embody actions that mitigate, disrupt, and dismantle the systemic oppression that they face as precarious instructors.

The Knowledge Principle of Reflexive Practice

By its nature, reflexivity interrupts normalized institutional traditions and allows questions to surface about capacities as adjunct instructors. It is a cerebral act with creative outputs such as journalling or storytelling guided by the individual's lived experiences. As Lyle and Caissie (2021, p. 221) purport, "reflexivity is not to be engaged casually. To be reflexive is to live with an empathic heart and redirect the onus of responsibility from I to we with the intent of fostering deeper debate and critical questioning." If adjunct instructors engaged collectively in reflexive practice and then shared their new insights and actions as a form of resistance, Alemán (2017) suggests, then previously invisible and silenced scholars could be heard. Collective reflexive practice could look like sharing artistic representations of the instructional work through media such as poems, sketches, sculptures, paintings, et cetera. It could be infused into monthly synchronous sessions during which fellow adjunct colleagues share their experiences through their artworks to create an anthology of reflexivity. Such actions serve as sources of "fulfilment and communal empowerment" (Alemán, 2017, p. 75) that could create brighter pathways for all that fracture the hegemonic system of casualized labour and perhaps foster and re-story a new space of professional equity and humanity. Following is a poem that I wrote about envisioning "a new story of humanity" as I explored my reflexive voice as an adjunct instructor.

A New Story of Humanity

Take all the worn-down educators
and rally them
together.
Wrap them in empathy,
shared understanding,
and a sense of belonging

that awakens and revitalizes
a new space of capacity.
Woke once more,
polish each other to a shine
that illuminates
a united, powerful voice
so that they cannot
help but to listen.

—Unity (Keith, 2022)

The Knowledge Principle of Counternarratives

A powerful tenet of critical race theory is the centring of counternarratives to unsettle majoritarian narratives (Ladson-Billings, 1998) about adjuncting, such as being invisible to tenured faculty members, preparation and meeting time as free labour, and instructors not considered researchers, among others (Truong, 2021). According to Blaisdell (2021, p. 4), there are four tenets of counternarratives in critical race theory: providing new (often untold) narratives to understand power, deconstructing majoritarian narratives, serving as a cure for silencing, and fostering activism. How could these tenets shift the inequitable and unjust conditions that adjunct distance instructors face? In the case of instructor leadership, this could be meeting regularly in a shared "affinity space" (Gee, 2004), whether face to face or online, to share views and experiences as sources of strength in supporting one another.

These spaces could serve as an empathetic, capacity-rich, communal area that invites women instructors to share their lived experiences, co-construct and advocate for new policies, highlight their unique leadership qualities, and help to restore a sense of professional harmony. Counternarratives are powerful stories reaffirming that "those who lack material wealth or political power still have access to thought and language, and their development of those tools . . . differs from that of the most privileged" (Matsuda, 1995, p. 65), such as tenured faculty members. Counternarratives can serve as efficacious disruptors that shed light on the colonial advantage of growing adjunct dependence, particularly for under-represented instructors, including women, racialized, and minoritized scholars, and the normalization of this polarizing trend in white-dominant higher education institutions (Blaisdell, 2021; Flaherty, 2016).

The Knowledge Principle of High Expectations

For the most part, adjunct instructors are assigned specific course-based teaching duties and teach in relative isolation from the academic faculty of the university (Webb et al., 2013). Although most universities have teaching and learning centres and professional development initiatives available for faculty members, there is little opportunity for distance adjunct instructors to share their experiences, collaborate, and embrace culturally responsive approaches to curriculum and pedagogy with fellow colleagues (Webb et al., 2013). Even if opportunities to do so arise, faculty members are financially remunerated for this learning, whereas adjunct instructors are not. Two considerations in support of adjuncts' professional learning to enhance the development of their critical consciousness are flexible communities of practice and high expectations of scholarly teaching and learning (Norman et al., 2020).

Flexible Communities of Practice

Given the multi-faceted teaching and professional lives of adjunct instructors, traditional communities of practice need to be re-envisioned (Luo et al., 2020). Gone are the days of after-class professional learning meetings at which educators are trained by subject experts who facilitate a one-and-done presentation. Current distance education instructors have varied amounts of knowledge pertaining to new pedagogies and equity understanding related to decolonization, critical engagement, and culturally and linguistically relevant teaching. Faculties are demanding this understanding and praxis from their adjunct instructors yet offer a one-size-fits-all approach to professional learning (e.g., a workshop facilitated by an external consultant) or none at all (Hudley & Mallinson, 2017). A re-envisioning of adjunct professional learning is possible through flexible communities of practice.

A flexible community of practice caters to the strengths of adjunct distance instructors since it is responsive to their professional development needs and circumstances. Specifically, it is grounded in sharing one's intersectional lived experiences and recognizes the unique expertise and skills of each community member (Webb et al., 2013). Flexible communities of practice are solidified through scholarly and professional interactions of both adjunct and permanent faculty to develop a deeper shared understanding and sense of cohesion. This could look like mentoring or active coaching partnerships by which the expertise of each group member, regardless of adjunct or faculty, is equally illuminated. Learning modalities are carefully considered for the community and can include blended or distance professional development opportunities with the strategic use of educational technology such as podcasts, webinars, online discussion posts, PDF readings, and other learning activities. Faculties should also reward adjunct members with incentives for their attendance, participation, and completion of various learning modules.

High Expectations of Scholarly Teaching and Learning

Adjunct instructors often carry the weight of program course loads across faculties, particularly teaching courses with larger enrolments (Dawson et al., 2019). In fact, the strength, or lack thereof, of their teaching skills becomes the fabric of the institutional culture of teaching simply because of the sheer number of adjunct scholars compared with tenured faculty members. An example from my adjunct experience is that, in some Canadian graduate programs, students may complete their entire two- or three-year degrees (e.g., MEd, EdD, PhD) without ever being taught by a tenured faculty member. This aligns with the Canadian trends mentioned earlier that 54% of all Ontario faculty appointments are sessional, with other provinces higher such as Quebec at 61% and British Columbia at 55% (CCPA, 2018, p. 6). Therefore, it is in the interest of a university to ensure that its adjuncts' teaching and learning praxis firmly aligns with its beliefs, policies, and practices and that they support scholarly, high-quality education (Dawson et al., 2019).

Recent shifts in higher education teaching philosophies and pedagogies include the use of a flipped classroom model by which students engage in generative dialogue and in-class activities based on the class readings of the day. Students are active learners engaged in critical thinking and discourse versus being passive listeners to instructor-led lectures. Other shifts include centring student learning in intersectional community spaces in face-to-face, hybrid, or online formats, which are relational and courageous, fostering pedagogies of care and wellness, ensuring culturally relevant and representative class resources, implementing equity audits, and decolonizing assessment practices (Dawson et al., 2019; Lopez, 2022; Ortiz et al., 2021). Learning these advancing scholarly teaching approaches will take time and commitment by the institution, faculty members, and adjunct instructors.

A greater emphasis on the value of teaching is also needed since most institutions are research driven and favour publications and grants over teaching competencies as evidence of effective scholarship (Dawson et al., 2019). Finding ways to celebrate and learn from one another regardless of rank is supported by Darling-Hammond's (2006, p. 305) argument that learning from each other is essential, especially since "the range of knowledge for teaching has grown so expansive that it cannot be mastered by any individual." Only when this culture of engaged vulnerability and collaboration is fostered and prioritized between distance education adjuncts and tenured faculty members will further scholarly teaching and learning innovation occur.

My Hope for Unity

As I continue to engross myself in Ladson-Billings' (2021b) enduring research, I am reminded that instructional leadership requires educators to "swim against the tide" and be vigilant about disrupting whiteness in distance education praxis that serves to fragment rather than unite faculty members. Ladson-Billings urges leaders in education to reimagine models of teaching that foster student curiosity and are driven by norms of intellectual capacity and excellence. Distance education instructors historically have been poorly served by higher education institutions (Dawson et al., 2019). By infusing decolonizing and culturally responsive and relevant pedagogies into distance education programs, not only students' voices and spirits but also those of adjunct instructors are celebrated. Transcendence, transformation, and humanity are possible when Ladson-Billings' frameworks of culturally relevant, sustaining, revitalizing, and reality pedagogies are embodied by all interconnected and valued members of distance education programs.

References

Akyildiz, S. T. (2019). Do 21st century teachers know about heutagogy or do they still adhere to traditional pedagogy and andragogy? *International Journal of Progressive Education, 15*(6), 151–169.

Alemán, S. M. (2017). A critical race counterstory: Chicana/o subjectivities vs. journalism objectivity. *Taboo: The Journal of Culture and Education, 16*(1), 73–91. https://doi.org/10.31390/taboo.16.1.08

Blaisdell, B. (2021). Counternarrative as strategy: Embedding critical race theory to develop an antiracist school identity. *International Journal of Qualitative Studies in Education, 36*(8), 1558–1578. https://doi.org/10.1080/09518398.2021.1942299

Canadian Centre for Policy Alternatives (CCPA). (2018). Contract U. Faculty appointments at Canadian Universities. https://policyalternatives.ca/sites/default/files/uploads/publications/National%20Office/2018/11/Contract%20U.pdf

Caretta, M. A., Drozdzewski, D., Jokinen, J. C., & Falconer, E. (2018). "Who can play this game?" The lived experiences of doctoral candidates and early career women in the neoliberal university. *Journal of Geography in Higher Education, 42*(2), 261–275. https://doi.org/10.1080/03098265.2018.1434762

CUPE (Canadian Union of Public Sector Employees). (2018, September 28). Sector profile: Post-secondary. https://cupe.ca/sector-profile-post-secondary-education

Darling-Hammond, L. (2006). Constructing 21st-century teacher education. *Journal of Teacher Education, 57*(3), 300–314. https://doi.org/10.1177/0022487105285962

Dawson, D., Meadows, K., Kustra, E., & Hanson, K. (2019). Perceptions of institutional teaching culture by tenured, tenure-track, and sessional faculty. *Canadian Journal of Higher Education, 49*(3), 115–128. https://ir.lib.uwo.ca/ctlpub/19

Donohoo, J., & Katz, S. (2020). *Quality implementation*. Corwin. http://dx.doi.org.proxy1.lib.uwo.ca/10.4135/9781544354217

Eidinger, A. (2021, April 15). Enough talk, it is time to take action to help precarious faculty. University Affairs. https://www.universityaffairs.ca/career-advice/careers-cafe/enough-talk-it-is-time-to-take-action-to-help-precarious-faculty/

Flaherty, C. (2016, August 22). More faculty diversity. Not on tenure track. Inside Higher Ed. https://www.insidehighered.com/news/2016/08/22/study-finds-gains-faculty-diversity-not-tenure-track

Gee, J. P. (2004). *Situated language and learning: A critique of traditional schooling*. Routledge.

Hudley, C., & Mallinson, C. (2017). "It's worth our time": A model of culturally and linguistically supportive professional development for

K–12 STEM educators. *Cultural Studies of Science Education, 12*(3), 637–660. https://doi.org/10.1007/s11422-016-9743-7

Joseph-Salisbury, R. (2018). *Black mixed-race men: Transatlanticity, hybridity and 'post-racial' resilience.* Emerald Publishing Limited. https://doi.org/10.1108/978-1-78756-531-920181012

Khalifa, M. (2018). *Culturally responsive school leadership.* Harvard Education Press.

Ladson-Billings, G. (1995). But that's just good teaching! The case for culturally relevant pedagogy. *Theory into Practice, 34*(3). http://www.jstor.org/stable/1476635

Ladson-Billings, G. (1998). Just what is critical race theory and what's it doing in a nice field like education? *International Journal of Qualitative Studies in Education, 11*(1), 7–24. https://doi.org/10.1080/095183998236863

Ladson-Billings, G. (2021a). I'm here for the hard re-set: Post pandemic pedagogy to preserve our culture. *Equity & Excellence in Education, 54*(1), 68–78. https://doi.org/10.1080/10665684.2020.1863883

Ladson-Billings, G. (2021b). Three decades of culturally relevant, responsive, & sustaining pedagogy: What lies ahead? *The Educational Forum, 85*(4), 351–354. https://doi.org/10.1080/00131725.2021.1957632

Lopez, A. (2016). *Culturally responsive and socially just leadership in diverse contexts: From theory to action.* Palgrave Macmillan.

Lopez, A. (2022, February 1). *Embedding & sustaining equity and decolonial praxis in higher education: Actualizing ProLovePedagogy* [Video file]. YouTube. https://youtu.be/kd-Kqt1-T7c

Luo, T., Freeman, C., & Stefaniak, J. (2020). "Like, comment, and share"—Professional development through social media in higher education: A systematic review. *Educational Technology Research and Development, 68*(4), 1659–1683. https://doi.org/10.1007/s11423-020-09790-5

Lyle, E., & Caissie, C. (2021). Rehumanizing education: Teaching and learning as co-constructed reflexive praxis. *LEARNing Landscapes, 14*(1), 219–230. https://doi.org/10.36510/learnland.v14i1.1034

Mason, O., & Megoran, N. (2021). Precarity and dehumanisation in higher education. *Learning and Teaching, 14*(1), 35–59. https://doi.org/10.3167/latiss.2021.140103

Matsuda, M. (1995). Looking to the bottom: Critical legal studies and reparations. In K. Crenshaw, N. Gotanda, & G. Peller (Eds.), *Critical race theory: The key writings that formed the movement* (pp. 63–79). New Press.

Norman, N., Robinson-Bryant, F., & Lin, Y. (2020). Examining adjunct faculty needs via a distance pedagogical framework in higher education. *Journal of Higher Education Theory and Practice, 20*(10), 113–122. https://doi.org/10.33423/jhetp.v20i10.3656

Ortiz, R., Rodesiler, C. A., Latz, A. O., & Mulvihill, T. (2021). Community college adjunct faculty: Picturing pedagogies of care. *New Directions for Community Colleges, 2021*(195), 23–35. https://doi.org/10.1002/cc.20464

Rose, D. (2020). A snapshot of precarious academic work in Canada. University of Guelph. *New Proposals, 11*(1), 7–17.

Shah, V. (n.d.). Culturally relevant and anti-racist leadership [Audio podcast episode 3]. In *UnLeading*. York University. https://www.yorku.ca/edu/unleading/podcast-episodes/culturally-responsive-anti-racist-leadership/

Shah, V. (2018). Leadership for social justice through the lens of self-identified, racially, and other-privileged leaders. *Journal of Global Citizenship and Equity, 6*(1), 1–41.

Smith-Carrier, T., Penner, M., Cecala, A., & Agócs, C. (2021). It's not just a pay gap: Quantifying the gender wage and pension gap at a post-secondary institution in Canada. *Canadian Journal of Higher Education, 51*(2), 74–84. https://doi.org/10.47678/cjhe.vi0.189215

Stoica, G., Eckert, J., Bodirsky, K., & Hirslund, D. (2019). Precarity without borders: Visions of hope, shared responsibilities, and possible responses. *Social Anthropology, 27*(S2), 78–96. https://doi.org/10.1111/1469-8676.12700

Truong, K. (2021, May 27). Making the invisible visible. Inside Higher Ed. https://www.insidehighered.com/advice/2021/05/28/why-and-how-colleges-should-acknowledge-invisible-labor-faculty-color-opinion

Webb, A., Wong, T. J., & Hubball, H. T. (2013). Professional development for adjunct teaching faculty in a research-intensive university: Engagement in scholarly approaches to teaching and learning.

International Journal of Teaching and Learning in Higher Education, 25(2), 231–238. https://files.eric.ed.gov/fulltext/EJ1016541.pdf

Zitko, P. A. & Schultz, K. (2020). The adjunct model as an equity crisis in higher education: A qualitative inquiry into the lived experience of "part-time" community college faculty in northern California. *Education Leadership Review, 8*, 1–19.

15 Carving Out Spaces

Jasmine Pham

My name is Jasmine Pham. I am a queer, Chinese Canadian woman born and raised in Edmonton, Alberta. I am currently a second-year PhD student in the Educational Leadership and Policy (ELP) program at the Ontario Institute for Studies in Education (OISE). In 2019, I started my studies at OISE as an MEd student in ELP and finished most of my program online and then went on to pursue a PhD.

Over the course of my doctoral journey, I dedicated a lot of my time to leadership positions in student groups with the goal of tackling anti-Asian racism and encouraging cross-racial solidarity among Black, Indigenous, and people of colour (BIPOC) community members. In these online groups, I often shared my experiences growing up as a visual minority in Canada. The more I shared, the more I realized the importance of having my voice heard, of having safe spaces in which to talk, and of carving out spaces, both online and in person, for others to share their experiences as well. And, as I gained additional leadership experiences alongside the theoretical knowledge from my courses, I realized how gender and racial stereotypes prevented me from chasing these opportunities sooner.

So why don't we go back a bit further? I would like to follow in the footsteps of the women before me and share my own narrative and counterstory (Solórzano & Yosso, 2002) as a student leader in online spaces (Bainbridge & Wark, 2023). I share my counterstory hoping to challenge the stereotypes associated with being a Chinese Canadian woman. And I share my narrative to demonstrate how it takes not an individual but a community to disrupt societal expectations and norms.

Early Years and Upbringing

My mother is an independent working mom who has been successful in balancing both her home life and her work life. My father is a wonderful stay-at-home dad who did most of the child rearing. Although this dynamic is no longer uncommon in Canadian households, at the time it defied both Canadian societal norms and traditional Chinese gender roles. The confidence that my parents had in their gender identities played a large role in the formation of mine; it also led to my subsequent passion for gender equality. In fact, as the oldest daughter in a family of four girls and one boy, I tended to be more outspoken than my peers and often took on leadership roles that my classmates found boring. I think that it came with the bit of extra responsibility of having four younger siblings. Either way, Jasmine Pham as an elementary student was headstrong and unabashedly herself.

Unfortunately, this meant that I had no idea that girls were expected to act one way and boys another. As a result, my first experience with gender norms left me distraught. I remember playing house with my classmates and being handed an apron and a broomstick despite asking for a hammer. I then watched in horror as another classmate was given the toy instead. The reason? Well, he was a boy, and I was a girl. This happened when I was five, and even at 28 I still remember how disappointed I felt. Sadly, this was the first of many more events that left me feeling both angry and confused. I had no idea why this was happening to me or how to articulate how I felt. All I knew was that gender norms did not matter in the safety and comfort of my own home but meant the world once I took a step outside my front door.

My Primary and Secondary Schooling Experience

The gender socialization that I experienced in the playground was distressing, and what I faced in the classroom was no better. I went to a Mandarin bilingual elementary school and took Mandarin classes in junior high school. Unfortunately, the texts used in my Chinese classes often highlighted traditional Chinese gender norms. The poems that I memorized in class had subtexts detailing the habits that a girl had to develop to become the perfect wife, and the fairytales that we read usually depicted male warriors rescuing damsels in distress. The cultural expectations that came with my ethnicity intersected with the oppression that came with my gender (Manion & Shah, 2019), and these experiences often left me feeling conflicted. Was it okay to be proud of my cultural roots while also hating the patriarchal norms that came with them? I had trouble understanding what it meant to be Chinese Canadian and what it meant to be a woman. From the hidden curriculum of my playground activities to the texts used in my Chinese classes, my experience with oppression was complex, and my feelings of resentment were compounded. I thought that I was expected to be obedient because I was a girl, doubly so because of the submissive nature associated with being a girl who was also Chinese.

By the time I reached high school, I faded into the background. I put my head down, did my homework, and chose to express only the most colourful parts of myself among my small group of friends. I stopped taking on leadership roles in school. I quit the student council after serving for two years in junior high school. I also stopped volunteering in roles that required public speaking. Why? I didn't want to be the "bossy" girl anymore. I wanted people to stop seeing me as some "smarty pants." It was tiring having to defend myself. Just because I was a girl did not mean that I was bossy or pushy when I was simply being assertive. But I was a child who did not have the vocabulary to express myself the way that I do now. I was a child who was angry, confused, and in some ways lonely. It felt like nobody else understood why I was so upset.

Looking back, I realize that my peers did not understand what they were doing either. They were also children growing up in a world where girls and boys were expected to "participate in gender-typed activities" (Orr, 2011, p. 272). Even now boys are encouraged to engage in more physical activities, whereas girls are expected to participate in nurturing activities (Orr, 2011). And, though gendered activities such as childhood games might seem to be trivial, these expectations and perceived differences continue to affect how people socialize as teenagers and adults (Baily & Holmarsdottir, 2015; Marshall & Young, 2006). These social expectations put constraints on what boys and girls can and cannot do, which then limits their vision of the future in terms of their education and career choices (Baily & Holmarsdottir, 2015). Despite having positive role models and being an outspoken, rambunctious child, I struggled with the power of gender socialization. So I spent the rest of my adolescent years grappling with the freedom of expression that I had at home and the social pressure that I had at school.

Unearthing My Voice

As I got older, I started to find bits and pieces of myself again. I started my undergraduate studies in September 2012 and noticed how the brilliant women in my classes spoke up and shared their insights. I took classes with both female and male professors who praised my work and offered suggestions for student clubs. I started to feel less afraid. There was always that voice in the back of my head telling me to stop being such a "smarty pants" or to stop "being so loud," but the voice became softer as the world around me evolved. And as I progressed in my undergraduate studies, the gender discussions that I had in class became more nuanced, enabling me to recognize that gender equality is not about pitting one gender against the other (Harris & Leonardo, 2018) but about embracing the multiple forms of masculinity and femininity. Equality means providing all genders with the option to choose what is best for them and what is best for me, the ability to speak up and speak out.

After receiving my Bachelor of Education in 2016, I flew halfway across the world to teach English as a Foreign Language in Seoul, South Korea. I spent two wonderful years as a native English teacher and learned a lot about myself. I became well known for going against the grain and pushing back against standards that did not sit right with me. Although I adored my students and most of my colleagues, I realized that being the lone person who spoke up was not enough. I soon developed an interest in policy studies that ultimately took me to Toronto, a diverse city composed of various cultures and ethnicities.

Becoming a Graduate Student Online

In 2019, I enrolled in the ELP program at the OISE with the hope not only of expanding my teaching pedagogy but also of developing my knowledge in educational policies. I wanted to know how I could disrupt a system that simply does not work for traditionally marginalized groups. Perhaps it was because I moved to a new city, or maybe it was because I went from being a teacher to being a student again, but I spent the first semester of my MEd with my head down. I had a crippling case of imposter syndrome (Clance & Imes, 1978) that made it hard for me to make friends and participate in student groups. Halfway through my second semester, though, things went online, and suddenly my nerves went away. As an independent learner who prefers to approach readings and discussions at my own pace, the shift to online learning gave me more flexibility in how I participated in class. Theoretically, I already knew that women are confident and independent learners online (Price, 2006) but experiencing it for the first time myself really solidified this point.

For one thing, seeing my classmates through a smaller screen was less intimidating. As a shorter woman, I no longer had to look up at 90% of my classmates. Another perk was that I no longer had to strain my voice to be heard. And, like other women who found that online learning offered them more control over their education (Gokool-Ramdoo, 2005), I also felt more control over how I engaged with my studies. Private chats as well as break-out rooms over Zoom meant having the ability to share more intimate discussions in smaller groups. It also meant having the opportunity to get to know my classmates more personally. Sometimes a pet cat would walk over someone's keyboard, or a child could be heard laughing in the background. Despite seeing one another only on the screen, something about break-out discussions and seeing my classmates show up in their pajamas felt more humanizing than attending classes in person. Really, online learning helped me to feel more, not less, connected to my classmates.

Finding Solace in Online Spaces

Discovering online spaces and joining student groups were other bonuses of online learning. BIPOC communities have long been engaging in practices that preserve their humanity in educational systems that continue to dehumanize and systemically oppress us (Abdi et al., 2020). Thus, it is no surprise that the shift to online learning has meant the creation of online spaces that cater to different demographics. And, though my previous experience with in-person learning meant that the classmates and colleagues whom I talked to depended on proximity, online learning meant that my network could expand beyond Toronto and North America.

By the time I entered the second year of my MEd, I had become a member of the Comparative, International and Development Education Student Association (CIDESA), which plans events for both students and faculty members. Our co-presidents at the time were two women of colour, and they acted as my mentors. They supported me during my studies and even offered me the position of administrative officer. As one of the core members of CIDESA, I soon became the person encouraging student participation and ensuring that student voices were heard through monthly check-ins. Despite the lack of in-person classes, CIDESA's events helped both students and faculty members alike to connect online. Being a part of CIDESA also enabled me to network with professors and students within the field of comparative, international, and development education. The costs that usually came with travel and in-person conferences were no longer a factor in whether I could afford to attend them or not. So I was able to present my own research at seminars and gain feedback from my colleagues.

As a member of CIDESA, I also connected with the OISE East Asian Interest Group, in which graduate students interested in East Asia came together to discuss their experiences as graduate students in Canada, celebrate cultural events, and present their research. This group was founded by Phoebe Kang, who realized that there were few spaces for East Asian students to talk about their experiences. She spearheaded the group and created a safe online space for us to gather. In 2020, our small team of 11 planned and hosted an Asian Heritage Month Symposium. At this online symposium, I was part of the graduate student panel and shared my experiences with gender socialization and anti-Asian sentiment in Canada. Other women who had similar experiences reached out after the event and thanked me for having the courage to be loud about and proud of my culture and being brave enough to share the sexism and racism that I had encountered.

I went on to join the OISE Student Experience Committee and became a mentor for the OISE mentorship program. In 2022, I also became the director of public relations for the University of Toronto's Chinese Graduate Student Association. As a member of these groups, I reconnected with my roots and realized that I am more than the stereotypes that came with being Chinese Canadian and queer. I came to realize that I can disagree with certain parts of my culture and still be proud of who I am. So too I can reject gender norms and still be a woman. And, really, it was through the sharing of my experiences at various virtual conferences and group meetings that helped me to realize just how important it is to have the space in which to talk through the gender- and race-related micro-aggressions that I faced (Kohli & Solórzano, 2012).

So I transitioned from a young girl confused by gender expectations to a young woman who wanted to dismantle our patriarchal system and break both gender and racial barriers. I did not have many opportunities to speak out and advocate for myself during my high school years, but I have been able to do so now as a doctoral candidate and student leader. It can be scary and daunting to share intimate details about yourself, but the online communities that I found helped me to open up. I'd like to thank the student leaders who came before me, the women who acted as my mentors, the women who listened to my concerns, and the women who celebrated my wins. Although I have yet to meet most of these women in person, the connections that we have built are no less valid.

Conclusion

Effective learning environments require the building of community to encourage students and faculty members alike to interact in meaningful ways (Santovec, 2010). I am just one voice, one educator, and one researcher who wishes to tackle both racism and sexism head on, but the communities of which I am a part and the brilliant mentors whom I have in my life are evidence that I am not alone. And, really, every time I present at a conference to share my work, I realize that the spaces that we have carved for ourselves have become bigger and will become bigger yet with time. As more women take on leadership roles in higher education and create communities in online spaces, other women who enter our respective fields will have the positive role models and support systems necessary to keep pressing forward. Although the misogyny and racism that we encountered in traditionally masculine and white spaces cannot be undone, we can make changes now for the future. I hope that we can offer the spaces that we needed as students to our students moving forward.

References

Abdi, N. M., Gil, E., Marshall, S. L., & Khalifa, M. (2020). Humanizing practices in online learning communities during pandemics in the USA. *Journal of Professional Capital and Community, 5*(3–4), 205–212. https://doi.org/10.1108/JPCC-07-2020-0066

Baily, S., & Holmarsdottir, H. (2015). The quality of equity: Reframing gender, development and education in the post-2020 landscape. *Gender and Education, 27*(7), 828–845.

Bainbridge, S., & Wark, N. (2023). *The encyclopedia of female pioneers in online learning*. Routledge.

Clance, P. R., & Imes, S. A. (1978). The imposter phenomenon in high achieving women: Dynamics and therapeutic intervention. *Psychotherapy, 15*(3), 241–247. https://doi.org/10.1037/h0086006

Gokool-Ramdoo, S. (2005). The online learning environment: Creating a space for women learners? *International Review of Research in Open and Distance Learning, 6*(3).

Harris, A., and Leonardo, Z. (2018). Intersectionality, race-gender subordination, and education. *Review of Research in Education, 42*(1), 1–27.

Kohli, R., & Solórzano, D. G. (2012). Teachers, please learn our names! Racial microagressions and the K–12 classroom. *Race, Ethnicity and Education, 15*(4), 441–462. https://doi.org/10.1080/13613324.2012.674026

Manion, C., & Shah, P. (2019). Decolonizing gender and education research: Unsettling and recasting feminist knowledges, power and research practice. *Gender and Education, 31*(4), 445–451.

Marshall, C., & Young, M. D. (2006). Gender and methodology. In C. Skelton, B. Francis, & L. Smulyan (Eds.), *Sage handbook of gender and education* (pp. 63–78). Sage.

Orr, A. (2011). Gendered capital: Childhood socialization and the "boy crisis" in education. *Sex Roles, 65*, 271–284.

Price, L. (2006). Gender differences and similarities in online courses: Challenging stereotypical views of women. *Journal of Computer Assisted Learning, 22*(5), 349–359. https://doi.org/10.1111/j.1365-2729.2006.00181.x

Santovec, M. L. (2010). Teach faculty to improve online learning success. *Women in Higher Education, 19*(1), 19. https://doi.org/10.1002/whe.10005

Solórzano, D. G., & Yosso, T. J. (2002). Critical race methodology: Counter-storytelling as an analytical framework for education research. *Qualitative Inquiry, 8*(1), 23–44. https://doi.org/10.1177/107780040200800103

16 Breaking Barriers and Leading from the Middle

A Racialized Woman Educator's Experiences

Afsaneh Sharif

My journey as a racialized woman educator in Canadian post-secondary education has been a testament to persevering, overcoming unique challenges, and advocating for change. In this chapter, I dive into the ever-evolving landscape of Canadian higher education, with a focus on distance education and online learning. I discuss the barriers encountered and the methods used to overcome them, the lessons learned on this transformative journey, and leadership insights for fellow educators navigating similar paths, particularly those dealing with the glass ceiling (Johns, 2013).

I believe that everyone has a role in effecting change in an organization. To me, leading from the middle means that anyone, no matter the position or job title, can be a leader. It means being collaborative in an environment in which everyone leads and follows. A leader in this context creates an environment in which people can shine, acknowledging and supporting others' achievements. Leading from the middle means leading by example, and doing what is right, even when facing resistance.

Background

I am a racialized support staff member and an uninvited settler working on the traditional, ancestral, and unceded territory of the xʷməθkʷəy̓əm (Musqueam) people. I was born and raised in Iran and did my undergraduate degree there. I immigrated to Canada in 1997 so that my daughter could grow up in a free country. Although I have not lived in my country of origin for almost 30 years and am now a citizen, I continue to follow the experiences of women in Iran with deep concern and hope. In many areas of life, women navigate cultural and legal expectations that influence their access to education, freedom of movement, and personal expression. Practices such as wearing the hijab in school, needing permission for certain legal processes, and restrictions on public performance remain part of the social fabric. Many women continue to advocate for greater opportunities, equity, and recognition of their rights. I have experienced war, revolution, civil unrest, Islamophobia, and racism throughout my life. I have been escorted to a plane, fingerprinted, separated from the crowd, and denied water, interviews, positions, and many other things because of my race and the colour of my hair.

My first job in Canada was in a part-time position at a postsecondary institution. While working in two different part-time roles, I applied for one of them when it became available full time but didn't get the job. I was told that, because English was my second language, I couldn't be put in that position full time. After changing positions in different postsecondary institutions and studying more in the field, I landed at the University of British Columbia (UBC) in 2006 with over seven years of experience in distance education and online learning. I have been in the same unit since, moving to a senior instructional designer position, based on my request for reclassification, and later to a faculty liaison/senior project manager position as part of a reorganization.

I completed my Master of Educational Technology at UBC and my PhD in Spain, both online; my doctorate was focused on the quality of online learning programs. After 20 years in distance education, I now co-chair the British Columbia Digital Learning Advisory Committee and serve on a few international editorial boards. I am a visiting professor at Rovira I Virgili University in Spain (where I completed my PhD), and I have served at the Canadian Network for Innovation in Education (CNIE) in different roles, including president. I am also considered one of the top Canadian researchers in online, blended, and distance education (Contact North|Nord, n.d.).

Challenges and Fewer Opportunities

Like many other women who seek advancement in an organization, I frequently encounter barriers or glass ceilings. I have faced cultural and structural barriers in gendered organizations and postsecondary systems in which hiring practices, wages, supervision, and informal interactions can lead to class, gender, and racial inequalities (Iverson, 2011).

Exploring the Absence of Belonging

As a new immigrant, my journey in the Canadian postsecondary education system was defined by the challenges of acclimatizing to both the workplace culture and the demands of my job while striving to establish a sense of belonging. To ensure job security and navigate this unfamiliar educational system, I rapidly adapted by refraining from discussing my family and the trials of being a new immigrant and avoiding raising questions about incorrect or unjust practices. Every time I introduced myself, my colleagues seemed to struggle with pronouncing my name, and a few asked if I had a nickname. Afy became my first nickname; at the time, I liked it since I didn't have to see their faces change and hear them make fun of my name. All of these adjustments were means of survival, allowing me to blend in and appear more assimilated within the workplace environment, even though they meant sacrificing parts of my identity and authenticity.

I also learned not to get too close and comfortable too soon. One day I joined colleagues for coffee shortly after being hired in a role, and I started opening up and sharing some of my challenges as a new immigrant. One of my colleagues told me to go back to my country to avoid the issues and didn't even let me complete my sentence. I soon found out that, no matter how determined and eager I was to learn and grow, I was treated as a second-class citizen. When I worked hard to show my potential, I was told "not to be a tall tulip in a field of tulips, or you will be cut." I have found that, for women of colour, self-doubt and the feeling that we don't belong can be even more pronounced in this field. As Tulshyan and Burey (2021) state, the intersection of race and gender often places us in a risky position at work. Many of us across the world are implicitly—in my case explicitly—told that we don't belong in white- and male-dominated workplaces.

Limited Representation in Senior Leadership and the Glass Ceiling

Another persistent challenge that I confronted was the striking lack of representation of racialized women in senior leadership positions within academic institutions and in the field of online learning and distance education. The glass ceiling (Johns, 2013) seemed to be almost impenetrable, maintaining a status quo that hindered diversity and perpetuated a cycle of inequity. Hiring practices present significant barriers for women and minorities when it comes to advancing to senior management positions.

My experience has been that most institutions promote employees from within. Even when women manage to overcome the recruitment obstacle, they often encounter organizational and cultural barriers, including various gender-related communication styles, behaviours, and socialization practices. Furthermore, numerous barriers in the career pipeline hinder women's attainment of top positions. These obstacles include a lack of mentoring, roles with limited growth prospects, differences in performance evaluation and hiring criteria, and limited access to informal communication networks (Johns, 2013).

Women continue to be systematically disadvantaged, and it is clear to me that it is the whole structure of an organization in which we work (Iverson, 2011) that holds women back. Previous life experiences showed me that getting to a leadership position in my field was almost impossible; my ceiling as a racialized woman was definitely lower, and it was made not of glass but of concrete.

After dedicating numerous years of hard work and feeling drained by the systemic obstacles and difficulties, I decided to explore alternative avenues for personal and leadership growth. I realized that a formal title wasn't a prerequisite for leadership. So I embarked on a journey to make strides and lead from within the organization, opting to volunteer with national organizations and engage in collaborative research and publication. Notably, all of my leadership roles in the field of distance and online learning were on a voluntary basis. In the following section, I elaborate how I successfully navigated these challenges and transitioned into a role of leading from the middle.

Leading from the Middle (Overcoming Challenges)

My journey toward embracing my identity and leading from the middle has been both a personal and a professional evolution. Initially, I faced the challenge of not always feeling fully seen or heard within educational spaces. I recognized that my unique perspective brought a valuable dimension to my role. To overcome the lack of belonging, I sought opportunities for self-growth and empowerment, committing to dialogues and initiatives that encouraged diversity and inclusion. By engaging in education and fostering open dialogue, I not only discovered my own voice but also transformed into a guiding source of encouragement and motivation for my peers. Embracing my identity allowed me to connect authentically with my colleagues and community members, particularly those from marginalized groups who saw in me a role model who had worked hard to overcome similar challenges. I have learned that leading from the middle is about being a bridge between community members and the institution, advocating for equitable opportunities, and fostering a sense of belonging for all. By embracing my identity and sharing my experiences, I have helped to create a more inclusive and empathetic educational environment in which everyone feels valued and empowered to succeed.

I think that to lead you do not need a leadership title but empathy, communication skills, vision, and multi-tasking abilities. Self-acceptance, self-development, and alliance building are a few strategies that have helped me to grow and lead from the middle. To lead, you need to be open to new experiences, listen to people, seek advice, heed criticism, and not give up.

I recognize the significance of seeking mentorship from pioneering women who have shattered the glass ceiling and are enthusiastic about mentoring the next generation. I find that, the more ways in which I develop myself, the broader my skill set and the greater my success. Finding opportunities to learn and connect with experts in my field was one of the most important factors for me to overcome my challenges. Looking upward for allies and mentors is crucial because those managers and executives regularly interact with other higher-level people and can sing your praises when the opportunity arises. However, I found it very difficult to find Black, Indigenous, and people of colour (BIPOC) allies when looking upward since there are just a few in those leadership positions.

Women who want to advance their careers and move into leadership roles must realize that the relationships they cultivate and nurture are among their most valuable assets in achieving their career aspirations. The effectiveness of alliances and mentorships depends on the influence that one can harness from them (Mackey, 2018).

Through unwavering dedication to my values and a commitment to accessible and inclusive teaching and learning, I had the honour of being named one of the recipients of the 2022 Envisioning Equality awards at UBC. This prestigious award, one of the first of its kind, was established to spotlight and celebrate the exceptional contributions of women and gender-diverse faculty and staff members at UBC.

My involvement in networking and volunteering has been particularly rewarding, providing me with more opportunities for leadership than traditional positions offered. Through collaboration across the university, I was able to co-create the UBC Instructional Design Community of Practice, facilitating regular meetings for instructional designers to discuss current topics and challenges. Furthermore, my volunteer work with the CNIE allowed me to establish connections and exchange knowledge with fellow educators across Canada. Specifically, I initiated enhancements in communication processes, including a website redesign and a regular monthly newsletter.

I also played a crucial role in a nationwide collaborative research initiative focused on blended and online learning and teaching in higher education, organized by the Collaboration for Online Higher Education and Research and Athabasca University. This experience further enriched my professional journey.

Additionally, I have served in various capacities, including as president, on the UBC Board of Directors for the Association of Administrative and Professional Staff, the largest employee group at UBC. Furthermore, I proudly contribute as a member of the BIPOC Connections Advisory Group at UBC, fostering a sense of community and inclusivity on campus.

Conclusion and Strategies

My journey as a racialized woman educator in Canadian post-secondary education has been marked by formidable challenges and an ongoing commitment to effective and positive change. Drawing from the experiences above, I will share a selection of strategies and lessons that I have learned, hoping to inspire women educators who navigate similar paths. These strategies are not unique, and they will not necessarily be primary considerations for all leaders in distance education and online learning, but they are the reminders that mean the most to me. Our collective voices and actions can reshape the landscape of education, making it more inclusive, equitable, and accessible for all. In the spirit of leading from the middle, we persistently strive for change and create pathways for others to follow in our footsteps, dismantling barriers one step at a time.

Embrace your identity. As an educator, particularly a racialized woman, recognize that your unique identity brings valuable perspectives to the educational landscape. Embrace your background, culture, and experiences as strengths that can enrich the teaching and learning of your students and colleagues.

Challenge the glass ceiling. Be a vocal advocate for breaking through the glass ceiling in academia. Encourage institutions to establish initiatives for diversity and inclusion that provide pathways for under-represented groups to ascend to senior leadership roles.

Seek mentorship and create alliances. Seek connections and mentors who are or have been successful leaders. To be impactful in your organization, connect with your community members and build alliances in support of your objectives. This can be with people in your own organization or outside it. Identify them, confirm their alignment with your objectives and values, and reinforce your similarities to strengthen connections. Staying connected with others in the field can also be a good way to keep updated on what is happening and what is changing.

Strive for continuous self-growth. The dynamic nature of education demands a commitment to continuous learning. Embracing this philosophy enabled me to adapt to new challenges and remain effective in navigating the ever-changing landscape of online education.

Empower those around you. Care for people and bring out the best in everyone. Take time to acknowledge and appreciate your colleagues' good work. While progressing in your career, it's essential to pause, observe your surroundings, and offer support to lift others up or help them to build their own paths to success. Encourage them to embrace themselves fully, support them, care for their well-being, provide opportunities for them to exercise leadership at whatever level they operate, and offer constructive feedback and mentorship.

Create safe spaces for women. To create safe spaces, it is important to provide environments in which women feel physically and emotionally secure. This involves setting up processes and structures to prevent harassment, discrimination, and bias. This can be achieved through clear policies and protocols, reporting mechanisms, and commitment to zero tolerance of any kind of discrimination. Work to create safer spaces to support growth and leadership and be vigilant about both deliberate and inadvertent bias.

Lead from the middle and embrace transformative leadership. Transformative leadership happens when your individual importance is overshadowed by the purpose that you serve. Transformative leaders embody deeply held values and strive to make a good impact: "They appeal to the higher ideals and values of their colleagues by modelling these behaviours, use symbols and coaching to focus efforts, instill pride, gain respect and trust, and promote teamwork and intrinsic motivation" (Kanwar et al., 2013, p. 12).

Do the right thing. Doing the right thing might not be easy; it means standing up for what you believe, which might not always be popular and can be met with resistance. This is riskier for some than for others, and it can be helpful for those with more security and privilege to support others as allies.

References

Contact North|Nord. (n.d.). Sharif, Afsaneh. Teachonline.ca. https://teachonline.ca/tools-trends/searchable-directory-canadian-researchers/sharif-afsaneh

Iverson, S.V. (2011). Glass ceilings and sticky floors: Women and advancement in higher education. In J. L. Martin (Ed.), *Women as leaders in education: Succeeding despite inequity, discrimination and other challenges*. (Vol. 1, pp. 79–103). Praeger. https://books.google.ca/books?hl=en&lr=&id=FFSNMCMGTvEC&oi=fnd&pg=PA79

Johns, M. L. (2013). Breaking the glass ceiling: Structural, cultural, and organizational barriers preventing women from achieving senior and executive positions. *Perspectives in Health Information Management*, 10(Winter), Article 1e. https://www.ncbi.nlm.nih.gov/pmc/articles/PMC3544145/:

Kanwar, A., Ferreira, F., & Latchem, C. (2013). *Women and leadership in open and distance learning and development*. Commonwealth of Learning. http://oasis.col.org/handle/11599/24

Mackey, Z. (2018). *Women in leadership: Finding and leveraging allies and mentors*. Berrett-Koehler Publishers. https://ideas.bkconnection

.com/women-in-leadership-finding-and-leveraging-allies-and-mentors

Tulshyan, R., & Burey, J. (2021, February 11). Stop telling women they have imposter syndrome. *Harvard Business Review*. https://hbr.org/2021/02/stop-telling-women-they-have-imposter-syndrome

17 The Leadership of Walking Alongside

Tammy Soanes-White

Women are the CEOs of their families, project managers of their communities, and mentors for tomorrow's leaders. Women go to school to improve their lives and become role models for their families, friends, and communities; they encourage, support, and sustain their ways of life. They have a deep tenaciousness that undergirds efforts necessary for self-improvement and strive to improve who they are and how they can make the world a better place. Women dream about improving their collective future and nurture thoughts of a better world, and this is done by leading from alongside one another.

This chapter contextualizes women who undertake postsecondary education in remote communities and discusses the leadership of alongside, a collaborative approach to supporting and improving remote postsecondary distance education. The chapter also addresses the importance of social and cultural contexts, the significance of relationality, and the duty of care to open up learning opportunities, remove barriers, and invite relational and dialogic connections between women on their learning journeys.

My Story

As a first-generation higher education student and a lifelong learner, I have spent most of my life living, working, and studying in rural and remote Canada. When our family moved north almost three decades ago, distance education became even more important to me as the separation from southern institutions was magnified. I continued to study throughout the years and earned three degrees and numerous certificates and diplomas at a distance during that time. I valued the supportive connections available to me and appreciated the opportunity to remain at home while earning my degrees. I realized the importance of institutional and relational supports as I navigated through learning at a distance, and I valued the support provided by my many tutors and instructors. From these experiences, I felt a deep desire to give back to my northern community and make our learning conditions here better through service to others who choose to learn through distance education.

Throughout my career, I have worked to connect students in remote communities to higher education. I have had the privilege of hauling a networked computer system up and down the Dempster highway in the High Arctic to offer cohort-based courses, connecting women across the North. I have also instructed quadriplegic students at a distance, supporting them through teleconferencing lectures and using voice-adaptive technologies, Padlets for visual supports, and Moodle course sites to improve access to courses. Communities also support their students, providing access to workable broadband connections so that students can attend virtual classes.

During one virtual lecture, a student needed to move to three separate buildings in her community because the connection to the virtual class was unstable; her screen would freeze, so she was unable to follow along or hear the lecture. To ensure that she was able to complete this final course in her program, I waited online 1,000 miles away until she reappeared on the screen in front of me. These are the conditions in which we work, requiring patience (both hers and mine) so that learning can happen. Adaptations can be frustrating and time consuming but are necessary as we walk together to improve learning conditions across the North. These examples illustrate the creativity, innovation, and persistence of northern women as they adapt while achieving their educational goals. These efforts have been successful because of the supportive and respectful relationships built among learners, community leaders, and instructors, each walking alongside the other to meet educational needs.

Contextualizing Remote Postsecondary Learning

There are many consistencies between traditional distance education students and those studying in remote regions. Many remote learners are separated geographically from bricks-and-mortar institutions (Moore, 2013). In addition, many remote learners are the first in their families to pursue postsecondary education and belong to under-represented groups such as Indigenous students (Government of the NWT, 2013). However, there are unique and distinguishable differences between remote distance education students and general populations who study at a distance. Remote distance education students in the Northwest Territories (NWT) are dispersed across 1.4 million square kilometres, making distance education one of a limited number of options available for postsecondary education. Inequitable access to secondary education (PK–12) in remote communities means that many women from smaller communities have limited access to prerequisite courses necessary to begin studies in their preferred programs. For example, because of teacher shortages and high educator turnover in smaller communities, many students experience delays or breaks in secondary education.

In 2022, there were over 100 jobs posted for teachers in remote NWT communities, leaving some communities with no teachers during parts of the academic year. A lack of applicants, delays in the hiring process, and the scarcity of available housing for teachers are some of the reasons that positions remain unfilled, leaving students without instructors or supports. These factors have a detrimental effect on remote learning. A loss of one day per week in the academic year means that 20% of the material might not be accessible to students, resulting in incomplete grade levels. When student placement tests are administered, many students discover the impacts that these breaks have on their education, resulting in necessary upgrading before they are allowed to access programs. Necessary bridging years require students to move to larger centres to access both developmental studies courses and parent programs.

Other barriers for remote postsecondary students include limited internet access and inconsistent broadband capacity across remote communities. Accessibility and stable broadband services are contingent on each community's location (Soanes-White, 2022). Given the lack of universal standards for internet speeds, there is disparity in students' access to various distance education options. Learners who live near larger centres have faster internet and consistent access to secondary schooling. In contrast, students in more remote communities (e.g., fly-in or limited road access) can be affected by their location, access to prior learning, or limited technological capacity. Therefore, the level of support required by learners will vary according to their unique circumstances (Government of the NWT, 2019). Increasing numbers of programs are creating distance education options for students, but many of these programs must rely on first- and second-generation distance education technologies (Anderson & Dron,

2011) to ensure equitable access by all students. Understanding each community's unique conditions is necessary and must be evaluated to ensure that the best distance education options are used to support each location. Each community represents another woman, another future, another connection extending across the North, creating an interconnectedness among women in their pursuit of education.

There is a culture of interconnectedness that strengthens women's distance education across the Northwest Territories. This culture can be expressed as a set of interconnected relationships corresponding to the needs and expectations of individuals and communities, coexisting in time, space, and land-based connections. Deep and meaningful social bonds originate from familial relationships, connection to the environment/land, and ties to others outside close families, expanding relational identity and interdependence with one another (Halfacree, 1993; Koziol et al., 2015; Waldorf, 2006). Personal identity related to familial ties and cultural identity creates a connectedness through lived experiences of physical, emotional, spiritual, and familial connections. These relationships extend our relations outward to include others with shared needs.

Being a leader in this educational environment means walking alongside others as we co-construct our experiences by valuing roles, responsibilities, and knowledge systems together. These shared responsibilities can include how a student connects to distance courses (e.g., by phone, mobile device, computer, Teams, Zoom, or videoconferencing). Shared decisions can include discussions on the format of course syllabi or on how students prefer to be assessed (e.g., open-ended assignments, presentations in students' native languages, oral or take-home exams, or peer-reviewed assessments). By allowing flexibility in the assessment of courses, students are empowered to demonstrate their learning from a strengths-based approach.

The Leadership of Walking Alongside

I did not set out to be a leader in distance education; in the beginning, I was pursuing my own educational goals. Through my experiences, I witnessed other students' efforts to access distance education programs, and I realized that I had the knowledge and capacity to help others. As people reached out to me, in my role as an academic, I shared what I knew to try to make their journeys a little easier. My academic positions also allowed me to act in and adapt to certain learning spaces. Requesting a portable computer lab that I could carry in the back of a three-quarter-ton truck was one step. Gathering women in their small communities, using a cohort-based, guided, independent study model, was another step. Connecting students through videoconferencing when we lost funding for our Inuvik campus was an important accomplishment in preserving access for High Arctic students, made possible through a partnership arrangement with the Business Development Investment Corporation, using its videoconferencing equipment in a pilot project. Two years later we were able to invest in our own conferencing equipment and connected the third campus in Fort Smith to the Yellowknife-Inuvik pilot project. Meeting child-care needs and respecting community events were also important in accommodating students. Hiring a female Indigenous lawyer to instruct a condensed two-week course was a game-changer and created energy and deep connection that I had not anticipated between students and instructor. These are examples of the leadership of walking alongside that include being present, empathetic, and connected to students.

One of the most essential parts of developing remote distance education programs is creating caring and responsive relationships. Connecting with others across the North built respectful relationships and improved our knowledge of what students needed. Asking people what they need and not making assumptions about what might work best for them require active listening and working together to improve learning conditions. Through listening, collaborating, and supporting one another, we can create a systemic approach to distance education that spans the territory. Leadership from alongside requires recognizing when educational gaps exist, listening for what is required, and adapting current practices to meet students' needs. Leadership from alongside requires relationship building, standing up when requests are made, and creating sustainable solutions with the resources that exist. It is about ensuring that everyone's needs are considered, connecting people with common needs, and sharing what we have. These relationships span distance and evolve over time; they ebb and flow depending on learners' needs and available resources.

The North is a big place with a small population, and because of this connection we need to live our lives in relation to each other. Creating these connections builds bridges and joins students to materials, students to students, and students to instructors, creating spaces for learners to connect the dots in their lives to the materials provided (Laurillard, 2012). Respect and reciprocity build strength through our shared relationships and reinforce that each of us has a vested interest in our shared paths and a responsibility to interact respectfully. This is how we live together in a good way. Developing trusting and supportive relationships is essential in remote distance education; respect also expands relational space for new connections and relationships.

Leading from alongside is a necessary approach to remote distance education because remote populations reside in a culture of relational interdependence, coexisting together while originating from diverse cultures. Remote distance education is first and foremost about making spaces for these connections and learning through leading from alongside one another. Leading from alongside is based on active engagement between students and instructors, to develop and inform a shared approach to distance learning, guided by a duty to assist and empower students. By collaborating with students and promoting their self-advocacy, educational environments become more relevant and richer spaces for learning.

Challenges for Women in Distance Education

There are layers of complexity, including environmental limitations and accessibility issues, that women in remote locations need to navigate to access higher learning. This is further complicated by the numerous challenges already revealed, including distance between communities, secondary education limitations, and broadband issues (Government of the NWT, 2013; Soanes-White, 2022). In addition, steep learning curves exist as women navigate new technologies, applications, and approaches in their distance learning environments. Sometimes it is necessary to adapt learning environments to environmental limitations. Many times multiple workarounds are necessary for each community within one course offering. For example, in one course, some students might need to connect via teleconferencing, whereas others might have access to Teams or Zoom for virtual lectures, given the variety of broadband connections available in each community. Some broadband limitations also mean that some students require print materials because the upload and download speeds will not accommodate online access to resources or supplies (Soanes-White, 2022). By using adaptive approaches to distance education, it is possible to connect each student across the Northwest Territories and improve their access to distance education courses.

Leading from alongside in remote distance education requires knowing our learners and understanding their educational expectations and limitations. This includes embedding a learning culture that aligns with the institutional culture while responding to and respecting diverse learner needs. Walking alongside students requires building bridges between cultures, creating trusting long-term relationships, and making spaces for growth and development. By providing a duty of care, by caring with and for our students, they sense our authentic desire to improve conditions and support them on their educational journeys (Noddings, 2016).

Commonality within Women's Stories

Through my relationships, I have witnessed a common thread that ties women's postsecondary education stories together; when these women begin their journeys, there is little that stops them. Their interest in pursuing education and their determination to meet their goals surpass many environmental limitations and accessibility issues. When asked why they persist to completion of their studies, many of these women state that their journeys are based on improving their lives and futures. They are focused on self-improvement and curious about their areas of study while remaining at home and sustaining their cultural and social ways of life. If women have children, then most express a desire to be positive role models through education. When asked how they make it through all of the existing barriers, they acknowledge their determination, persistence, and tenacity. Each is aware of environmental limitations and prepared to navigate known and unknown challenges as they arise; the women focus on the ends in sight with courage and connection. Because women in remote communities are tenacious and determined, it is important to meet them where they are at, to listen to and respect their experiences, and to work with them to improve environmental conditions that will not only sustain but also promote supportive environments.

What I have come to understand over the years by listening to women's stories is that getting an education is as much about the connections within a woman's life as it is about a woman's educational goals. These connections are to their children, families, and communities. Some women are driven by their desire to be mentors and role models for their children. For others, their aspirations are for self-improvement and the capacity to provide for themselves and their families. For others, education is an opportunity to continue to grow and nurture themselves through deepening professional relationships and improving their communities. Finally, for others, it is about a second career after raising their children and wanting to continue to contribute and nurture others. By walking alongside others, I have been able to see the common threads that bind our stories together. Women's distance education might begin as a sole journey, a path forged by each woman to satiate her own personal goals, but for many of us what begins as an individual journey becomes, throughout the years, our soul's journey, and that knowledge deepens connections to our common goals.

Practical Recommendations

Accessing postsecondary learning through distance education means that we do not need to leave behind our identities or our homes; we can imagine and reimagine differences from our own spaces through our connections to others who might think, feel, and behave in new and different ways. This is something that we are good at in the North; we have a capacity to listen, to learn, and to make space for each other. This approach to learning respects differences among us and honours our unique identities.

Summary

Leadership from alongside begins with the classroom of one: one student, one need, one future. By walking alongside students, I have been able to learn and understand the strengths and limitations of each learning environment. By respecting that students are the experts of their own learning conditions, we work together to respond to their needs and improve distance education conditions and experiences. Working with students invariably improves our understanding of educational conditions, expands options through creative collaboration, and empowers students to assist in the development of their own learning environments. Women grow and flourish through their experiences in distance education; challenges become more manageable when shared with others, and opportunities expand as women walk alongside one another. We live, we grow, and we expand our interrelationships by embodying our shared reality as northern women, supporting one another, and living in a good way.

References

Anderson, T., & Dron, J. (2011). Three generations of distance education pedagogy. *International Review of Research in Open and Distributed Learning, 12*(3), 80–97. https://doi.org/10.19173/irrodl.v12i3.890

Government of the NWT. (2013). *Directions for change: Education renewal and innovation.* Government of the NWT.

Government of the NWT. (2019). *Highest level of schooling.* NWT Bureau of Statistics.

Halfacree, K. H. (1993). Locality and social representation: Space, discourse and alternative definitions of rural. *Journal of Rural Studies, 9*(4). 23–37.

Koziol, N. A., Arthur, A. M., Hawley, L. R., Bovaird, J. A., Bash, K. L., McCormick, C., & Welch, G. W. (2015). Identifying, analyzing, and communicating rural: A quantitative perspective. *Journal of Research in Rural Education, 30*(4), 1–14.

Laurillard, D. (2012). *Teaching as a design science building pedagogical patterns for learning and technology*. Routledge.
Moore, M. G. (2013). The theory of transactional distance. In Moore, M. G. (Ed.). *Handbook of distance education,* (3rd ed.), 66–85. Routledge.
Noddings, N. (2016). *Philosophy of education*. Routledge.
Soanes-White, T. L. (2022). Defining and exploring broadband connections and education solutions in Canada's Northwest Territories. *Canadian Journal of Learning and Technology, 48*(4), 1–18.https://cjlt.ca/index.php/cjlt/article/view/28262/20621
Waldorf, B. (2006, July 3–26). A continuous multi-dimensional measure of rurality: Moving beyond threshold measures. Paper presented at the annual meeting of the American Agricultural Economics Association, Long Beach, California. https://ageconsearch.umn.edu/record/21383?v=pdf

18 Leading at a Distance

Insights and Practical Advice for Early Career Women in Higher Education Leadership

Connie (Levina) Yuen

What is leadership, and what does it mean to lead in distance education? To answer this question, I draw from other voices in higher education (e.g., Nicklin & Segool, 2022; Selzer & Robles, 2019) as well as my experiences as an early career academic and educational technologist. Although there is a range of effective leadership approaches in higher education (Dopson et al., 2019), leadership is fundamentally about serving others through guidance, knowledge sharing, and capacity building, with the primary aim of creating solidarity to achieve collective goals (Oreg & Berson, 2019). To lead means to be actively involved in communication, resource management, and organizational change (Oreg & Berson, 2019) while empowering individuals to be motivated, effective, and focused. Thus, leaders work best by making decisions *with* others by consulting with stakeholders and experts, coordinating resources, and inspiring their teams to act in line with shared priorities or approaches affecting organizational change at both the micro- and the macro-level. By making well-informed decisions, leaders can quickly address necessary changes or concerns.

This narrative is divided into three parts recounting my journey and lessons learned about the importance of leadership as an early career professor at a Canadian online university. In the first part, "Becoming a Great Leader," I recount my experiences of cultivating leadership skills by establishing visibility, capacity, and credibility in the field. I reflect on my evolving identity as a young scholar in emerging technologies, traditionally male dominated. Then I elaborate how I developed effective communication skills and an intentional focus to empower myself and affect others. I next delve into insights into the optics, struggles, and considerations of women who pave the way in their respective research fields. In the second part, "On Climbing the Ivory Tower," I detail the decisions, triumphs, and challenges of advancing my career as a minority moving up the ivory tower of higher education. These lessons address the planning process and internal conflicts that I encountered while pursuing a professional career and balancing other commitments or needs. This section also offers practical advice and solutions to women who aspire to develop leadership capacity or move into leadership roles. In the third part, "Leading the Way in Distance Education," I reflect on the outlooks and implications of women who take on leadership roles in distance education. This section includes an examination of leadership strategies to mobilize others and effect change in an organization from a position of strength and sustainability.

Despite progress in women's working conditions and an increase in equity practices in Canadian higher education, there is still a prevalence of bias against and resistance to women in leadership positions (O'Connor, 2020; Oleschuk, 2020). Although more women are studying and working in higher education, it is well known that they are under-represented in leadership positions (Momani et al., 2019). O'Connor (2020, p. 212) describes this paradox in higher education as a "hierarchical cul-de-sac . . . [in which men occupy] the majority of senior positions" because of persistent beliefs and evaluation practices that favour the employment of men as being more strategically important or skilled in the labour market. Exacerbating these inequitable leadership practices and beliefs are the expectations that both men and women hold regarding the career woman often because of traditional gender roles reflected in both media and history (e.g., Oleschuk, 2020; Tandrayen-Ragoobur & Gokulsing, 2022). This inequity is observed in the working-woman paradigm—particularly during the COVID-19 pandemic—in which women reported taking on the majority of domestic and caregiver responsibilities while working full time (Fisher & Ryan, 2021).

Academic women are often expected to commit to more internal service roles rather than their own research and career pursuits (Allen et al., 2021). Thus, they are perceived as supporters rather than individuals with their own goals. In addition, women are compensated less and often seen as less competent leaders regardless of their accomplishments (Malisch et al., 2020). For example, academic women are faced with limited advancement opportunities as well as unfavourable work policies, including those related to tenure and promotion (Oleschuk, 2020). I have encountered scenarios in which male and female leaders made the same decision but were spoken about differently by colleagues. In one instance, a male leader who implemented a new work policy was said to be setting clear expectations, whereas a female leader who did the same was described as micromanaging. Others have commented that women are less dedicated and hard-working, more likely to leave a job for personal reasons, or too easily influenced by external factors to be fair, competent, or representative leaders. These implicit biases are not only demoralizing to hear but also problematic in that they lead women to be overlooked as viable choices—both by others and by themselves—for leadership positions, particularly when there is no precedent or role model. This contributes to the disproportionately few women in leadership or administrative positions in higher education even though women make up the primary population of faculty members and learners. If a university aims to grow as an educational institution and serve a diversified student population, then it needs to demonstrate its ability to identify and provide equitable opportunities for growth for its own staff. I have found that, when assembling team members for a project, the more diversified the members, the more perspectives and values are considered when evaluating the needs and trajectories of research.

Becoming a Great Leader

It is never too early to begin cultivating leadership skills, even as an entry-level academic. All people possess skills or knowledge that they can impart to others based on their previous experiences with both competent and incompetent leadership. By stepping into leadership roles, women can become beacons of hope reflecting equitable treatment or opportunity, diverse representation, and contemporary vision. Below I describe my experiences while developing a leadership mindset and how I came to embrace my role in leading others in distance education.

You Are Your Best Advocate

In my early career as an analyst in the field of technology, I recall, I barely made ends meet financially, but I had not yet realized the importance of self-advocacy. It took several years before a senior colleague mentioned that an intern's starting pay was higher and had been adjusted further to meet inflation, and I finally mustered the courage to ask the manager for a raise. My manager responded swiftly and favourably, telling me that I was the first woman there to ask for a raise and that she hoped to see more young women like me with the courage to negotiate their compensation as readily as our male counterparts. To this day, her words of wisdom resonate with me: you are your own best advocate. Each time you advocate for yourself, you also learn how to advocate for the well-being of others. As women, we need to recognize and value our self-worth and then have the courage to act.

Internalizing Self-Worth and Being Clear about Your Purpose

An important component of becoming a leader is building capacity and developing a focused mindset. Although I had the necessary experience and capabilities to carry out my responsibilities in research, teaching, and service, as a new faculty member I had to be strategic in managing all three areas to set myself up for success (and proactively prevent burnout). As academics and leaders, we need to internalize our self-worth and recognize the significance of actively promoting our work and ourselves. This is a necessary step in establishing our reputations as scholars and as advocates of change. Be clear and direct in asking questions and speak with conviction when you have ideas that could support the betterment of the organization.

One of the expectations of being a scholar is that you become an expert in the field, and for many scholars it also means being well read on many interdisciplinary topics. As a result, I have often observed other early career academics being overworked: they push themselves to understand every detail of a topic, yet when it comes time to write or publish they still feel insecure about having others review their work. With the plethora of information readily accessible, and with limited time, scholars realize that there is much more to learn, and there is a belief or doubt that can settle in about whether we truly deserve to be recognized as researchers equal to our senior colleagues. This kind of thinking seems to be especially true for those who transitioned quickly from graduate school to a tenure-track position or for colleagues who thought that they had fewer publications and research writing skills. This imposter syndrome, surprisingly, takes hold early in one's career and remains throughout one's career—even for well-established, tenured scholars as the field and expectations grow. This deconstructive mindset tends to linger because of the unspoken power relations that one perceives, and it is more prevalent in women, particularly women of colour (Manongsong & Ghosh, 2021). Perhaps a colleague seems to have a long-standing co-authorship relationship or seems to know a lot about the field in which one is supposedly an expert. However, this is a self-limiting perception that needs to be counteracted quickly. Being cognizant of self-doubt, we can then re-evaluate improvements or changes over which we have control to address them.

One way to accomplish this is by consolidating your beliefs about success and establishing a clear vision for the value that you contribute with your work. You must be clear on your purpose: why you are in academia, why your field or topic is important, and what you seek to change or improve. What is the higher-level aim and impact of what you seek to do? Who is your audience, and for whom do you advocate? For example, my goal is to challenge the status quo and find adaptive, meaningful ways to address problems affecting technology use in education and society. I work toward this goal by constantly reviewing and writing about the current state of technology implementation and research in education. I hope that by sharing my consolidated knowledge in accessible, innovative ways, I can inspire others to do the same. As long as we keep our personal mission in focus, we can push past self-doubts and comparisons.

On Climbing the Ivory Tower

Before accepting a faculty position at an online university, I worked for a decade as an educational technologist at several campus-based universities. Much of my work focused on developing and applying my technological and instructional design skills to help others carry out their projects. As I continued working in higher education, I became more interested in academic and research-based activities. Soon I began formulating my own research ideas and aspired to exercise my creative energy, thus transitioning into a faculty position.

Although taking on a faculty position was an exciting and new experience, it soon became apparent that leadership was a significant element of my work. As a course instructor, I led students on a constructive path to learning. As a researcher, I led teams of research assistants, instructional designers, and staff to carry out university initiatives. Developing leadership competence and enabling others to carry out their work effectively are essential factors of the institution's success as well as my own. I am fortunate to have observed examples of great leadership at the university, and it became evident that leadership is a decisive factor in individual and collective success in higher education. Following are a few lessons that I learned about developing leadership capacity as an early career academic.

Be Discerning and Intentional about Your Work

Although faculty citizenship is important, remember to protect your time and energy from extra research, teaching, or service commitments beyond your manageable workload. As an early career academic, you will have ongoing opportunities to contribute to the university community, and it is important to delegate tasks appropriately. Being a leader does not mean micromanaging or being involved with every task; rather, it means recognizing the expertise of others and enabling them to work better.

Manage Time and Well-Being for Active Online Engagement

In distance education, it is vital to learn how to develop online connections with limited to no face-to-face opportunities. This meant changing my conception of how to initiate and nurture collegial relationships, knowing that I might have few opportunities to meet informally or socialize virtually with colleagues depending on the university's existing practices and sometimes because of actual physical or time barriers. Also, because a typical workday for an academic in distance education includes numerous activities and conference calls conducted while sitting in an office chair, amplified by a reduced presence online, it requires capable management of the workload, timelines, and well-being. For example, be cognizant of screen fatigue, the pressure to be online all the time (i.e., colleagues and learners have access to you through email 24/7) and added responsibilities such as learning to set up a home office or technologies conducive to a distraction-free, quiet, and ergonomic space. Safeguard your personal time from your work obligations beyond virtual office hours to prevent burnout.

Support Others' Work and Success Often

Partake in your colleagues' lectures or workshops at conferences, co-teach in different courses, and promote their successes at meetings and public forums. Their successes are intertwined with your success.

Be Realistic about Your Progression and Timelines

Sometimes unexpected delays or challenges occur, and you need to be flexible and revise your schedule to adapt to these changes. Also understand that occupational ambitions can align with or support your personal goals and that you do not necessarily need to choose between one or the other. This idea is supported by Nicklin and Segool (2022), who discuss the application of self-determination theory and work-family balance for women in higher education. I frequently reviewed my career and personal goals and broke them down into the smaller steps needed to accomplish them. At other times, research commitments or grant application deadlines were at odds with the timing of personal priorities, such as starting a family. Current statistics reveal that most permanent academic positions are appointed to people around 34 years of age (O'Connor, 2020), which can coincide with women's timelines for child-bearing and -rearing. In fact, this was my case as I found myself embracing the role of a new parent and primary caregiver to two young children over the course of my pre-tenure. A day in my life included a combination of holding academic interviews, undertaking research projects, teaching courses, feeding babies, and changing diapers. During this time, I honed my productivity and time management skills and discovered the positive impact of spending just 10 minutes at various intervals throughout the day to do research. It also helps to be surrounded by understanding colleagues and continually to build your support network so that you can delegate tasks to others and remind yourself to practise self-compassion.

Co-Shape Work Practices

Part of being a good leader is understanding the "bigger picture" and co-shaping practices through collective action (By, 2021). This means being cognizant of the group dynamics among people, seeking perspectives from diverse members, and always learning with others. Seek mentors for advice and become a mentor for others. By doing so, you will be more attuned to the available resources, processes, and creative solutions to address future challenges. For example, if you are planning to go on parental leave, check for published documentation and work with human resources to clarify policies that support you while away on leave (e.g., coverage, benefits, the tenure clock).

Understand the "Business" of Education

Take time to learn your organization's distinct characteristics and strategic plan and then align your activities with your role and responsibilities as an academic within the university. Reflecting on these processes and reviewing university policies will enable you to identify gaps in your own workflow and uncover solutions to recurring barriers. Over time, you will become more adept at working with other teams, managing resources, delegating tasks, evaluating proposals, and handling the complexities of university bureaucracy and politics—all of the elements that contribute to informed decision making and the making of a great leader.

Leading the Way in Distance Education

Leaders are emblematic of an organization's vision, priorities, policies, future trajectory, and most of all how the organization treats and values people. As such, leaders need to have reach and impact when it comes to motivating or influencing others. Women can lead in distance education by promoting gender and diversity awareness and serving as role models for young women or marginalized persons—particularly visible minorities who might not feel represented or well understood in their careers. In this way, women can amplify an organization's capacity to create supportive, inclusive environments in which others feel comfortable expressing their ideas, which in turn can prevent rapid employee turnover and career burnout (Thomas et al., 2020).

Leadership in distance education is unique in that it is situated predominantly—and often solely—in virtual settings. This context provides both unique opportunities and challenges that a leader must navigate in order to coordinate and sustain meaningful relationships with colleagues and students. One persistent challenge to leading at a distance involves reliance on online communication: nuances are lost through the written word (especially email), and other factors—such as eye contact, body language, and network latency—can affect one's online presence. In my leadership work, I familiarized myself with the processes involved in facilitating virtual collaborative activities such as pacing content sharing in anticipation of technology latency issues, providing brief technology overviews at the beginnings of meetings, as well as implementing mindfulness health breaks throughout. The inherently blurred boundaries between work life and home life—particularly in post-pandemic times—necessitated an adjustment to my expectations regarding meaningful, online-based relationships and their effects on work productivity and time flexibility.

This understanding and expectation must also extend to leaders themselves. Leaders must be highly self-aware, open to new developments or solutions, and flexible with their time to address urgent but necessary organizational or human issues that occur (Herbst & Conradie, 2011). They lead by example, being courageous and earnest in sharing their perspectives (even when they are unpopular), seeking and applying feedback, spending time and energy to collaborate effectively with others, and always looking to facilitate growth or innovation. In this way, leaders act as strong advocates of change and continually evaluate individual and organizational activities to help meet diverse student needs (e.g., By, 2021; Samuelson et al., 2019).

Conclusion

Ultimately, being a leader means empowering others and ensuring access and equity for the betterment of the organization. The challenges described in this chapter are just some of the difficulties that women face given pervasive biases in society, such as those with which I am familiar. With consistent reflection and self-appraisal, women in early career academic positions can become more influential and valued leaders in their workplaces. As organizations adopt increasingly equitable policies (O'Connor, 2019), women are empowered to step into higher leadership roles and set new precedents for professional practice in distance education.

References

Allen, K. A., Butler-Henderson, K., Reupert, A., Longmuir, F., Finefter-Rosenbluh, I., Berger, Grove, C., Heffernan, A., Freeman, N., Kewalramani, S., Krebs, S., Dsouza, L., Mackie, G., Chapman, D., & Fleer, M. (2021). Work like a girl: Redressing gender inequity in academia through systemic solutions. *Journal of University Teaching & Learning Practice, 18*(3). https://doi.org/10.53761/1.18.3.3

By, R. T. (2021). Leadership: In pursuit of purpose. *Journal of Change Management, 21*(1), 30–44. https://doi.org/10.1080/14697017.2021.1861698

Dopson, S., Ferlie, E., McGivern, G., Fischer, M. D., Mitra, M., Ledger, J., & Behrens, S. (2019). Leadership development in higher education: A literature review and implications for programme redesign. *Higher Education Quarterly, 73*(2), 218–234. https://doi.org/10.1111/hequ.12194

Fisher, A. N., & Ryan, M. K. (2021). Gender inequalities during COVID-19. *Group Processes & Intergroup Relations, 24*(2), 237–245. https://doi.org/10.1177/1368430220984248

Herbst, T. H., & Conradie, P. D. (2011). Leadership effectiveness in higher education: Managerial self-perceptions versus perceptions of others. *SA Journal of Industrial Psychology, 37*(1), 1–14. https://doi.org/10.1080/13678868.2020.1779911

Malisch, J. L., Harris, B. N., Sherrer, S. M., Lewis, K. A., Shepherd, S. L., McCarthy, P. C., Spott, J.L., Karam, E.P., Moustaid-Moussa, N., McCrory Calarco, J., Ramalingam, L., Talley, A.E., Cañas-Carrell, J.E., Ardon-Dryer, A., Weiser, D.A., Bernal, X.E., & Deitloff, J.

(2020). In the wake of COVID-19, academia needs new solutions to ensure gender equity. *Proceedings of the National Academy of Sciences, 117*(27), 15378–15381. https://doi.org/10.1073/pnas.2010636117

Manongsong, A. M., & Ghosh, R. (2021). Developing the positive identity of minoritized women leaders in higher education: How can multiple and diverse developers help with overcoming the impostor phenomenon? *Human Resource Development Review, 20*(4), 436–485. https://doi.org/10.1177/15344843211040732

Momani, B., Dreher, E., & Williams, K. (2019). More than a pipeline problem: Evaluating the gender pay gap in Canadian academia from 1996 to 2016. *Canadian Journal of Higher Education, 49*(1), 1–21. https://doi.org/10.47678/cjhe.v49i1.188197

Nicklin, J. M., & Segool, N. K. (2022). Work-family thriving for women in higher education. In B. Cozza & C. Parnther (Eds.), *Voices from women leaders on success in higher education* (pp. 121–132). Routledge. https://doi.org/10.4324/9781003219897

O'Connor, P. (2019). Gender imbalance in senior positions in higher education: What is the problem? What can be done? *Policy Reviews in Higher Education, 3*(1), 28–50. https://doi.org/10.1080/23322969.2018.1552084

O'Connor, P. (2020). Why is it so difficult to reduce gender inequality in male-dominated higher educational organizations? A feminist institutional perspective. *Interdisciplinary Science Reviews, 45*(2), 207–228. https://doi.org/10.1080/03080188.2020.1737903

Oleschuk, M. (2020). Gender equity considerations for tenure and promotion during COVID-19. *Canadian Review of Sociology, 57*(3), 502–515. https://doi.org/10.1111/cars.12295

Oreg, S., & Berson, Y. (2019). Leaders' impact on organizational change: Bridging theoretical and methodological chasms. *Academy of Management Annals, 13*(1), 272–307. https://doi.org/10.5465/annals.2016.0138

Samuelson, H. L., Levine, B. R., Barth, S. E., Wessel, J. L., & Grand, J. A. (2019). Exploring women's leadership labyrinth: Effects of hiring and developmental opportunities on gender stratification. *The Leadership Quarterly, 30*(6), 101314. https://doi.org/10.1016/j.leaqua.2019.101314

Selzer, R. A., & Robles, R. (2019). Every woman has a story to tell: Experiential reflections on leadership in higher education. *Journal of*

Women and Gender in Higher Education, 12(1), 106–124. https://doi.org/10.1080/19407882.2018.1534246

Tandrayen-Ragoobur, V., & Gokulsing, D. (2022). Gender gap in STEM education and career choices: What matters? *Journal of Applied Research in Higher Education, 14*(3), 1021–1040. https://doi.org/10.1108/JARHE-09-2019-0235

Thomas, R., Cooper, M., Cardazone, G., Urban, K., Bohrer, A., Long, M., Yee, L., Krivkovich, A., Huang, J., Prince, S., Kumar, A., & Coury, S. (2020). *Women in the workplace 2020*. McKinsey & Company. https://wiw-report.s3.amazonaws.com/Women_in_the_Workplace_2020.pdf

19 Female Leadership in Online Education in Canada

Reflecting and Forging the Future

Lorraine Carter, Diane Janes, and Katy Campbell

Canadian women have always undertaken complex roles as caregivers and navigators of change in the workplace. They have also been key members of emergency health and remote learning teams that emerged in recent global shifts. With respect to education and doing things a little differently, women in postsecondary settings were influential in online learning long before 2023. In this chapter, as early leaders in online education, we will highlight how we and other women have made important contributions to the practice of online and distance education from 1990 to 2023. We will also reflect on the future of female leadership in the sustained development of this educational approach.

LORRAINE CARTER

My journey into online education involves connections to geography, continuing education, and the grit of extraordinary women.

My career began in Sudbury, northern Ontario, where life, work, and education are influenced by long winters, a small population, and service limitations. Not surprisingly, these variables affect the learning experiences of adults in the North, a reality that became stark in my work as an instructional designer in continuing education (CE) at Laurentian University beginning in the early 1990s. Composed principally of women, the CE team worked tirelessly to develop course materials and support instructors and students. Reaching our objectives was challenging with instructional designers and learning technologists hired on soft money, inadequate staff to carry out operational tasks and respond to learners' questions, and a small leadership team to work with the faculties and guide the unit. The bilingual nature of the university meant that many courses were prepared in both English and French. Despite these variables, there was a determination among the CE staff influenced by the leadership of John Daniel, who served as the university's president from 1984 to 1990. After leaving Laurentian University, he went on to be a global leader in distance and open learning.

During this time, I worked closely with the director of the School of Nursing, Dr. Ellen Rukholm, and other nursing and CE colleagues on the university's first federally funded online programs called Cardiac Care on the Web and Nursing Health Assessment on the Web. Although none of us had experience designing and delivering online programs, we were strongly motivated and brought a "how hard can this be?" attitude to the process. We needed that attitude.

These projects cultivated my research acumen since, in addition to doing design work, I served as a co-investigator on two studies of online education involving working nurse-learners. I was also the lead designer of online courses for post-diploma nurses seeking degree status before it became an entry-to-practice requirement in Ontario in 2005. Complementing my reading of nursing literature was work by Liz Burge and Margaret Haughey (2001) about women leaders in distance and early online education. This portfolio of work served as the basis of my doctoral work in education, completed in 2006. Working with the late Dr. Larry Morton from the University of Windsor, I investigated the critical thinking, writing, and online learning experiences of post-registered nurses whose complex professional lives were augmented by their families, community responsibilities, and inability to attend in-person classes. Both Larry and Ellen were exceptional mentors, with Larry seeing the access that online education affords and Ellen recognizing how online nursing education was a game changer for the profession. She and I presented and published in many national and international contexts as champions of online nursing education.

I likewise had the chance to work with motivated women as part of the launch of the Northern Ontario School of Medicine. Although the senior leadership of the school was male dominated, women played a major role in designing and developing courses for medical students distributed across northern Ontario. Later I became the education manager for the Ontario Telemedicine Network, a provincially funded organization that uses technology to support clinical consultations across distance and to respond to the continuing educational needs of health professionals. Again, the Ontario Telemedicine Network "doers" were principally female. The same pattern continued in my faculty days when I joined the School of Nursing at Nipissing University and served as director of the Centre for Flexible Teaching and Learning. In each setting, women—and particularly those in nursing faculties—saw the potential of online education and were committed to actualizing it.

Throughout my career, I have learned a great deal from female leaders with the Canadian Network for Innovation in Education (CNIE) and the Canadian Association for University Continuing

Education (CAUCE). Eventually, I served as president of each organization. The CNIE and CAUCE tend to attract women who understand that online education is vital to the achievement of educational access and accessibility. In a recent informal count of deans and directors representing university continuing education units belonging to CAUCE, 70% of these leaders were female (CAUCE, 2023).

Recently I retired as director of McMaster University Continuing Education, a unit that has more than 90 years of history in adult education and a staff that is 75% female. As part of my core work, assuring others in the academy that teaching and learning accomplished "a little differently" is a valid educational methodology, and advocating for services afforded to undergraduate and graduate students for adult learners were no easy tasks. I continued to be an actively engaged scholar in the online and continuing education sectors since not doing so would have been negligent in advancing the credibility of both fields. This work followed my editorship and co-editorship of the *Canadian Journal for University Continuing Education* and the *International Journal of e-Learning & Distance Education*, respectively.

DIANE JANES

I stumbled into instructional design and online learning at a time when it was open to women from different backgrounds and histories. I was also the first person in my family to finish high school and pursue postsecondary learning. Along the way, I took every course in every discipline that I could and still graduate. This became the metaphor for my life's work: exploring and drawing "outside the box."

I discovered a Master of Educational Technology program at Memorial University of Newfoundland and Labrador in the late 1980s. Taught by Dr. M. F. (Mary) Kennedy and others, the degree program was one of the first in the country to focus on instructional design, educational technology, and distance education. My thesis evaluated the first course offered by the university via distance education (paper, email, and audiotaped lectures). Mary had completed her doctoral studies at Indiana University with some of the biggest names in educational technology. She was the first Canadian to intern as a graduate student at the Association for Educational Communications and Technology (Ives et al., 2023). In turn, she influenced me and the next generation of educational technologists and educators.

In 1996, I went to the University of British Columbia (UBC) under the mentorship of Dr. A. W. (Tony) Bates, who had joined UBC from the Open University in the United Kingdom the previous year. I was his first hire for the new department, Distance Education and Technology. Working with other UBC colleagues, we moved distance learning from correspondence to technology-enhanced to fully online. At UBC, I was a member of the team with Tony and Dr. Mark Bullen that, with Mexican colleagues, created the post-graduate certificate in Technology-Based Distance Learning—a collaboration between Tecnológico de Monterrey, Mexico, and UBC. One of the first certifications in online learning offered to academics and practitioners globally, by 2002 it had become the Master of Educational Technology, the first online master's program at UBC and a program in which Mark and I continue to teach. I completed my PhD at UBC, where a key member of my doctoral committee was Dr. Jean Barman, an amazing mentor in engaging graduate learners and a mentor in writing, having been an award winner for her own academic writing. I have been writing ever since. Between our time at UBC and other new ventures, such as serving as president of the CNIE, Mark and I edited *Making the Transition to E-Learning: Strategies and Issues* (Bullen & Janes, 2007).

My first faculty position at the University of Saskatchewan in 2003 was the beginning of the pathway to where I am today. After I was tenured and promoted, the university closed my division, and I went on to teach graduate students at a distance for six universities. By 2009, I had moved to Cape Breton University to become the inaugural chair of the new Department of Education and to establish a new BEd, one of the first to incorporate educational technology methodology into its core offerings. In 2013, I joined the Donald School of Business as its inaugural associate dean. There I led the creation of the first provincial post-baccalaureate blended credential in international business. After faculty roles at the University of Alberta and the Southern Alberta Institute of Technology, I returned to British Columbia in 2021 to join Thompson Rivers University in Kamloops as a coordinator for the Centre for Excellence in Learning and Teaching. There I mentor colleagues in teaching, design, and the scholarship of teaching and learning. Most of my current work involves blending traditional university face-to-face delivery methods with online and design thinking in addition to co-editing the *International Journal of e-Learning & Distance Education*.

Over my years in distance education, I have discovered a few things about myself and the influences that these different institutions and the women and men within them have had on my life and career in online and technology-enhanced learning. Mentoring and supporting women as they accomplish their goals has been the mainstay of my work. To teach means to understand design, flexibility, and scholarship. These core areas guide all of my work. Finally, teaching and learning are political acts. To bring this work into the spaces of others, especially when working with new faculty, is to change how they engage with and even see the world. This work is transformative in all ways imaginable.

KATY CAMPBELL

My career path from instructional designer to dean was fashioned from disorienting dilemmas. It was Dr. David Mappin who declared me an instructional designer and had me lead design teams in the Faculty of Education at the University of Alberta. There I had two epiphanies: first, I had no idea what an instructional designer was, although I knew that the practice described in the theoretical literature was embedded in masculinist traditions; second, instructional design was a social process of storytelling. My doctoral supervisor, Dr. Jean Clandinin, encouraged me to reshape instructional design as relational practice, and I began to see instructional design as a strategy for social action. Dr. Margaret Haughey further encouraged my identity transformation into a scholar of instructional design, and I began to shape a feminist instructional design practice. After my PhD, I began working with Dr. Rick Schwier and others to develop a "theory" of instructional design as socially agentic practice, and in 1992 I accepted my first academic position at the State University of New York, where I was expected to lead technology integration in the teacher education college. This was my first exposure to the World Wide Web, and I linked elementary school students around the state with my pre-service practicum students. It was awkward, but it opened up possibilities in our teacher education program, particularly with students from vulnerable communities.

In 1995, I moved to Keewatin Community College in Manitoba as a distance education coordinator. Sadly, the college was not ready for this vision, and my daughter and I were bullied mercilessly. I was not welcome as an agent of change and deeply suspect as an academic. The president's goal to make the Thompson campus a distance education centre did not sit well with faculty members, although the community was enthusiastic. I struggled to build rapport and launch programs. Ultimately, the "distance" in "distance coordinator" meant visiting fly-in communities to talk with First Nations leaders about the learning needs of their communities, very few of which, such as child care, we could meet (see Kirkup & Von Prümmer, 1990). I was faced with the realities of colonization; from that time on, I actively sought ways to be an ally in my academic roles, especially as a dean.

By 1996, I was recruited as an instructional designer and later a tenure-track academic in the Faculty of Extension at the University of Alberta by Dean Dennis Foth. The faculty had taken a plan for the Distance Learning Initiative (later the Academic Technologies for Learning) to the provost, who agreed to fund it as a "skunkworks" for faculty members interested in exploring learning technologies. As the lead designer, I was challenged to change the culture of "face to face is always best." For several years, we worked to change the discussion, and most of the time I was in a zone of proximal development, until our director, Dr. Terry Anderson, accepted a position at Athabasca University. I became the interim director, but I struggled. I was resented by staff in the Academic Technologies for Learning, not respected by peers who doubted my technical chops, and discounted by the male-dominated central administration. Like other women who aspired to leadership, I was never named as the permanent director. With budget cuts in the mid-1990s, our funding was discontinued.

Although we developed our first graduate distance degree, the Master of Arts in Communications and Technology, the Faculty of Extension always struggled for credibility as a degree-granting faculty. I became the associate dean, charged with bringing new credentials forward, and I became more passionate about the access to learning upon which the faculty was built. In 2007, because of a failed deanship, I was appointed dean of the faculty (again in an interim capacity) as it moved to the city's core. The move escalated the chaos that faculty members felt, and the feelings of marginalization were strong. Yet the crisis opened up creative space in which to build social capital in new communities.

The newly appointed associate dean, Dennis Foth, and I led the faculty through an intensive reorientation and revisioning and alignment with the evolving "movement" of engagement scholarship (see Boyer, 1996). As a "boundary organization" or an "experimental incubator" since 1912, the faculty's research and teaching were intended to promote innovation in engagement, including prioritizing Indigenization in our programs and activities. In 2017, the faculty established the Master of Arts in Community Engagement, to our knowledge the first graduate program of its kind in the world.

Despite the growing academic reputation of the Faculty of Extension, deans of other faculties (a.k.a. predatory deans) protested the development of for-credit engaged programs in various formats, the establishment of two related research centres, efforts to secure donors, and the tiny budget from central administration. In 2013, with severe budget reductions, all faculties were pressured to prioritize revenue generation. Faculties that had worked collaboratively with our faculty to develop accessible programs were now encouraged to develop their own. Other deans thought that engagement scholarship was not a legitimate intellectual domain and that our learners were not university-level students. The faculty would be "decommissioned." Although my intensive lobbying and overt resistance resulted in the acting provost reversing the decision, it was merely forestalled. In the fall of 2019, the new provost moved to disperse the faculty's academic staff and research centres to other faculties. The University of Alberta deinstitutionalized the academic mission of community-engagement scholarship, conceiving of it as a community relations and advancement function. The emotional labour of over 20 years, in many ways the "women's work" of relationship building, did not diminish the precarity of a marginalized practice (online learning) and scholarship (of engagement) in a faculty committed to access for adult learners.

Shared Findings

Through the act of reflecting on our experiences, we perceive six principal themes. We provide some summative remarks on each theme below.

Instructional Design

The term "instructional design" came of age in the online domain. Fundamentally, it is about team-based development of a learning experience because of the complexities involved in online learning and the criticality of including multiple perspectives. Since many early instructional designers were women, including the three of us, we argue that women laid important groundwork for how instructional design is practised today as a critical, agentic form of social action (Burge & Haughey, 2001; Campbell et al., 2005). Did we know what we were doing at the outset? Not always, but we learned along the way.

The Politics of Acceptance

The politics of the acceptance of online learning are important for women who have been in the field for some time. Both rich and poor learning experiences can occur in any context, including technology-supported and in-person settings. We know, though, that thoughtful instructional design, strong support systems, and engaged instructors can enable top-tier online teaching and learning experiences (Carl, 2017).

A Scholarly Tradition

Each of us has a strong scholarly identity in online education. In our early and mid-career days, we knew that what we were doing with different communities and in different settings was important and that not to share it would be counter to the social justice principle of access to education that we treasure. Although the following statement is about adult education, it is equally true of the scholarship of online education: "Scholarly journals play a pivotal role in the life of any academic field. . . . This is particularly relevant in a comparatively new and diverse academic and practitioner-oriented field" (Nesbit, 2011, p. ii). Although there are people today who see online and technology-supported education as a new field, those of us who have engaged in its scholarship over time know that is untrue. It has existed for decades. Knowing the scholarly tradition of online education can only lead to better decisions in the present and for the future.

Women as Leaders and Mentors

If one studies the leadership of organizations such as CAUCE and CNIE, then one sees a distinct history of female leaders. Women also tend to be active in communities of practice that advance teaching and learning in ways that push boundaries. The idea of necessity being "the mother of invention" holds merit here. At the same time, as early leaders in online and distance education, we came to experience issues of culture, including those related to Indigenous contexts and the broader masculinist academy. Regarding the latter, though we did not always win, we certainly spoke up and advocated for values that reflect feminist thinking (Bainbridge & Wark, 2023).

Access and Accessibility

As women, we continue to see the access that online education can facilitate in our country. This access moves beyond borders, makes learning possible during busy lives, and defeats variables such as weather and distance. Accessibility for those who live with health and other realities that limit ability to attend classes on a campus is greatly enhanced by online education models.

More than 30 years ago, Haughey (1990, pp. 35, 43) identified that the "development of community and the recognition of the ethnic, political, historical and gendered context of learners" are key components of distance learning and society as a whole. Although these ideas might not have been recognized as singularly important at the time, they are relevant today. Thinkers such as Daniel (2019) and Bates (2022) have also championed the value that online and open educational models can bring not only to Canada but also to countries around the world where education is not as accessible as it is in this country.

Continuing Education

As the past few years have shown, online learning can occur at all levels and be implemented quickly (although quickness is rarely a sign of good practice). One area in which online education has made valuable inroads over time is continuing education. In such units, flexibility is the mantra because of the diverse challenges that adult learners face. Perhaps not surprisingly, the staff and leaders in these units tend to be women guided by feminist thinking and action. The learner base in the continuing education unit represented in this chapter consistently skews female at just over 70%. In the same unit, the programs offered represent a cross-section of professional practice areas, including health care (Carter & Rukholm, 2008), business, communications, and emerging technologies (McMaster University Continuing Education, 2023). In the simplest terms, women are looking to advance their careers, and online learning enables this goal.

The Future

As we hypothesize the future of online education in Canada, the metaphor of forging with women in doing and leading roles emerges as a fitting choice. Forging as "heating and hammering" evokes the idea of tenacity among female online educators and administrators who deal with the many complexities of bringing education to diverse individuals and communities. Although some might argue that today's technologies hold potential for reducing these complexities, those who have lived and continue to live with today's changes know that this is an overly simplistic understanding of the challenge. Female grit, problem-solving skills, and commitment to a mission grounded in educational access must remain central to the evolution of meaningful online education.

Forging has also been associated with the act of developing new relationships and conditions, tasks that women are gifted to accomplish. Women will also be essential to navigating partnerships as online education becomes increasingly crowded with corporate entities. Strong women will be needed to counter the corporate mentality that could well dominate the online field without their presence.

Based on our experiences and reflections, we propose that feminist thinking and acting as well as strong female leaders are essential to the evolution of online education in Canada. Indeed, the next 30 plus years will tell the tale.

References

Bainbridge, S., & Wark, N. (2023). *The encyclopedia of female pioneers in online learning.* Routledge. https://www.routledge.com/The-Encyclopedia-of-Female-Pioneers-in-Online-Learning/Bainbridge-Wark/p/book/9781032230351

Bates, A. W. (2022). *Teaching in a digital age: Guidelines for designing teaching and learning* (3rd ed.). Tony Bates Associates. https://pressbooks.bccampus.ca/teachinginadigitalagev3m/

Boyer, E. L. (1996). The scholarship of engagement. *Bulletin of the American Academy of Arts and Sciences, 49*(7), 18–33. https://doi.org/10.2307/3824459

Bullen, M., & Janes, D. P. (2007). *Making the transition to e-learning: Strategies and issues.* IGI Global. https://www.igi-global.com/book/making-transition-learning/703

Burge, E. J., & Haughey, M. (Eds.). (2001). *Using learning technologies.* Routledge Falmer.

Campbell, K., Schwier, R. A., & Kenny, R. F. (2005). Agency of the instructional designer: Moral coherence and transformative social practice. *Australasian Journal of Educational Technology, 21*(2), 242–262.

Carl, D. R. (2017). Bridging the gap: The contributions of individual women to the development of distance education to 1976. In K. Faith (Ed.), *Toward new horizons for women in distance education* (pp. 316–337). Routledge.

Carter, L., & Rukholm, E. (2008). A study of critical thinking, teacher-student interaction, and discipline-specific writing in an online educational setting for registered nurses. *Journal of Continuing Education in Nursing, 39*(3), 133–138.

Daniel, J. S. (2019). Open universities: Old concepts and cost challenges. *The International Review of Research in Online and Distributed Learning, 20*(4). https://www.irrodl.org/index.php/irrodl/article/view/4035

Haughey, M. (1990). Trends and issues in distance education with implications for northern development. In D. Wall & M. Owen (Eds.), *Distance education and sustainable community development: Selected articles from a Conference on Distance Education and Sustainable Community Development* (pp. 29–37) Canadian Circumpolar Institute. https://files.eric.ed.gov/fulltext/ED400150.pdf

Ives, C., Janes, D. P., & Crowley, C. (2023). *MemoryKeepers—Profiles and interviews: AMTEC History Project—Dr. Mary F. Kennedy* [Video]. YouTube. https://www.youtube.com/watch?v=VZvtaYIO4Eo

Kirkup, G., & Von Prümmer, C. (1990). Support and connectedness: The needs of women distance education students. *Journal of Distance Education, 5*(2), 9–31.

McMaster University Continuing Education. (2023). https://continuing.mcmaster.ca

Nesbit, T. (2011). Editorial: Keeping the flame alive. *Canadian Journal for the Study of Adult Education, 23*(2), ii–vi. https://cjsae.library.dal.ca/index.php/cjsae/article/view/949

Conclusion

As we introduced at the beginning of this book and as illustrated across the three sections, leadership is an evolving, multi-faceted, and dynamic process. We began by describing the inspiring feminist and literary traditions of women in distance education. Then we identified specific and relevant leadership approaches to situate our thinking. In a collection of stories, the chapter authors share their unconventional journeys to leadership, often noting that they had a responsibility that few wanted or, in some cases, recognized was needed. Threaded throughout this book are post-heroic narratives that illuminate women's desire for relational and inclusive leadership practices and demonstrate the need for thoughtful communication and collegial support. In these examples, we see an opportunity for future theorists and scholars to consider the nuanced ways that women demonstrate leadership in higher education, potentially to advance a theory of distance education leadership.

We turn now to a summary of the themes emerging from the chapters. The first section is a multi-dimensional representation of the contexts within which distance education leaders work. The voices in "Planning Learning" resonate with some of our own experiences with leadership in higher education. Authors describe their work in course and program development, instructional design, and faculty development. Research supports this pathway to leadership. For example, Pollard and Kumar (2021) recognized the contribution potential of instructional designers. Although they did not use the word *leadership* for this uniquely positioned group of professionals with deep and wide influences in the academy, they pointed out that "instructional designers are beginning to be recognized for the deeper, more expansive, and more transformative potential they offer to institutions: the potential to support strategic missions and bring change at the organizational level" (p. 8). Other scholars have identified instructional design competencies as unique skills and approaches valuable for leadership functions. However, instructional designers do not always identify themselves as leaders. Schwier et al. (2006) articulated multiple levels of agency among instructional designers with interactions among operational and organizational areas of focus and pointed out that opportunities for transformative agency exist in the very nature of their work and processes of communication. In other words, by creating environments for effective learning, designers influence the performance of others in their communities. The chapter authors describe their contributions as agentic.

The chapters in "Communicating and Collaborating" also include the voices of those who identify as middle-level leaders. These stories confirm that, supported by effective communication and collaborative action, leadership involves strategic, thoughtful design and innovative solutions to ill-structured and often externally imposed problems. Research supports the need for these competencies in the management and leadership of distance education (Ashbaugh & Piña, 2014; Nworie, 2012). The narratives add to the literature of design thinking (Schön, 1987; Zenke, 2014) in which designers address "wicked," complex problems creatively. Branson and colleagues (2016) contended that, though power and authority are not necessarily features of middle-level leadership, influence and persuasion often are. In these narratives, women report enacting leadership from a multidirectional relational stance. They portray perseverance and innovation in response to challenges. Their stories illustrate that distance education approaches can serve as a continuity model during times of disruption and crisis, often because of weather-related events, emergencies, or pandemics. Abrupt changes in their environments provided leadership opportunities, creating conditions that disrupted the status quo or inspired leadership action.

In "Reflecting on Experiences," the chapter authors share deeply personal, evocative stories of their leadership journeys. We are inspired by the courage and resilience that these narratives highlight, and we identify with expressed feelings of under-representation and imposter syndrome. For those who identify as members of marginalized or racialized communities—including women—the foundational values of distance education that promote and facilitate access to knowledge and social mobility are evident. This theme lingers in the trust demonstrated by the authors, who with their words advocate for change, especially reconciliation, decolonization, and employment equity. The authors not only write about their experiences but also share insights and learning that emerged from their reflections and meanings negotiated between self and others (Lyle, 2013). These reflective narratives illustrate the importance of safe spaces, both physical and virtual. The experiences lead to an understanding of the power of conversation and grassroots networking, sharing stories of personal and systemic discrimination and injustice, and ultimately offering alternative approaches to leadership. This gives us hope for the future.

References

Ashbaugh, M. L., & Piña, A. A. (2014). Improving instructional design processes through leadership-thinking and modeling. In B.

Hokanson, & A. Gibbons (Eds.), *Design in educational technology: Design thinking, design process and the design studio,* (pp. 223–247). Springer.

Branson, C. M., Franken, M., & Penney, D. (2016). Middle leadership in higher education: A relational analysis. *Educational Management Administration & Leadership, 44*(1), 128–145.

Lyle, E. (2013). From method to methodology: Narrative as a way of knowing for adult learners. *Canadian Journal for Studies in Adult Education, 25*(2), 17–24. https://cjsae.library.dal.ca/index.php/cjsae/article/view/1213

Nworie, J. (2012). Applying leadership theories to distance education leadership. *Online Journal of Distance Learning Administration, 15*(5). https://ojdla.com/archive/winter154/nworie154.pdf

Pollard, R., & Kumar, S. (2021). Instructional designers in higher education: Roles, challenges, and supports. *The Journal of Applied Instructional Design, 11*(1). https://dx.doi.org/10.51869/111/rp

Schön, D. A. (1987). *Educating the reflective practitioner: Toward a new design for teaching and learning in the professions.* Jossey-Bass.

Schwier, R. A., Campbell, K., & Kenny, R. (2006). Instructional designers' perceptions of their agency: Tales of change and community. In M. J. Keppell (Ed.), *Instructional design: Case studies in communities of practice* (pp. 1–18). IGI Global.

Zenke, P. F. (2014). Higher education leaders as designers. In B. Hokanson & A. Gibbons (Eds.), *Design in educational technology: Design thinking, design process and the design studio,* (pp. 249–259). Springer.

Contributors

Amy Burns is a professor and dean of the Faculty of Education at Queen's University in Kingston, Ontario. Her previous role was as associate dean of the Undergraduate Programs in Education with the Werklund School of Education at the University of Calgary. She is currently the president of the Canadian Association for the Study of Women in Education.

Katy Campbell is a professor of women's and gender studies at the University of Alberta. She joined the Faculty of Extension at the university in 1996, served as the dean from 2007 to 2019, and facilitated a new academic plan for the faculty, emphasizing university-community engagement and the scholarship of engagement.

Lorraine Carter is the former director of McMaster University Continuing Education. From northern Ontario, she has worked in distance and online education since 2000, principally in health-related education contexts. She is also a champion of educational initiatives serving the general public, including equity-deserving groups.

Elizabeth Childs is a professor and the head of the Master of Arts in Learning and Technology program at Royal Roads University in Colwood, British Columbia. Her research focuses on exploring open education practices, online learning communities, and design thinking. Recent publications include co-authored essays in distance education and chapters in the *Handbook of Distance Education* (4th ed.) and *Open(ing) Education: Theory and Practice* (2020).

Lynn Corcoran is a registered nurse and an associate professor in the Faculty of Health Disciplines at Athabasca University. She occupied leadership positions in the Bachelor of Nursing Program at Athabasca University for six years. Her research and scholarly interests include issues related to women's health as well as innovations in teaching and learning in nursing education and the digital environment.

Kristine Dreaver-Charles is a member of the Mistawasis Nêhiyawak Nation located in Saskatchewan. She grew up in Prince Albert and taught in northern Saskatchewan and online. She is a PhD candidate focusing on decolonization in distance education. Kristine has worked at the University of Saskatchewan since 2013 as an instructional designer, a sessional lecturer, and currently an academic innovation specialist.

Patti Dyjur is an educational development consultant at the University of Calgary. During the early days of the COVID-19 pandemic, she led a team of instructional designers and educational developers tasked with supporting the campus in the move to emergency remote teaching. She took her first distance learning course about 25 years ago and has been teaching online for over a decade.

Cynthia Eden is a daughter, sister, life partner, mom, aunt, friend, and scholar-practitioner who has 28 years of experience working in Canadian and Asian higher education contexts. She has experience in international education, international student equity, online quality assurance, and program and curriculum development.

Margaret Edwards is a registered nurse and professor in the Faculty of Health Disciplines at Athabasca University. She has provided leadership within the faculty as a Graduate Program director, associate dean, and dean. Her leadership is recognized through awards from the Canadian Association of Schools of Nursing, the Alberta Nurse Educators Association, and the College and Association of Registered Nurses of Alberta.

Natalie Green has worked in higher education for 20 years. She is passionate about working with teams and collaborating with educators and industry experts to create high-quality learning experiences that effectively leverage technology and visual design practices. Natalie holds a Master of Educational Technology from the University of British Columbia and is a certified instructional designer with the Canadian Association of Instructional Designers.

Michelle Harrison is an associate professor of practice, instructional design, at the Learning Design and Innovations department at Thompson Rivers University in Kamloops. Her recent research has focused on exploring the role of open educational practices in various contexts, including institutional perspectives, textbooks, and care.

Jenni Hayman is a consultant and curriculum designer at the Waterloo Climate Institute. Prior to this she was chair of the School of Business (Online) at Conestoga College in Ontario. She has spent the past 15 years exploring research and practice in open and online teaching and learning with colleagues across the globe.

Rebecca E. Heiser is an adult and distance educator and recipient of the 2024 Governor General Gold Medal at Athabasca University for her academic achievements in the Doctor of Education in Distance Education program. Her leadership experience spans diverse educational contexts and emerges from learning design and evidence-based approaches to inform local, national, and international policies and practices. She serves as the interviews editor for the *American Journal of Distance Education*, and her research interests include quality dimensions in transnational distance education, internationalization strategies, and systems perspectives of online and distance education.

Christina Hendricks is a professor of teaching in philosophy at the University of British Columbia and the academic director of the Centre for Teaching, Learning, and Technology. Her recent research focuses on open educational resources and practices. She has participated in designing and facilitating several open online courses and has been a learner in many more.

Sandy Hughes has almost 40 years of experience working in educational leadership and online course development. Currently, she is an educational consultant, working in online course development and project management with various postsecondary institutions.

Cindy Ives is a distance educator with academic and administrative experience at four Canadian universities. During her career at Athabasca University, she inspired and supported innovative online and open initiatives, including MOOCs, open educational resources, course and program development and evaluation, new learning designs, digital learning resources, and learning analytics. She is now a retired professor emerita of distance education, still teaching and supervising graduate students and conducting research on organizational and learning issues.

Diane Janes is a tenured faculty member of the Centre for Excellence in Learning and Teaching at Thompson Rivers University in Kamloops. In her role, she coaches and mentors faculty, especially in the scholarship of teaching and learning. Her career has spanned five provinces, incorporating teaching, administration, and leadership in both in-person and online environments (well before the pandemic).

Erin Keith is an assistant professor at Cape Breton University who obtained her Doctor of Education from Western University. She has worked for over 16 years in public education. Her teaching and research focus on decolonizing inclusive and educational leadership, equity literacy related to well-being and heartwork, and culturally responsive and relevant pedagogies.

Victoria Kennedy has worked in roles supporting course design and development in higher education since 2018. Leveraging her PhD in English Literature and Film Studies, she is passionate about using narrative and visual design to create impactful learning experiences.

Jennifer Lock is a professor and the vice-dean in the Werklund School of Education at the University of Calgary. Her area of specialization is in the learning sciences. Her research interests are learning in technology-enabled learning environments, change and innovation in education, scholarship of teaching and learning, and learning in maker spaces.

Sarah MacRae is interim assistant dean in the School of Arts and Social Sciences and a senior lab instructor in the Department of Communication and Languages at Cape Breton University, where she also coordinates the Dr. Mary A. Lynch Communication Lab and teaches in the Department of Experiential Studies in Community and Sport.

Kathleen Matheos has been involved in distance and online learning for over 35 years in college and university systems. She is the director of the Centre for Higher Education Research and

Development at the University of Manitoba, having served as the associate dean of Extended Education for 11 years.

Michelle Mitchell is the dean at Northern Lakes College in Canada. She is passionate about supporting faculty members in providing quality online student experiences. Most of her 25-year career has been focused on distance education. She leads the Centre for Teaching and Learning and serves as chair of the Educational Technology Committee at her institution.

Tannis Morgan is the associate vice-president of academic innovation at Vancouver Community College. Her research and publications have focused on open education practices, educational technology, and distance education.

Kim Myrick is the co-director of the Centre for Innovation in Teaching and Learning at Memorial University. She is responsible for the planning and oversight of the centre. She is also an adjunct professor in the Faculty of Business Administration at Memorial. With a doctorate in business administration, her research interests have focused on vision and leadership in strategic management, co-leadership in higher education, and the scholarship of teaching and learning.

Sophia Palahicky is the executive director of online learning and educational resources with the Ministry of Education and Child Care in the BC Public Service. She is also an associate faculty member at Royal Roads University in Colwood, British Columbia. She teaches entirely online in the School of Education and Technology in a sessional capacity.

Jasmine Pham is a PhD candidate at the Ontario Institute for Studies in Education. She studies educational leadership and policy in the Department of Leadership, Higher and Adult Education. Her MEd is in educational leadership and policy.

Megan Pickard is an instructional designer who has worked with faculty, instructors, and authors to create engaging, inclusive, and meaningful pedagogical experiences for over 15 years. She is currently the Manager of Digital Learning Design and Innovation at the University of Guelph.

Sherry Rose is an associate professor at the University of New Brunswick. She teaches critical studies, early literacy, feminist theories, assessment, and curriculum. With Dr. Kim Stewart, she is a founding member of the university committee that developed and orchestrated the online, asynchronous Bachelor of Education in Early Childhood Education designed to create educational opportunities for early childhood educators with an early childhood diploma from an accredited community college.

Anne-Marie Scott is vice president at the Commonwealth of Learning. She is an internationally recognized expert in digital, online, and open education, with over two decades of leadership experience across higher education and the non-profit sector, including senior roles at Athabasca University and the University of Edinburgh in the UK, where she led major digital and open education initiatives.

Afsaneh Sharif is a researcher, consultant, instructional designer, e-learning specialist, and senior project manager and faculty liaison at the University of British Columbia. With over 25 years of experience in project management and instructional design, she brings extensive expertise in online and blended learning. She currently serves as co-chair of the BC Digital Learning Advisory Committee.

Tammy Soanes-White completed her EdD in distance education at Athabasca University. She is a researcher and adult learning specialist in the Centre for Learning and Teaching Innovation at Aurora College in the Northwest Territories. She makes and sustains connections with women in remote communities interested in sharing stories about their journeys and development as learners and leaders.

Kim Stewart is an associate professor at the University of New Brunswick. Through the theoretical frameworks of new materialism, posthumanism, and critical feminism, her research investigates ways to reconceptualize literacies and early childhood teaching and learning. With Dr. Sherry Rose, she is a founding member of the university committee that developed and orchestrated the online, asynchronous Bachelor of Education in Early Childhood Education designed to create educational opportunities for early childhood educators with an early childhood diploma from an accredited community college.

Denise Stockley is a professor and scholar of higher education at Queen's University, in the Office of the Provost (teaching and learning portfolio) and the Faculty of Health Sciences. With a doctorate in educational psychology, she studies how people learn across the lifespan, with a focus on adult learning, professional education, and inclusive teaching. Her work advances access through distance and blended learning, particularly for non-traditional and equity-deserving learners.

Lori Wallace is a dean emerita and senior scholar at the University of Manitoba. Her previous roles included professor and academic administrator (dean of Extended Education, director of Distance and Online Education), and senior instructional designer. She remains active in program design and evaluation, quality assurance and governance.

Pamela Walsh has worked in the post-secondary education sector for over 35 years, holding senior leadership positions at two Canadian Colleges and serving in an executive leadership role at

Athabasca University for six years. A distance educator with AU since 2008, she retired in 2024 and continues to contribute to the academic community as an adjunct professor.

Connie (Levina) Yuen is an associate professor in FHSS at Athabasca University. She has a decade of experience in educational technologies and learning assessments. She previously served as a K–12 educator, instructional designer, technology analyst, program evaluator, and lecturer in higher education.